IMAGES
of America

POWELL

I0792885

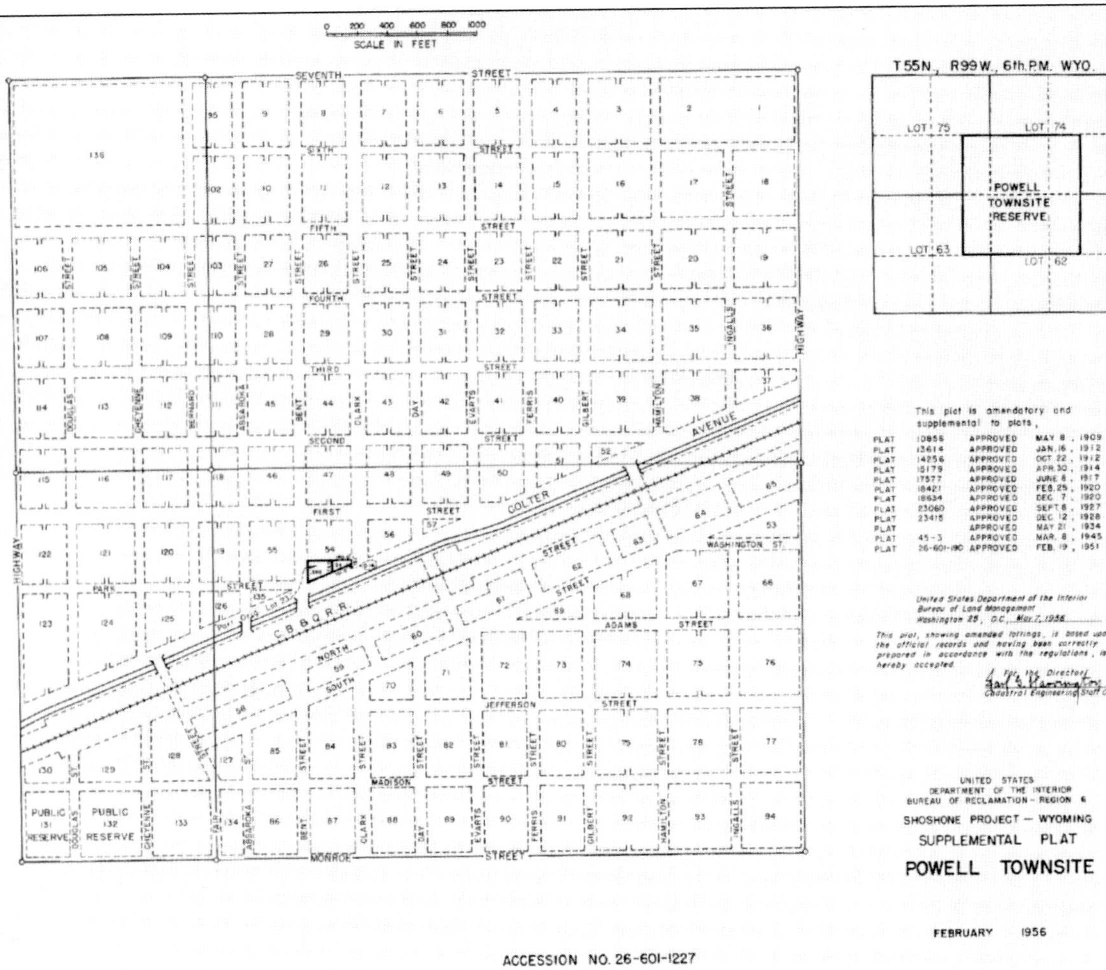

This map depicts the city streets of Powell in 1956. Coulter Avenue, originally Colter, follows the Burlington and Missouri River Railroad line. The streets running from north to south are named after early western explorers, various historical figures, and local residents. The streets running east to west are numbered north of the tracks; however, south of the tracks the east to west streets are named after the first American presidents. (Shoshone Irrigation District Archives.)

ON THE COVER: Powell residents gather on Bent Street around 1949 to enjoy the Park County Fair parade. A marching band follows a parade float celebrating the positive transformations resulting from the Bureau of Reclamation's Shoshone Irrigation Project. (Park County Archives.)

IMAGES
of America

POWELL

Jeremy M. Johnston

ARCADIA
PUBLISHING

Copyright © 2009 by Jeremy M. Johnston
ISBN 978-0-7385-6917-8

Published by Arcadia Publishing
Charleston, South Carolina

Printed in the United States of America

Library of Congress Control Number: 2009920015

For all general information contact Arcadia Publishing at:
Telephone 843-853-2070
Fax 843-853-0044
E-mail sales@arcadiapublishing.com
For customer service and orders:
Toll-Free 1-888-313-2665

Visit us on the Internet at www.arcadiapublishing.com

This book is dedicated to all past, present, and future residents of Powell and its countryside.

Contents

Acknowledgments

Many people are responsible for bringing this book to completion. First of all, I would like to thank Kelly Reed of Arcadia Publishing and Lynn Houze for encouraging me to write this book. Thanks to Rowene Weems, curator of the Homesteader Museum, for granting access to a variety of museum collections and her suggestions. I would also like to thank the staff of the Homesteader Museum, Brandi Wright, Darleen Carroll, and Judith Skinner, for their assistance. Marylin Schultz and Rhonda Spaulding of the Park County Archives also provided a number of photographs. Lori Nordland and Bryant Startin of the Shoshone Irrigation District granted me access to the archives and allowed me to acquire a great number of images pertaining to the reclamation project. Dave Reetz of First National Bank allowed me access to study and copy many photographs.

I also need to thank Susan Richards, Diane Martin, Deb Kelly, and Nancy Miller of the Hinckley Library for finding photographs, articles, books, and other useful information. Thanks to Gregg Randall who granted me permission to reprint his wonderful image of Boxcar Murphy. Laurel Vredenburg and David Vaughan assisted me in acquiring a number of Northwest College photographs. I would like to thank Scott Horton, Dustin Dicks, and Cole Assay for providing me technical assistance. I would also like to thank Sharon Earhart and the members of the Powell Centennial Committee for sharing with me their memories of Powell and encouraging me to complete this book. Thanks to my colleagues at NWC, especially those in the Social Science Division, for putting up with me the last 14 years. I especially want to thank Beryl Churchill and Bob Bonner for their wonderful books and stories detailing Powell's history. And last but not least, a special thanks to my family for instilling in me a love of history. Mandy, Jaxon, Sam, and Alexa, thank you for love and patience. Your encouragement and ability to live in the same house with a stressed out author will forever be appreciated. I extend to all of these individuals my eternal gratitude for their advice, assistance, and patience.

The courtesy abbreviations for the images are:

JTHL: A. G. Lucier Collection, John Taggart Hinkley Library, Northwest College
HM: Homesteader Museum, Powell, Wyoming
FNB: First National Bank Lucier Collection
PCA: Park County Archives, Cody, Wyoming
SIDA: Shoshone Irrigation District Archives, Powell, Wyoming
NWC: Wolsborn Collection, Northwest College, Powell, Wyoming

INTRODUCTION

On April 27, 1908, the Garland Canal brought water to the land surrounding the developing town of Powell, Wyoming, located in the central region of the Bighorn Basin. Soon a number of homesteaders and businessmen poured into the region hoping to establish new lives for themselves and their families in this newly irrigated landscape. Before long, these settlers transformed the arid lands of the Bighorn Basin into rich farmland. Thousands of acres where sagebrush flats and buffalo grass once grew now became irrigated farmland, producing wheat, alfalfa, beans, potatoes, and sugar beets. And in the middle of all this newly opened farmland stood the new community of Powell, Wyoming.

These former desert lands previously were home to the Crow and Shoshone, who viewed the Bighorn Basin not as a desolate, arid landscape, but as a productive region that provided them with countless bison. The bison herds grazing on the grasses of the Bighorn Basin supplied these early residents with food, shelter, and clothing. Other Plains Indian nations such as the Blackfeet, Nez Perce, and Bannock also hunted within the basin, some traveling from far distances, using well-traveled trails such as the Bannock Trail to reach these hunting grounds. These Plains Indian nations soon encountered various fur traders and hunters traversing the region in search of rich hides. Men such as Francois Laroque, John Colter, and George Drouillard became the first Europeans to traverse the region hoping to establish trading partnerships with the residents of the basin. Other traders and trappers soon followed these early explorers and the Bighorn Basin became a thoroughfare for the American fur trade. Using established trails, fur traders scurried all around the mountains that fringe the Bighorn Basin, the Bighorn Mountains, the Owl Creek Range, and the Absaroka Mountains, trapping and trading. On the heels of the trappers came bison hunters, also hoping to make money by procuring hides.

After the decimation of the beaver populations and the bison herds in the Bighorn Basin, various ranchers and homesteaders traveled through and settled within this arid landscape to create a ranching economy within the area. Beginning in the late 1870s, daring men such as John Chapman and Peter McCulloch drove cattle into the Bighorn Basin to graze the grasses once devoured by now depleted bison herds. These men soon attracted other ranchers and by the end of the 1880s, cattle grazed on lands throughout the Bighorn Basin. Some ranchers diverted water to small plots of land to grow feed for their livestock hoping to avoid disastrous losses caused by severe winter weather.

By 1894, promoters such as "Buffalo Bill" Cody advocated and promoted various reclamation projects under the Carey Act, an act that gave arid states up to one million acres of federal public domain, if the state ensured the land would be irrigated and settled. Working with the State of Wyoming, various entrepreneurs constructed dams, canals, and ditches, hoping to create new economies, new communities, and new fortunes for themselves and the state. After some limited success and many failures, proponents of irrigation hoped the federal government could complete massive reclamation projects in the West, an idea originally suggested by John Wesley Powell in the 1870s. The Newlands Act of 1902 created the Reclamation Service under the Department of the Interior, later renamed the Bureau of Reclamation in 1923. This new government agency used federal revenue generated from public land sells to develop various reclamation projects. Soon the Reclamation Service acquired Buffalo Bill's claim along the Shoshone River, formerly named the Stinking Water River, and began working on the Shoshone project's first reclamation division, the Garland Division. After successfully completing the Corbett Dam, the Corbett Tunnel, and the Garland Canal, all of which brought water to the Garland Division, the community of Powell emerged to provide goods and services to newly arrived homesteaders, who hoped to establish new lives as farmers on these irrigated plots of land.

On May 25, 1909, the Reclamation Service offered the first town lots for sale in Powell, formerly known as Camp Colter. Citizens considered this event the "birth" of Powell, which was officially incorporated by the State of Wyoming on May 10, 1910. The community of Powell slowly grew despite various obstacles such as town fires, unstable crop prices, and crop failures. Residents of Powell worked to establish a variety of social organizations, community events, churches, and schools to ensure an active community life. The Park County Fair found a home in Powell in 1923 and every year it continues to attract people from all over the Bighorn Basin.

By the 1930s, Powell boasted of having the largest school district and bus system in the state. To this day, hundreds of alumni return every year to celebrate their graduation from Powell High School. In 1946, community members advocated the establishment the Northwest Center of the University of Wyoming. Later this extended campus developed into Northwest Community College, now named Northwest College, which attracts over 1,700 students a year. Strong community institutions such as these, in addition to active community events, ensured Powell in 1923 would weather through booms and busts in oil, ranching, and farming.

Powell also provided a home to a variety of individuals that added to the rich tapestry of the community. W. Edward Deming resided in Powell as a young boy before attending the University of Wyoming. Working under Gen. Douglas MacArthur, Deming's theories of business management restored Japan's economy from the ashes of World War II. Town resident Earl Durand became well known as "Tarzan of the Tetons," a moniker he received after escaping from jail, killing four lawmen, and shooting up the downtown bank in a failed robbery attempt. Durand took his own life after a posse of townsmen wounded him and killed a teller in the process during the shoot-out at the bank. Another resident of Powell, Roy Barnes, became a popular cowboy musician with the stage name the Rocky Mountain Cowboy. Barnes's songs would play daily on KPOW, Powell's local radio station, and on other stations across the nation. Even the hobo Boxcar Murphy found Powell to be a welcoming community. Boxcar Murphy rode the rails into town and made it his new home, living day to day by bumming drinks and raffling off a variety of rifles he owned. Thousands of Japanese American residents found themselves living a few miles west of Powell, but not by their own choice. During World War II, the Relocation Authority established the Heart Mountain Relocation Canal to intern over 11,000 Japanese Americans for the duration of the war. The relocation center became the third-largest city in Wyoming, and its citizens greatly contributed to the agricultural development of the area by bringing in new crops and working on the Heart Mountain Division, an extension of the Shoshone Project. All of these individuals made Powell into an attractive and lively community that proudly celebrated its centennial year in 2009.

One

THE EARLY HISTORY OF THE BIGHORN BASIN

Thousands of years before the founding of Powell, hunting cultures flourished in the Bighorn Basin. Near Cody, Wyoming, archeologists discovered the Horner Site, where over 10,000 years ago a group of prehistoric Plains Indian hunters killed and butchered a number of bison. After the introduction of horses to the Great Plains, the Shoshone and Crow lived and hunted bison in the Bighorn Basin. Beginning in the early 1800s, European fur traders entered the basin to find potential trading partners and acquire beaver pelts. Thomas Laroque crossed over the Bighorn Mountains and explored the Bighorn River and Canyon with his Crow guides in 1805. In 1806, John Colter, a member of the Lewis and Clark Expedition, trapped and traded along the Clarks Fork of the Yellowstone River. He returned to further explore the region in the winter of 1807–1808 to establish trade relations for his new boss, Manuel Lisa. George Drouillard, another trader working for Manuel Lisa, later followed and mapped Colter's route.

Drouillard's map and Colter's information found its way to William Clark, who added the geographical material to the Lewis and Clark map. Clearly identified on this map were the Stinking Water River (later renamed Shoshone River in 1902); the boiling springs in the Shoshone Canyon, later identified by mountain men as Colter's Hell; and Heart Mountain. In the following years, trappers and hunters crossed the Bighorn Basin in search of pelts and hides. By the late 1870s, hunters decimated most of the bison herds in the basin, leaving vast areas of unused grazing range that attracted ranchers to the area. In 1878, John Chapman explored the area with a group of soldiers who were chasing the Bannock Indians. Chapman returned with a herd of cattle the following year and established a ranch near the claim of an old trapper named Pat O'Hara. That same year, Peter McCulloch herded cattle and established a ranch on the south fork of the Stinking Water River for Judge William A. Carter of Fort Bridger, Wyoming. The names of Judge Carter, Pat O'Hara, John Chapman, and Pete McCulloch soon identified a number of geographical features in the Bighorn Basin.

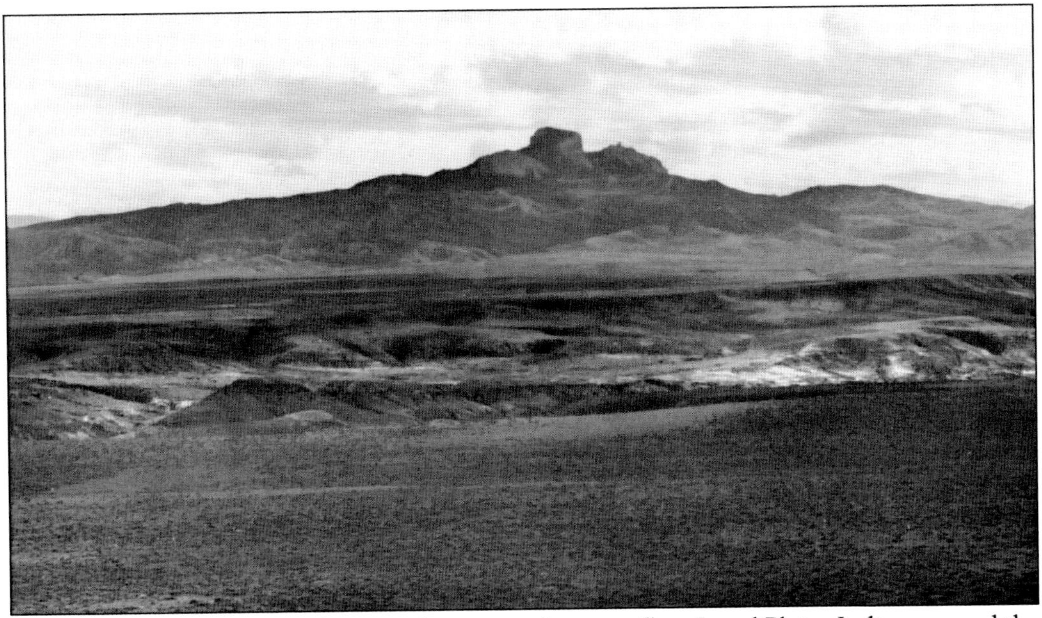

Heart Mountain clearly stands out in the surrounding sage flats. Local Plains Indians named the mountain Heart Mountain because of its similarities to a bison's heart. European explorers used this distinctive mountain as a landmark to orient themselves during their travels through the region. William Clark correctly located Heart Mountain on his manuscript map; unfortunately, on the published map, the mountain incorrectly appeared south of the Stinking Water River. (PCA.)

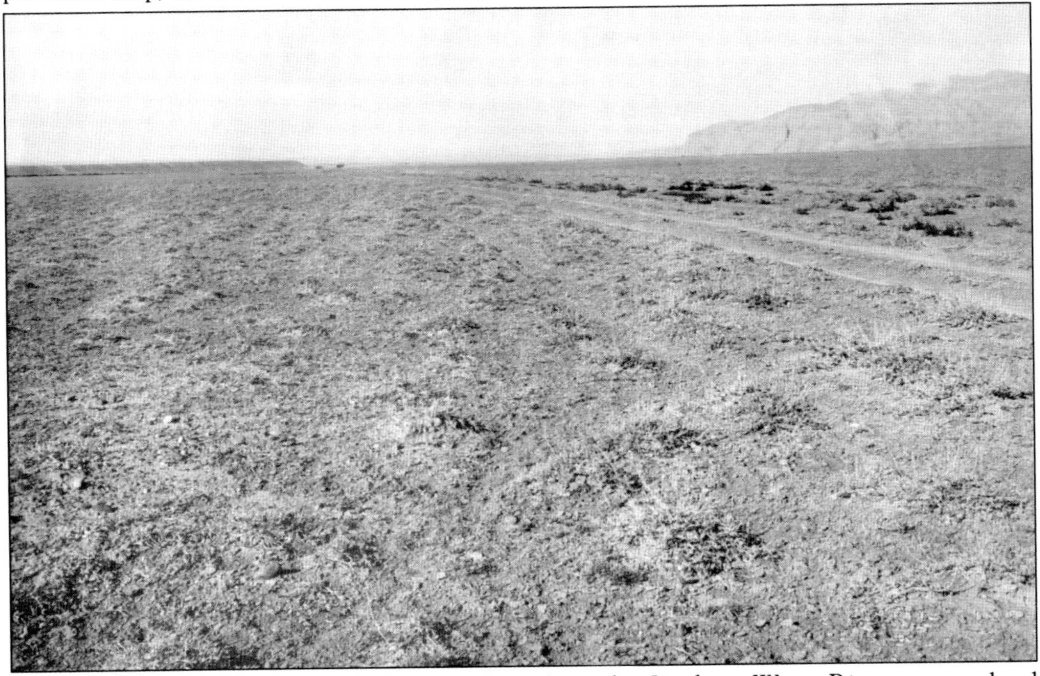

Early homesteaders viewed the sagebrush flats along the Stinking Water River as wasteland awaiting reclamation. To the Crow, Shoshone, and other Plains Indian nations, these arid lands productively fed thousands of bison. In turn, the bison provided Plains Indians all the basic elements to survive: food, clothing, tools, and shelter. (PCA.)

Hot springs boil up in the Stinking Water River. John Colter noticed these geothermal features during his visit in the winter of 1807–1808. Later travelers referred to the site as Colter's Hell. The sulfur smell resulting from these springs gave name to the Stinking Water River. William Clark included these boiling springs on the Lewis and Clark map. (SIDA.)

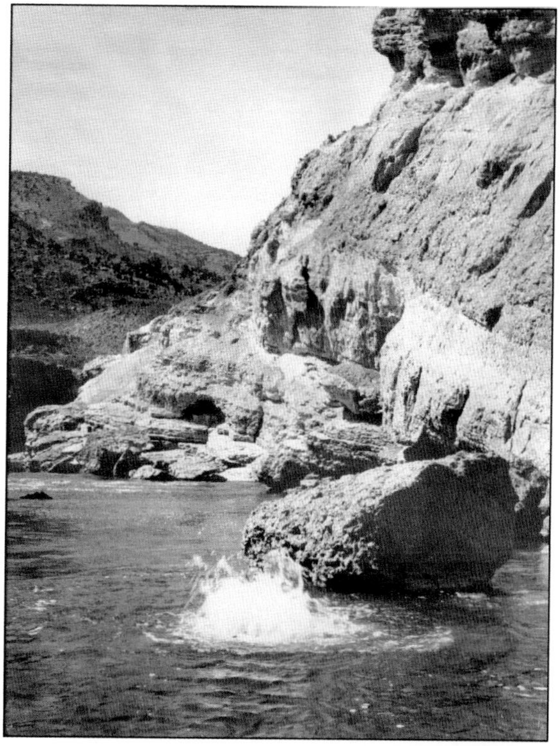

A solitary figure stands on the crater's edge of an extinct geyser. The presence of such features reminds one of the tremendous geothermal activities that once existed along the Stinking Water River. Today that activity is much less volatile, yet the smell of sulfur clearly indicates why the area became known as Colter's Hell. (SIDA.)

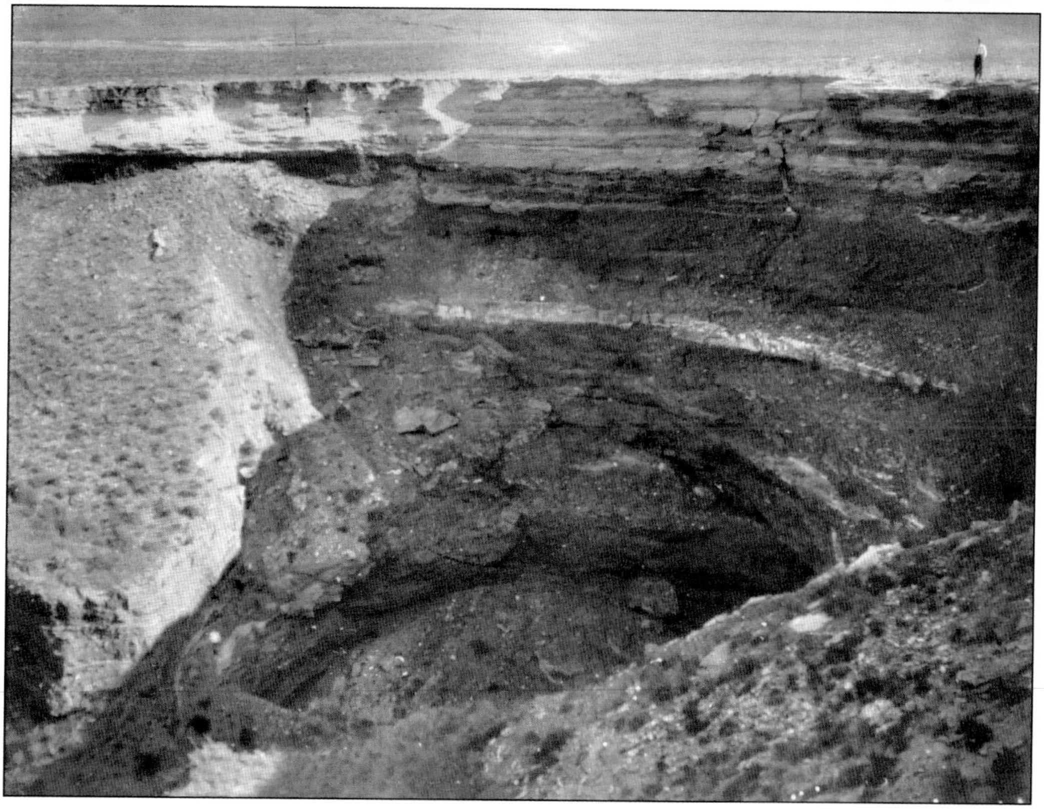

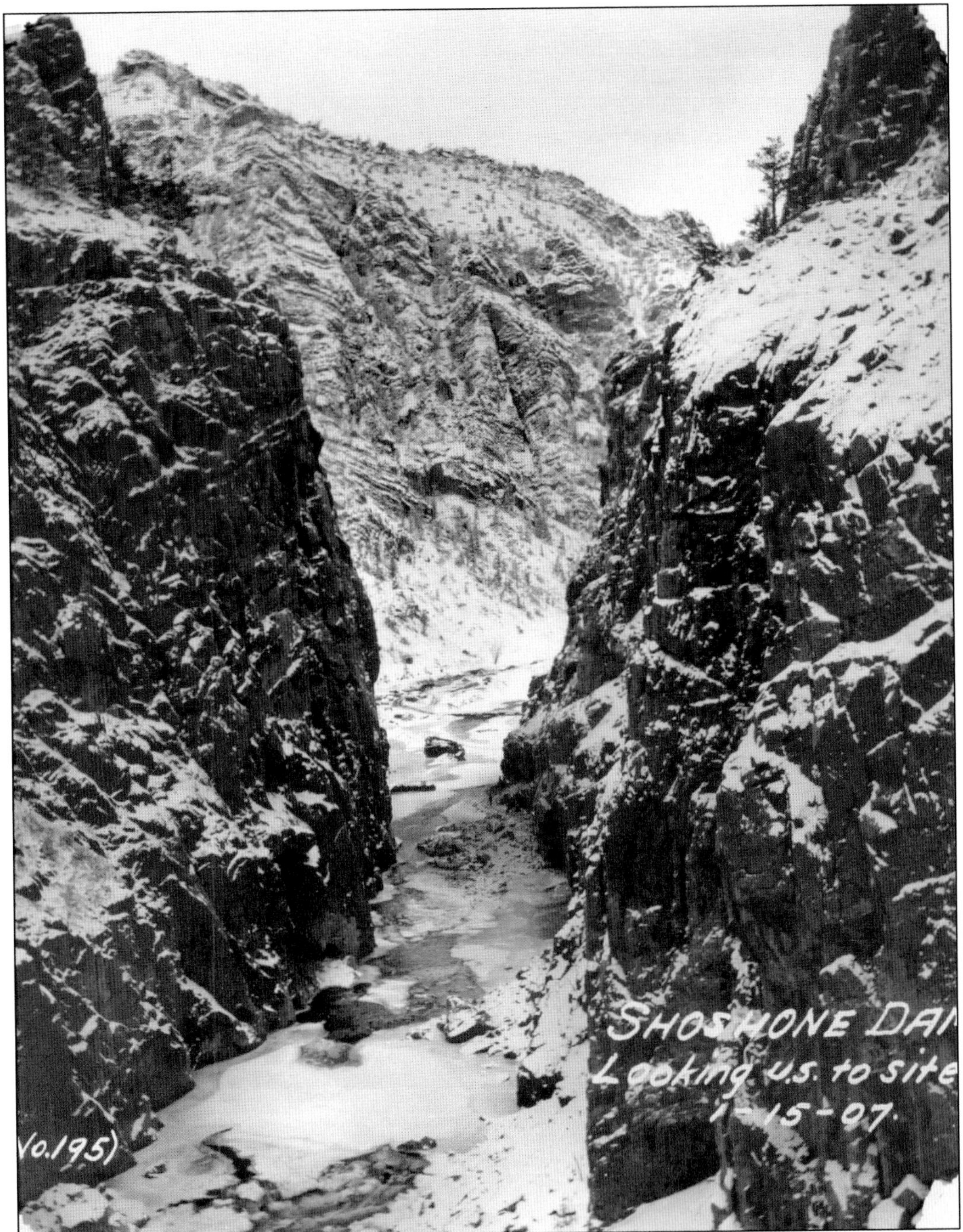

Snow covers the exposed ledges within the steep granite cliffs of Shoshone Canyon. The canyon divides Rattlesnake Mountain and Cedar Mountain. The name the Crow gave this landmark translated into "Like a Tipi Doorway." This spot later became the location of the Shoshone Dam, later renamed the Buffalo Bill Dam. Barely visible at the bottom of the canyon is the beginnings of a temporary diversion dam, which would divert water from the dam construction site. The faint impression of a road and a bridge are also visible. The steepness of the canyon walls and the cold winters proved to be very challenging for the workers constructing the Shoshone Dam. (PCA.)

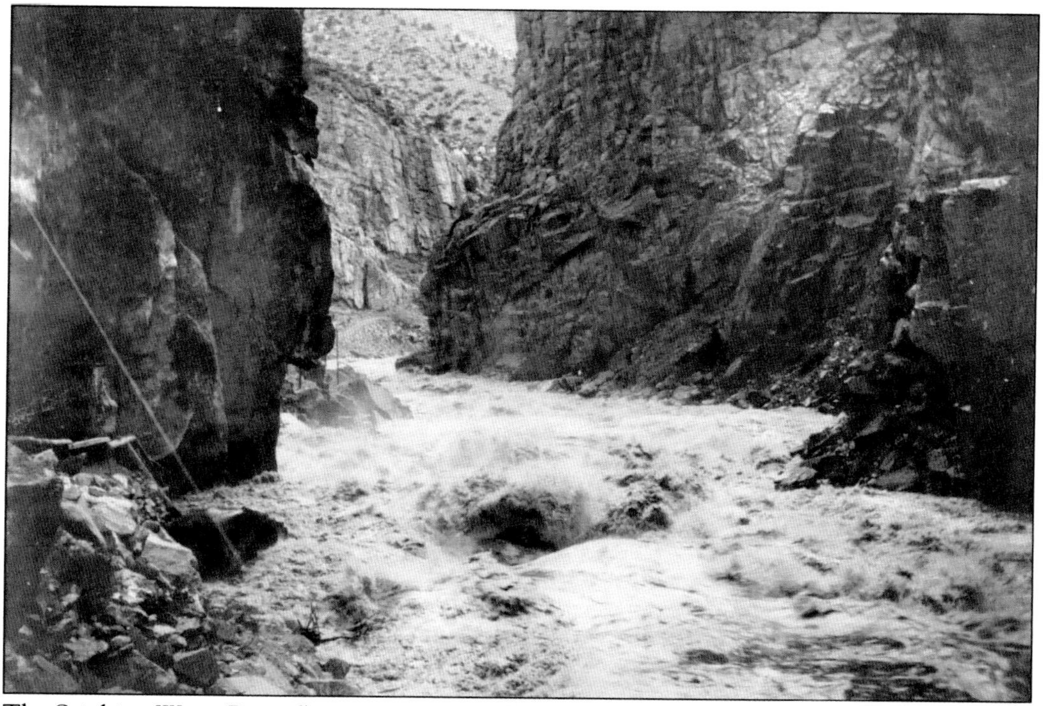

The Stinking Water River flows through the narrow Shoshone Canyon. Crow Indians believed the canyon to be the home of supernatural beings. The sound of loud rapids within the canyon walls, in addition to the sulfurous smell from the hot springs, certainly does give this location an eerie feeling. Today the Buffalo Bill Dam regulates the flow of the river running through the canyon, yet Shoshone Canyon remains a rugged place. (Both SIDA.)

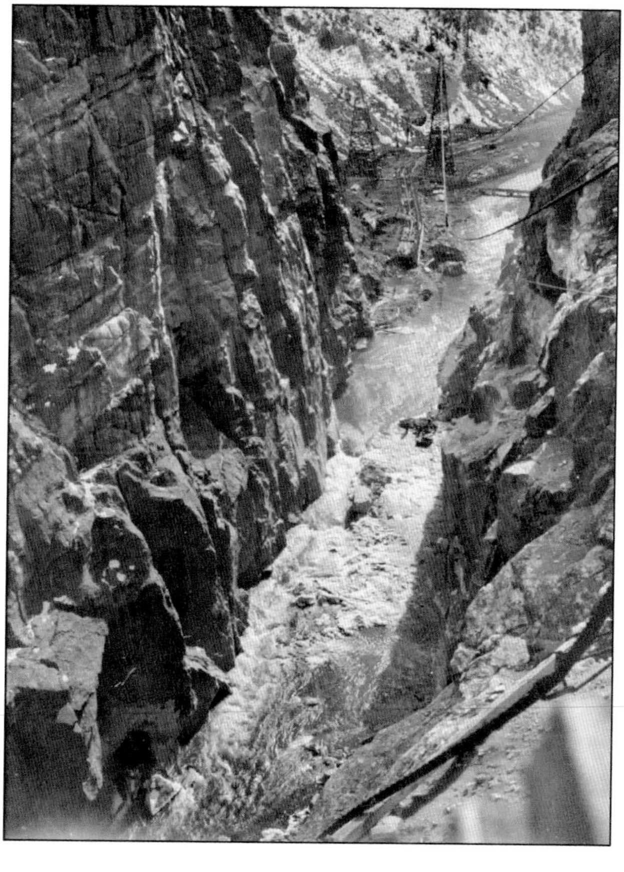

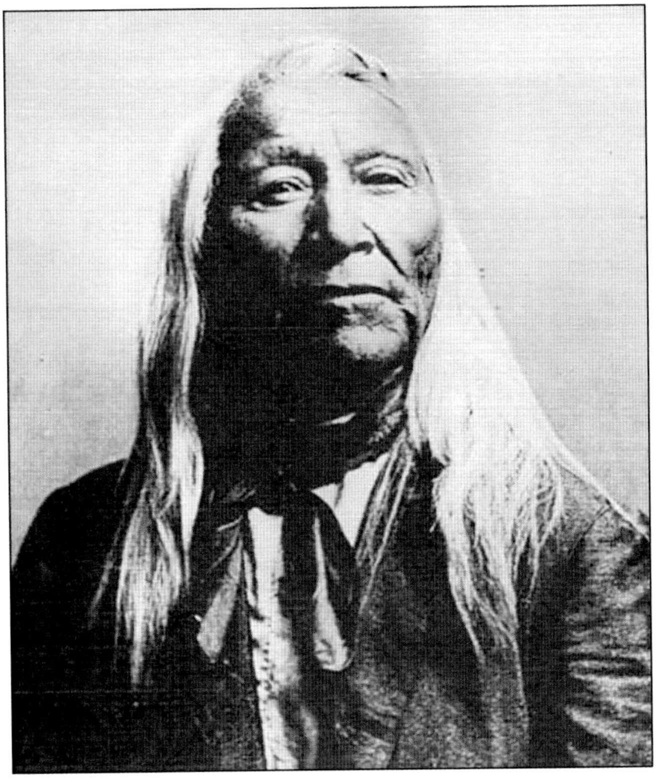

Chief Washakie, chief of the Wind River Shoshone, proudly poses for a portrait. Washakie signed the Fort Bridger Treaty of 1868 to reserve the lands of the Wind River Reservation, located south of the Bighorn Basin. In October 1874, Washakie led his band up to the Stinking Water River for the annual Shoshone buffalo hunt. Washakie died in 1900. (PCA.)

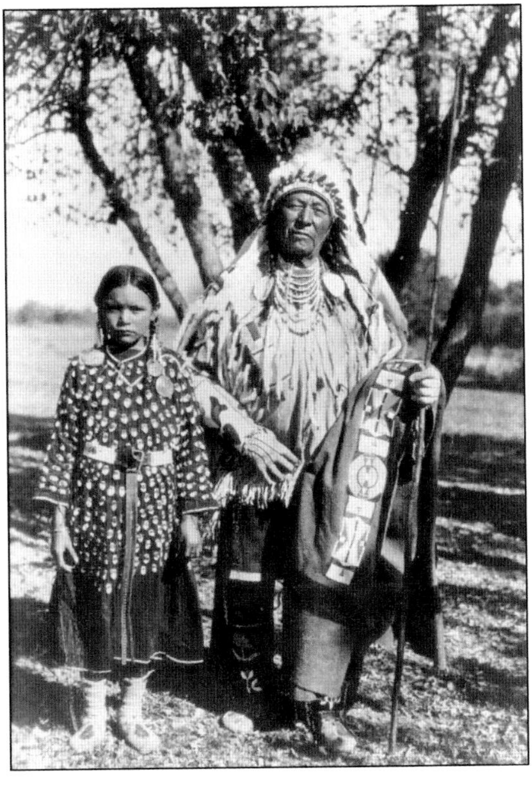

Chief Plenty Coups, a Crow leader, poses with his daughter. As a young Crow warrior, he fought his enemies and hunted bison in the Bighorn Basin. Plenty Coup's vision foretold the loss of the bison and revealed "the white men will take and hold this country and that their spotted-buffalo will cover the plains." This vision helped him to better prepare his people for the changes to come. Plenty Coups passed away in 1932. (PCA.)

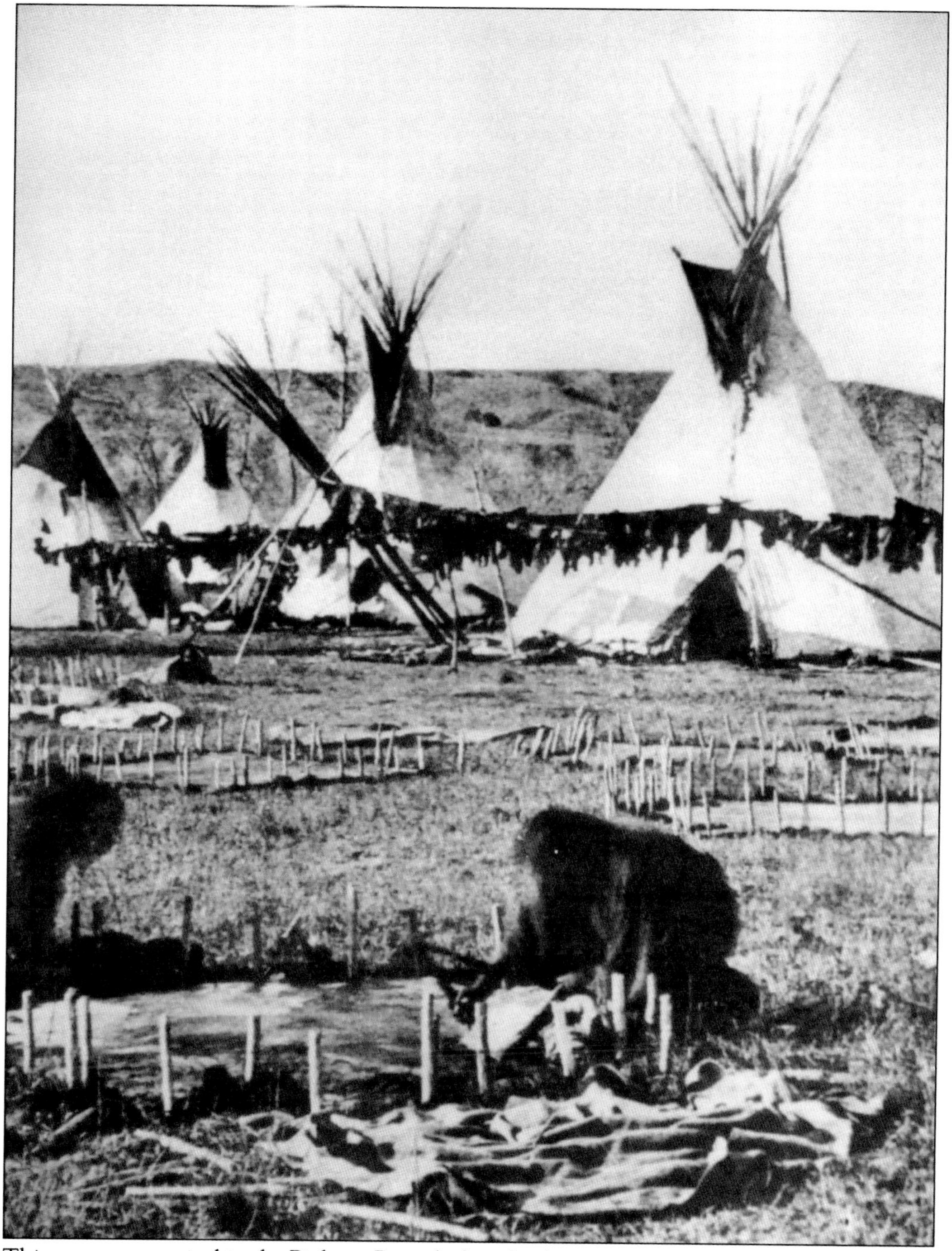

This scene was typical in the Bighorn Basin before the decimation of the bison herds. The bison provided the American Indians with food, shelter, and clothing. The bison herds attracted various Plains Indian nations such as the Crow, Shoshone, and Arapaho. Other nations traveled vast distances to hunt bison in the basin, including the Nez Perce, Bannock, Lakota, Cheyenne, and Blackfeet. Clearly the Bighorn Basin, despite its arid landscape, was seen as a plentiful land by a number of Plains Indian nations. (PCA.)

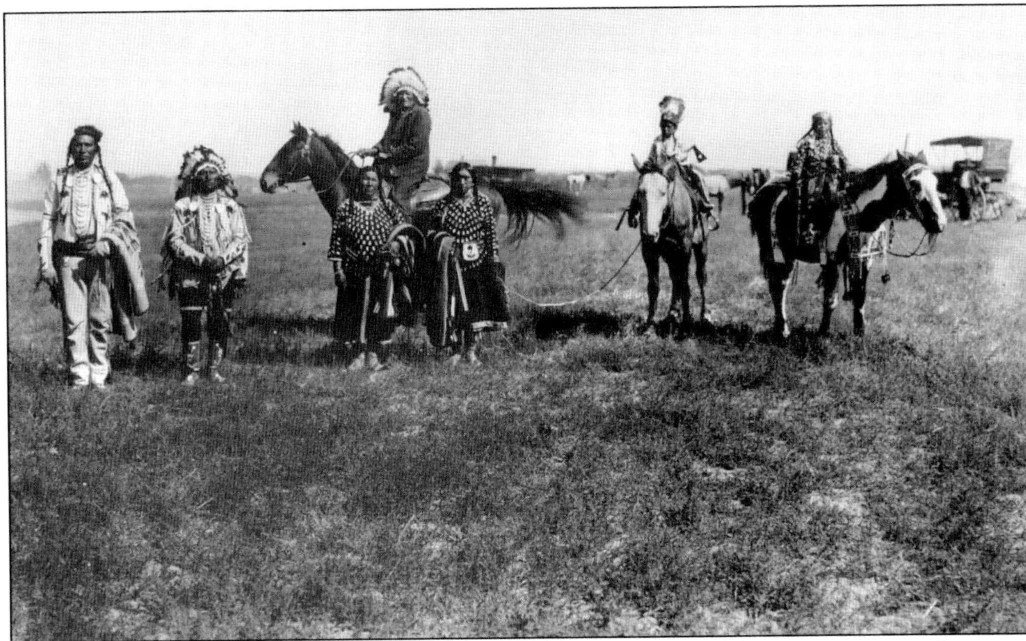

Crow chieftain Arapooish told fur trader Robert Campbell, "The Crow country is a good country. The Great Spirit has put it exactly in the right place; while you are in it you fare well; whenever you go out of it, whichever way you travel, you will fare worse." By 1884, the Crow were limited to a reservation that held just a small portion of their former lands. As white settlers moved into Crow country, the Crow continued to travel through their former lands near present-day Powell to assist in harvesting crops and to attend the Northwestern Wyoming Fair, hosted in Powell. These two images depict one such visit to the Northwestern Wyoming Fair in 1921. (Both SIDA.)

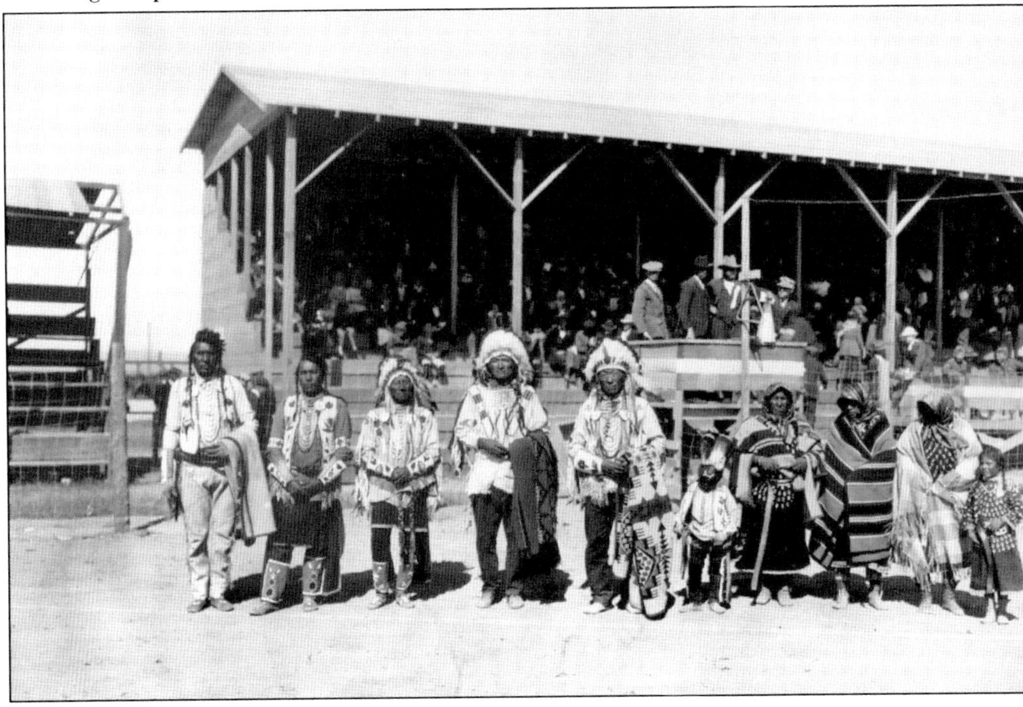

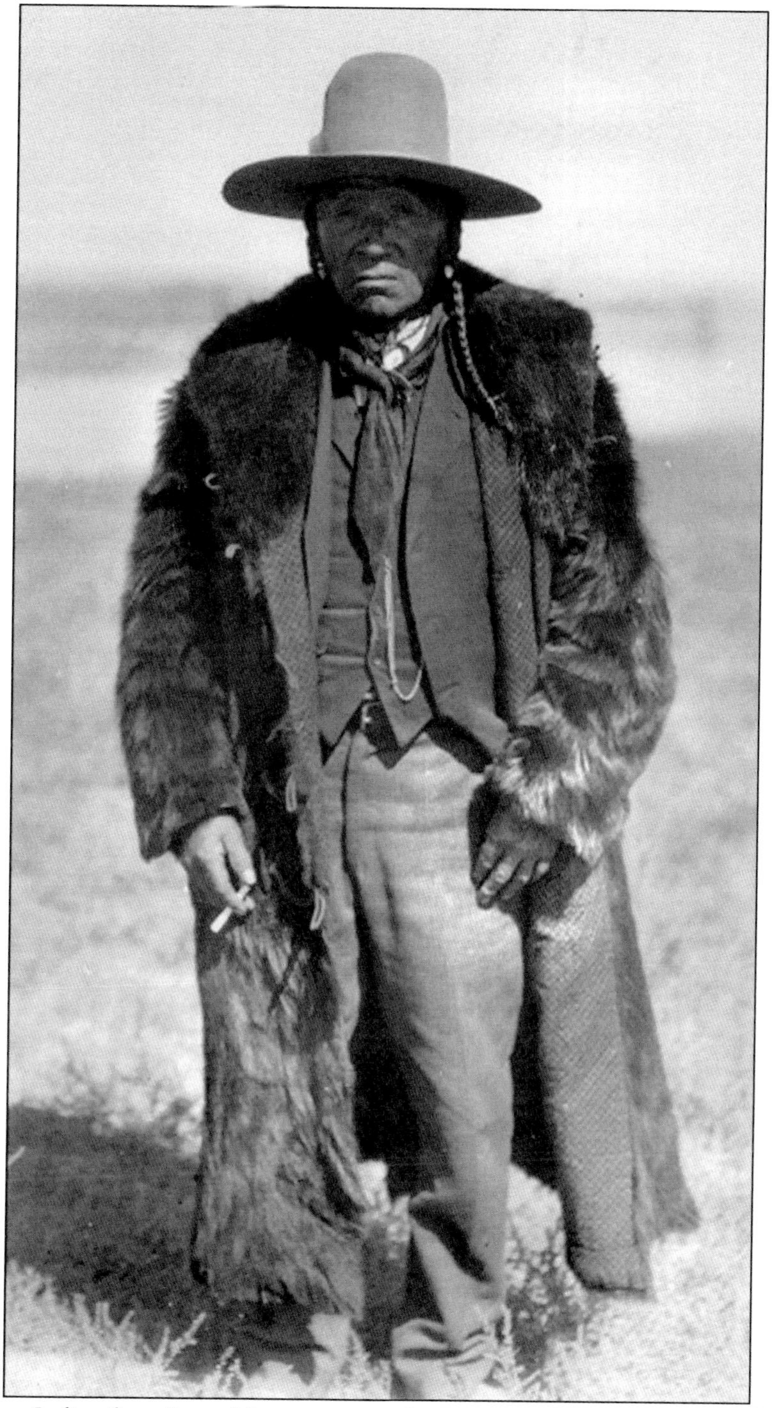

Birdhat, a Crow Indian from Pryor, Montana, poses for a picture while smoking a cigarette. Birdhat visited Powell with a group of Crow Indians to participate in the 1921 Northwestern Wyoming Fair. This photograph captures the mixing of the Crow culture with the white culture. Birdhat's fur overcoat, suit jacket, vest, pocket watch, and hat are clearly not traditional Crow clothing, but he continued to wear his hair in braids in the customary Crow fashion. (SIDA.)

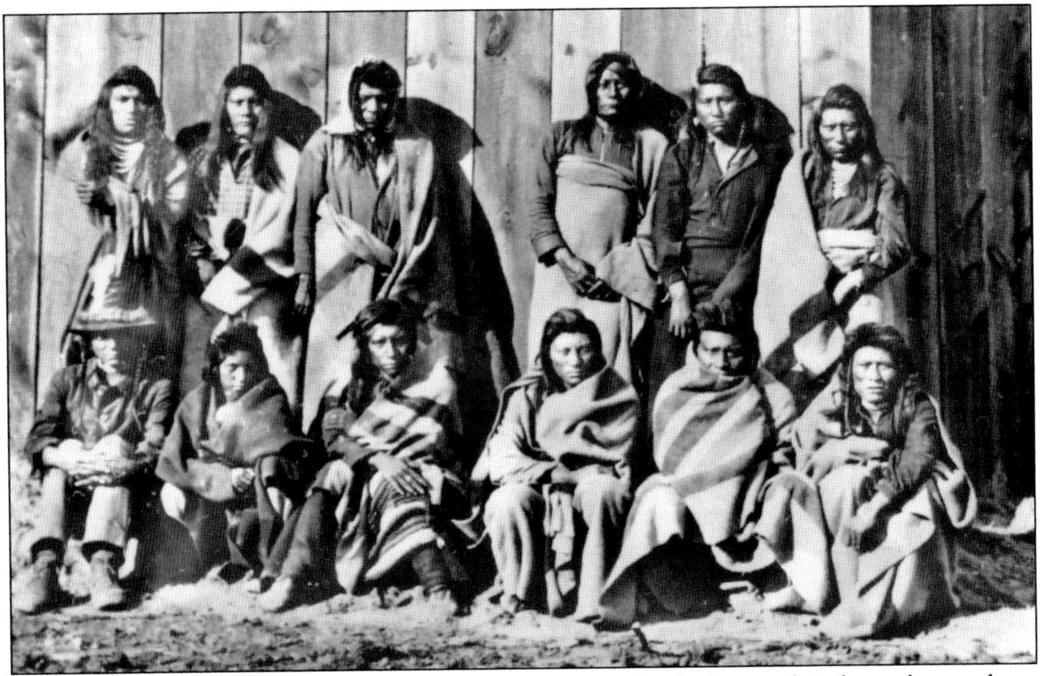

In 1878, a year after the Nez Perce attempted to flee to Canada, the Bannock Indians also sought to escape conflict with white soldiers by following the Bannock Trail from Idaho through Yellowstone National Park into the Bighorn Basin. Gen. Nelson A. Miles and his soldiers, accompanied by Crow scouts, surprised the Bannock encampment on the Clarks Fork River, near present-day Clark, Wyoming. Lt. Andrew S. Bennett was killed in the battle and a local creek now bears his name. This image depicts a group of captured Bannock Indians. (PCA.)

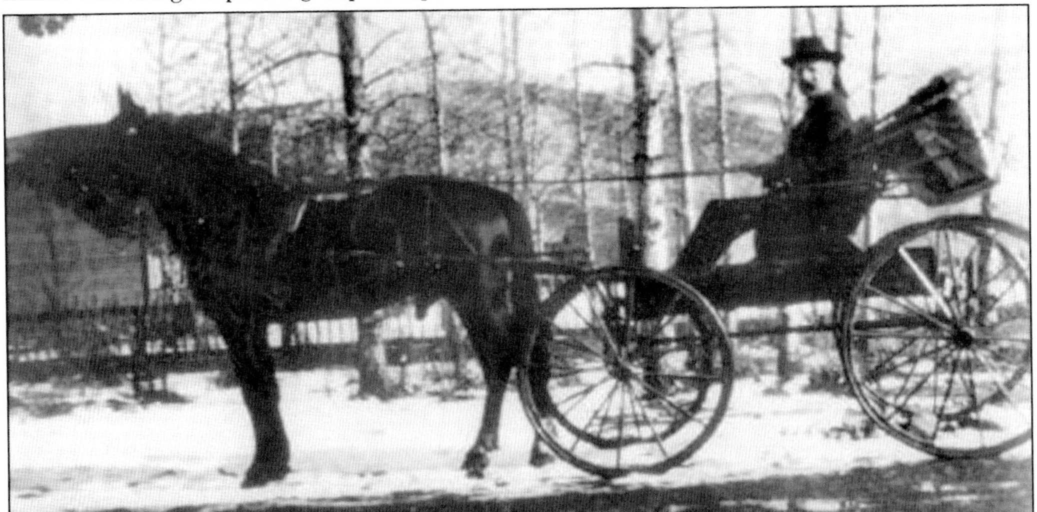

At the time of the Bannock War, Oregon cattleman John Chapman, pictured here in his wagon, explored the Bighorn Basin for potential ranch land. He found a suitable area on Pat O'Hara Creek, named after a local trapper. In 1879, Chapman trailed a herd of cattle to this location and established a successful ranching operation. In 1881, he returned to Oregon and married Affie Chapman. The newlywed couple honeymooned on the trail back to Wyoming. Chapman passed away in 1933. (PCA.)

In 1879, another cattleman drove his herd into the Bighorn Basin. Peter McCulloch, pictured here with his wife, Margaret, established a ranch along the Stinking Water River for Judge Carter of Fort Bridger, Wyoming. McCullough Peaks, located southwest of Powell, bear his name, although spelled incorrectly. McCulloch worked as Carter's foreman until 1889 when he moved to Iowa to be closer to his family. (PCA.)

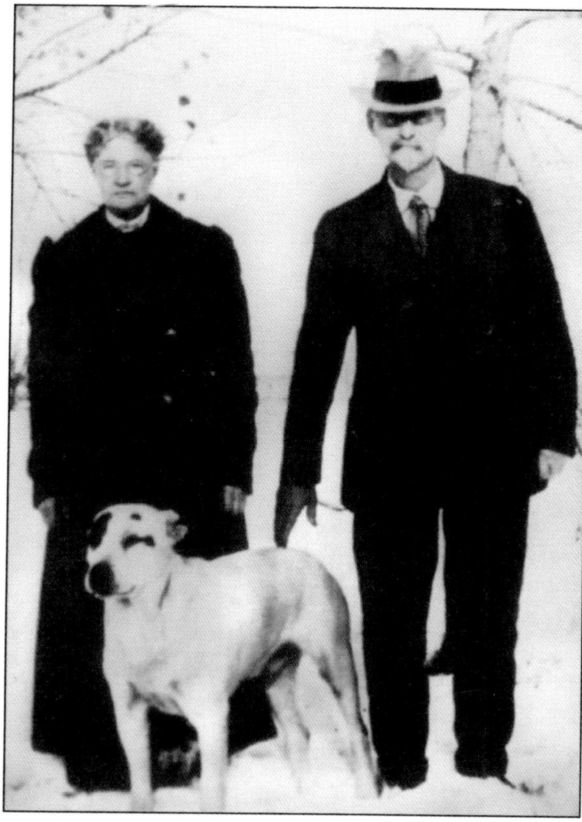

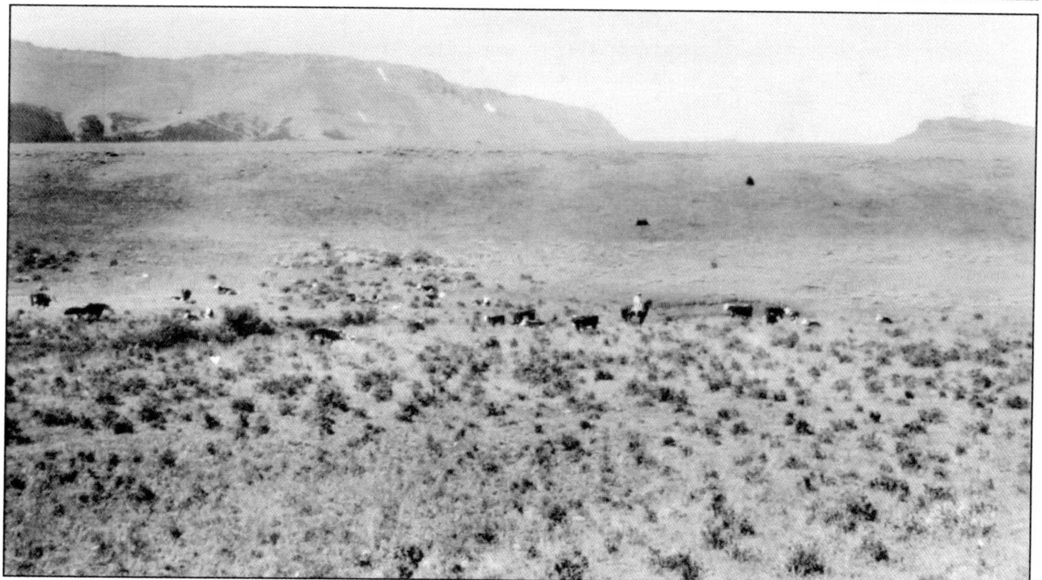

A herd of cattle graze on the open range. By the mid-1880s, many ranchers, following Chapman and McCulloch's examples, claimed ranches on every tributary of the Bighorn River. Severe winters and overgrazing of the range soon brought an end to many of the large ranching outfits. Judge Carter's son W. A. Carter reported, "Our heavy losses on Stinking Water were not in the winter of 1886–1887. We lost the greater part of our herd there in the winter of 1887–1888." (PCA.)

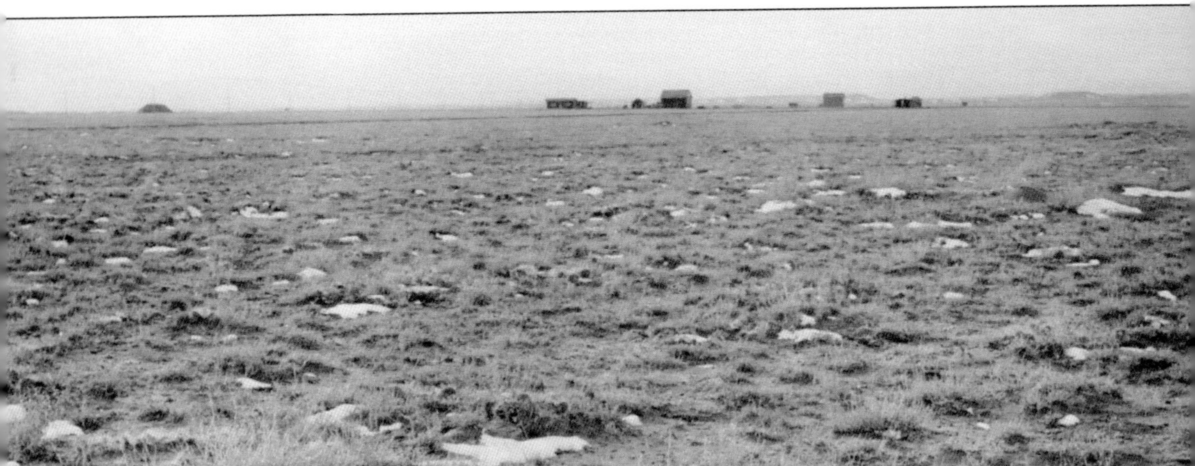

This early-1900s photograph illustrates the number of environmental changes that occurred in the Bighorn Basin during the 19th century. Far into the distance is Heart Mountain, a landmark for the early explorers. The bison skull in the foreground clearly indicates that the traditional Plains Indian uses of the land are now gone forever. The few buildings seen across the sagebrush-covered open range are the early settlement that would become Powell. This marks the beginnings of a farming economy. The bison skull seen here was used as a prop in other Reclamation Service photographs (see page 42). (PCA.)

Two

Bringing Water to the Arid Lands

The success of open range ranching in the Bighorn Basin lured other homesteaders to the region. Settlers established small claims along the banks of rivers, hoping to divert the much-needed water to small plots of land that produced hay for their livestock. The success of these small ranches attracted the attention of promoters who hoped to construct larger irrigation systems and bring even more arid land under cultivation. John Wesley Powell, a government surveyor renowned for his exploration of the Grand Canyon, warned that only the federal government could reclaim the vast amounts of arid land in the West. Private companies did not have the financial resources or the willingness to risk their money on such massive projects.

In 1894, Congress passed the Carey Act, named after Joseph M. Carey, the senator from Wyoming. This act granted up to 1 million acres of the public domain to each 10 arid states in the West, providing the state oversee the reclamation of the land. William F. Cody, the famed "Buffalo Bill," along with George T. Beck and other investors, contracted with the State of Wyoming to irrigate the lands along the Stinking Water River. Buffalo Bill and his partners began work on the Cody Canal in 1895 and, in the following year, founded the town of Cody, Wyoming. After years of struggling to build a canal through difficult terrain, in addition to financial problems, the Cody Canal finally brought water to the lands surrounding the new town. In 1899, Buffalo Bill and Nate Salsbury acquired 60,000 acres of arid land previously claimed under the Carey Act and then abandoned by Wyoming congressman Frank Mondell. Due to Salsbury's death and the inability to lure investors, Buffalo Bill did not finish the project. Despite the renaming of the Stinking Water River to the Shoshone River by the State of Wyoming, Buffalo Bill's project floundered. He did turn some of his claim over to the Mormon Church and Mormon settlers completed the Sidon Canal to water the lands on the lower section of the Shoshone River. By this time, Theodore Roosevelt signed into law the Newlands Act in 1902, which granted the secretary of the interior the power to use funds from public land sales to construct reclamation projects throughout the West. The new Reclamation Service now took on the task of the reclamation of arid lands. Buffalo Bill transferred his rights to the Reclamation Service and President Roosevelt approved the Shoshone Project on February 10, 1904. Four divisions of the Shoshone Project resulted in the reclamation of 96,000 acres. Lured by the possibilities of irrigated farms, many homesteaders now settled in the Bighorn Basin.

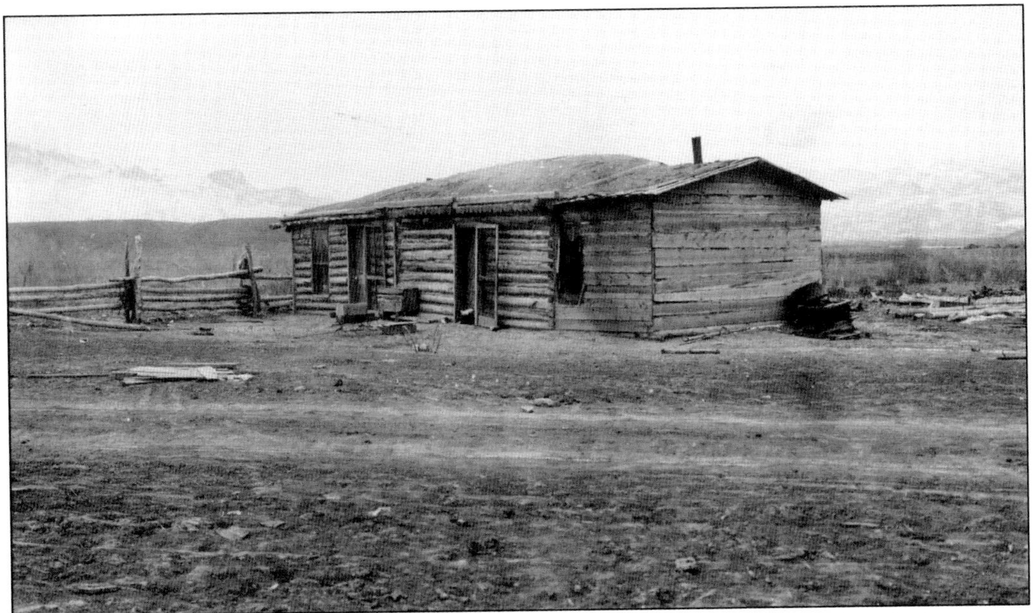

Before the completion of the Shoshone Dam, settlers lived, ranched, and farmed on the lands that would later be flooded. These settlers also established the small community of Marquette, which contained a store, saloon, and post office. The Reclamation Service portrayed these buildings as primitive dwellings standing in the way of progress that would follow the completion of the Shoshone Project. The cabin pictured above belonged to Edward Grinder. Grinder received $17,000 from the Reclamation Service for the loss of his property. The cabin in the photograph below belonged to B. F. Martin, who received $18,000 for the loss of his land. The buildings in the town of Marquette and these dwellings were removed before the filling of the reservoir. (Both SIDA.)

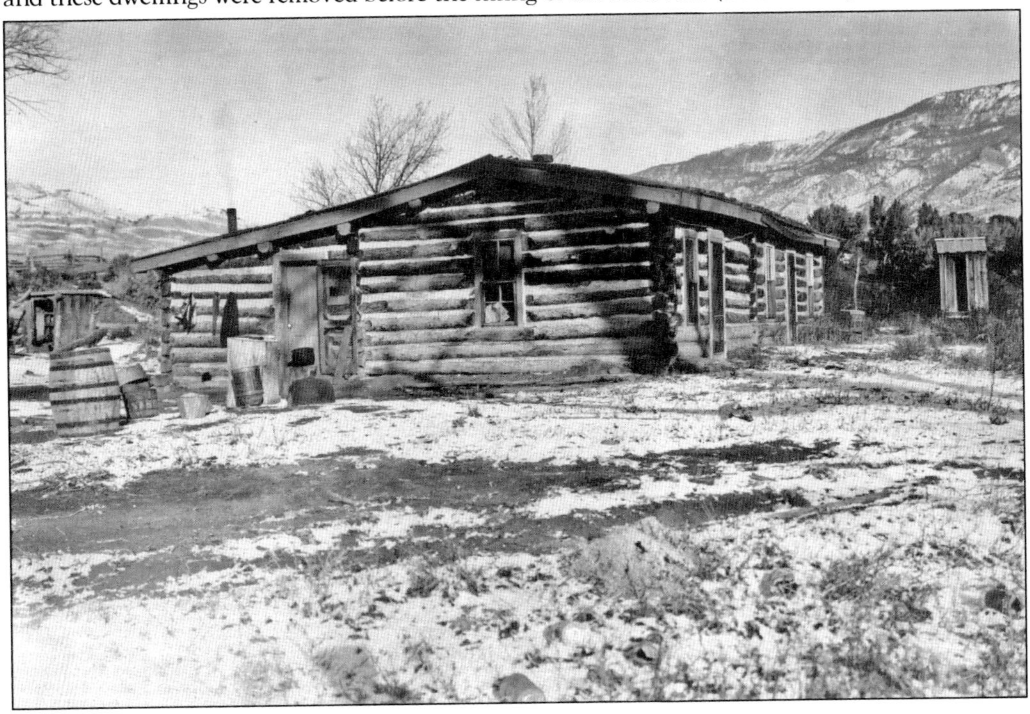

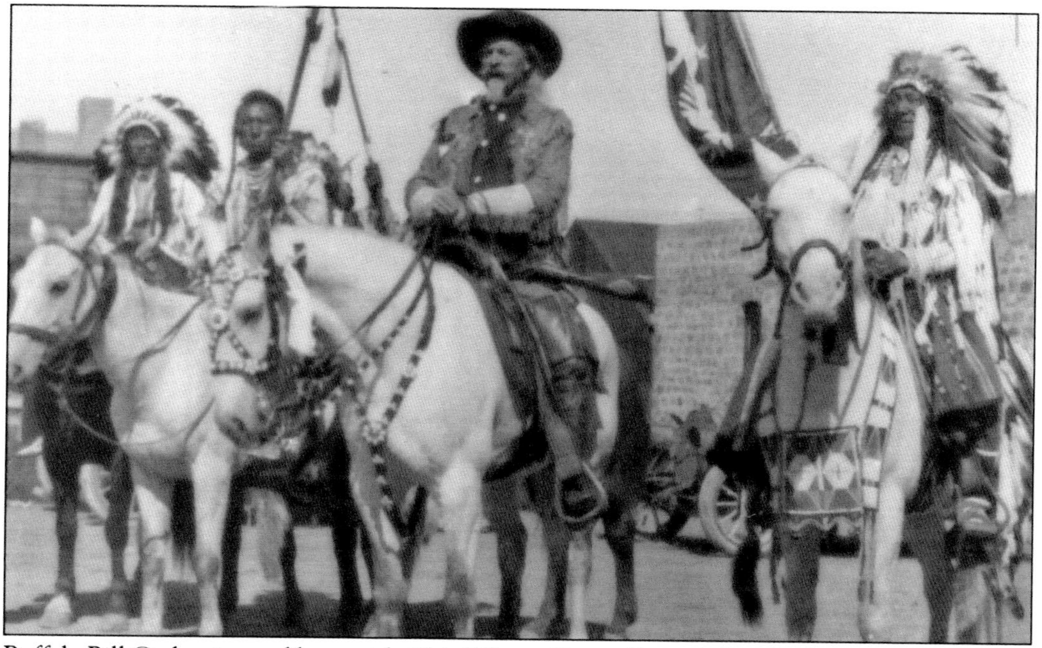

Buffalo Bill Cody, pictured here with Chief Plenty Coups (far right) and other Crow dignitaries, promoted various irrigation schemes in the Bighorn Basin. In 1896, the town of Cody, pictured below, was founded and named in his honor. After struggling to complete the Cody Canal, which irrigated the arid lands around Cody, Buffalo Bill hoped to develop a reclamation project to irrigate the region around present-day Powell. He later turned a portion of his acreage over to Mormon settlers, and the remaining acres were returned back to the federal government. (Both PCA.)

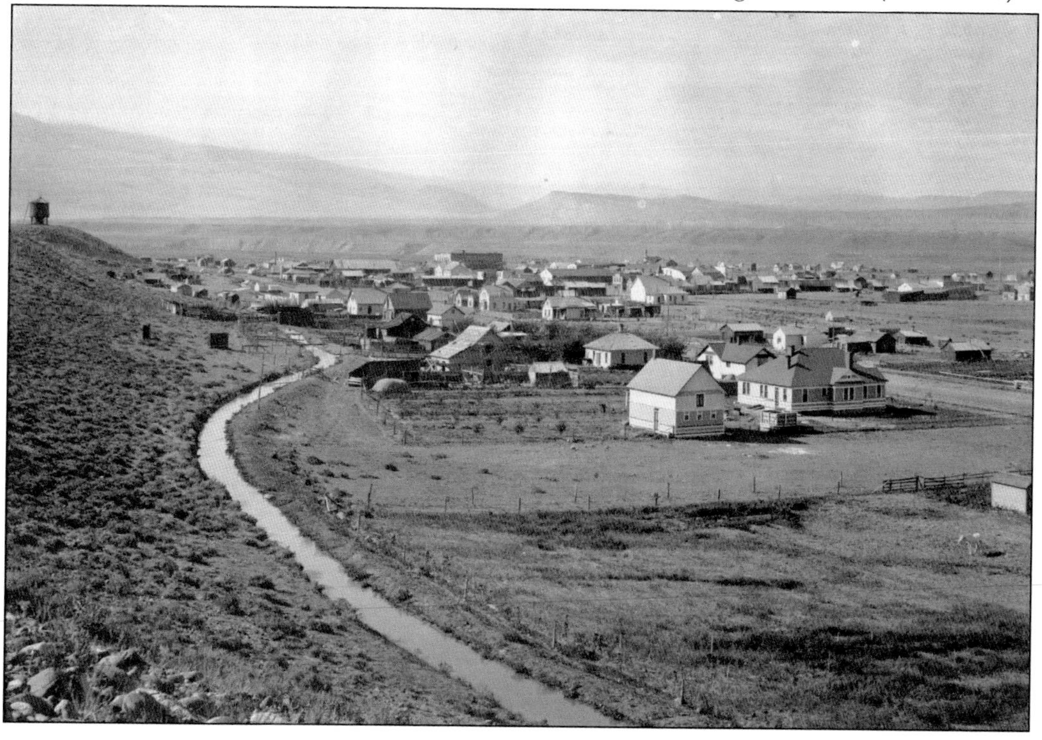

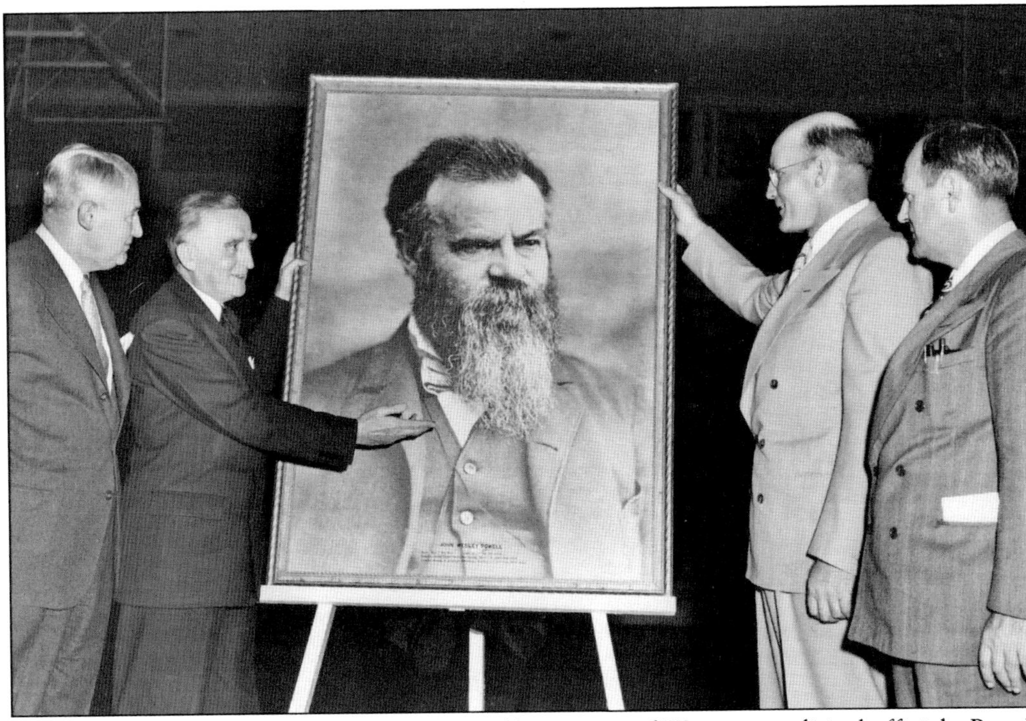

John Wesley Powell's portrait is being admired by a group of Wyoming political officials. Powell became famous after his rafting trip down the Colorado River in the Grand Canyon in 1869. Although he never visited the Bighorn Basin, Powell, Wyoming, was named in his honor because of his recommendation that the federal government fund and develop reclamation projects in the West. (PCA.)

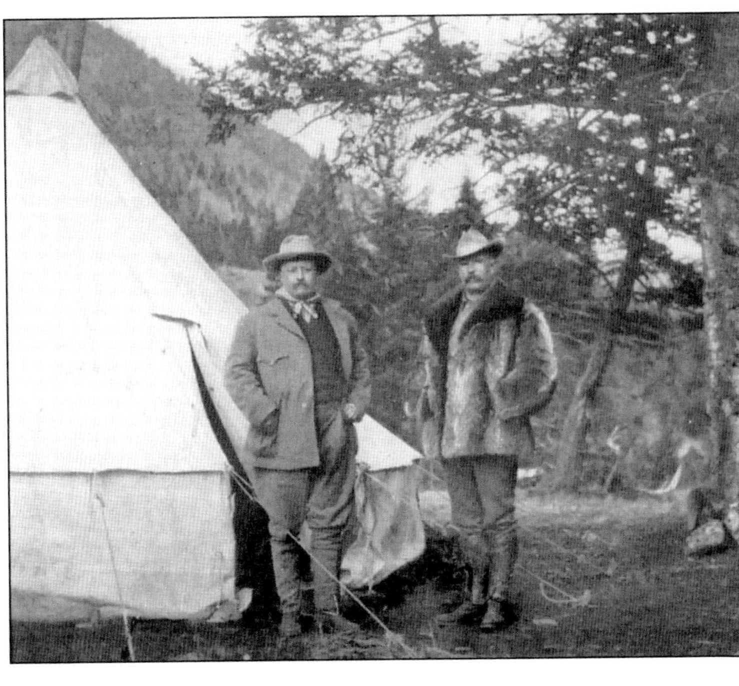

In 1902, Theodore Roosevelt signed into law the National Reclamation Act, named the Newlands Act after the sponsor of the bill, Francis Newlands. The Newlands Act generated the Reclamation Service, later to be named the Bureau of Reclamation, and the funding necessary to begin the Shoshone Project in 1904. Roosevelt is pictured here with Maj. John Pitcher on a trip through Yellowstone National Park in 1903. (Author's collection.)

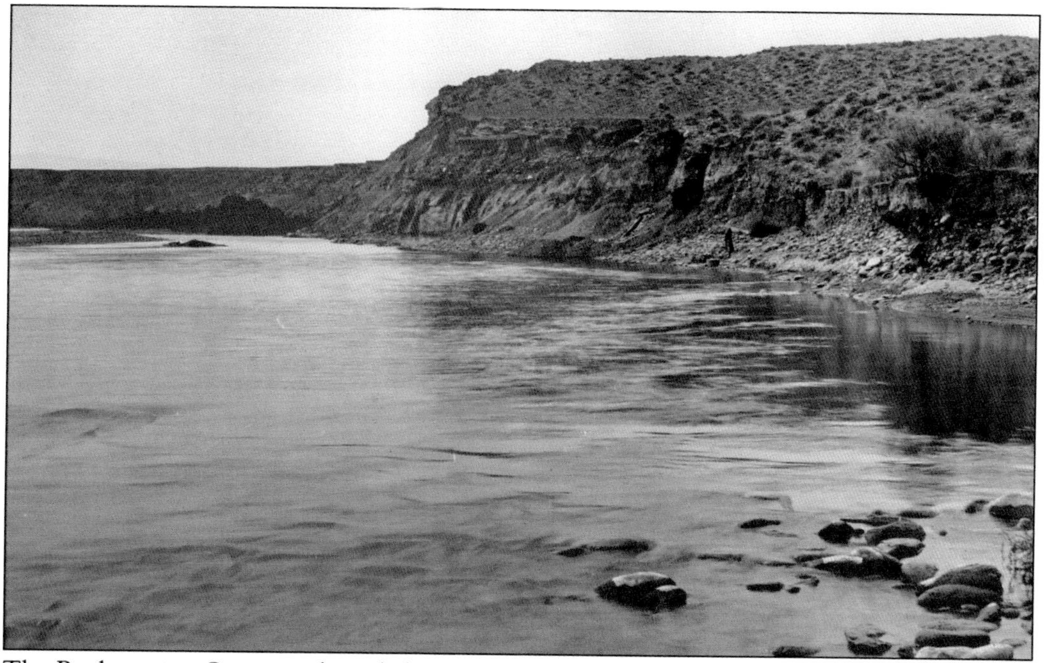

The Reclamation Service selected this site on the Shoshone River in 1904 to construct the Corbett Dam. The dam would divert water from the river into a 3-mile-long tunnel that would pour into the Garland Canal for the Garland and Frannie Divisions. Water from the canal would be spread across the arid lands through ditches. (SIDA.)

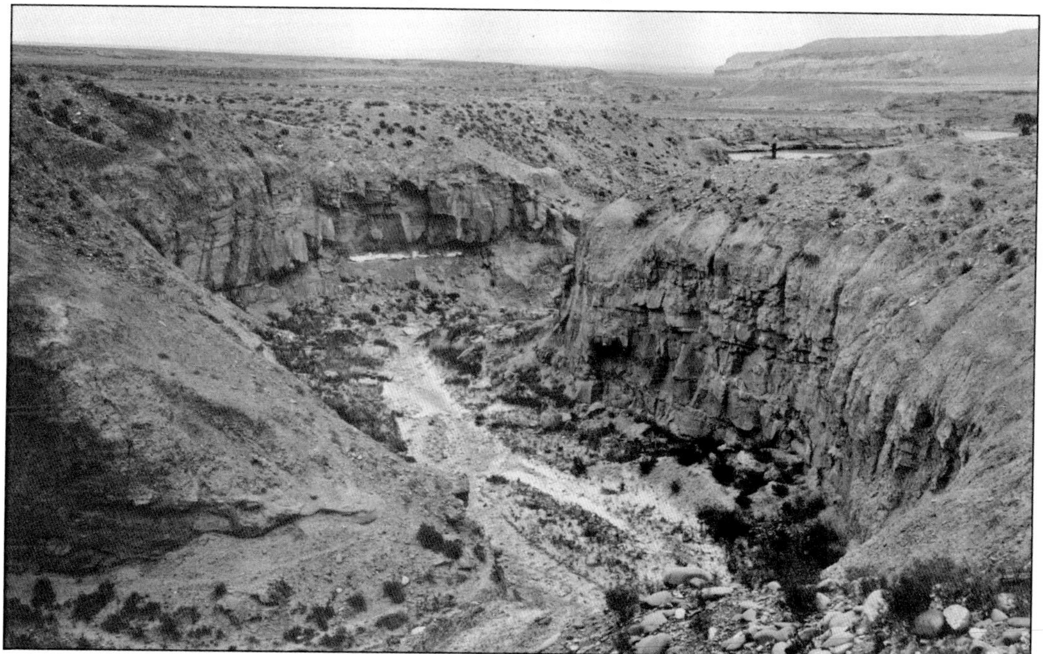

The Reclamation Service decided this natural outlet would make a good settling basin for the Corbett Dam. This image also illustrates the arid nature of the lands along the Shoshone River. The name Corbett came from John Corbett, who ran a roadhouse located 1 mile upstream from the dam site. (SIDA.)

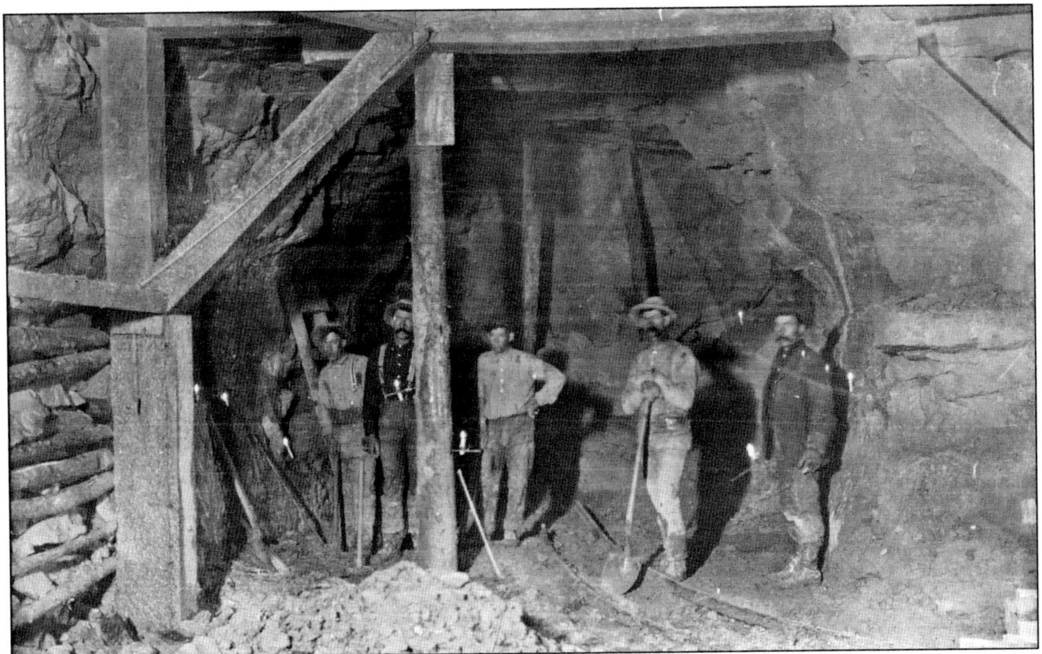

Working for $2.50 to $3 per day, workers excavated the 3-mile-long Corbett Tunnel, which diverted water from the Shoshone River for the Garland Division. In the above photograph, workers clean up the rubble in an adit using only shovels. In 1906, a photographer captured a piece of equipment known as the "Park Ore Loader" used to excavate more dirt from the tunnel. The sound of this machinery echoing off the tunnel walls must have been deafening. (Both SIDA.)

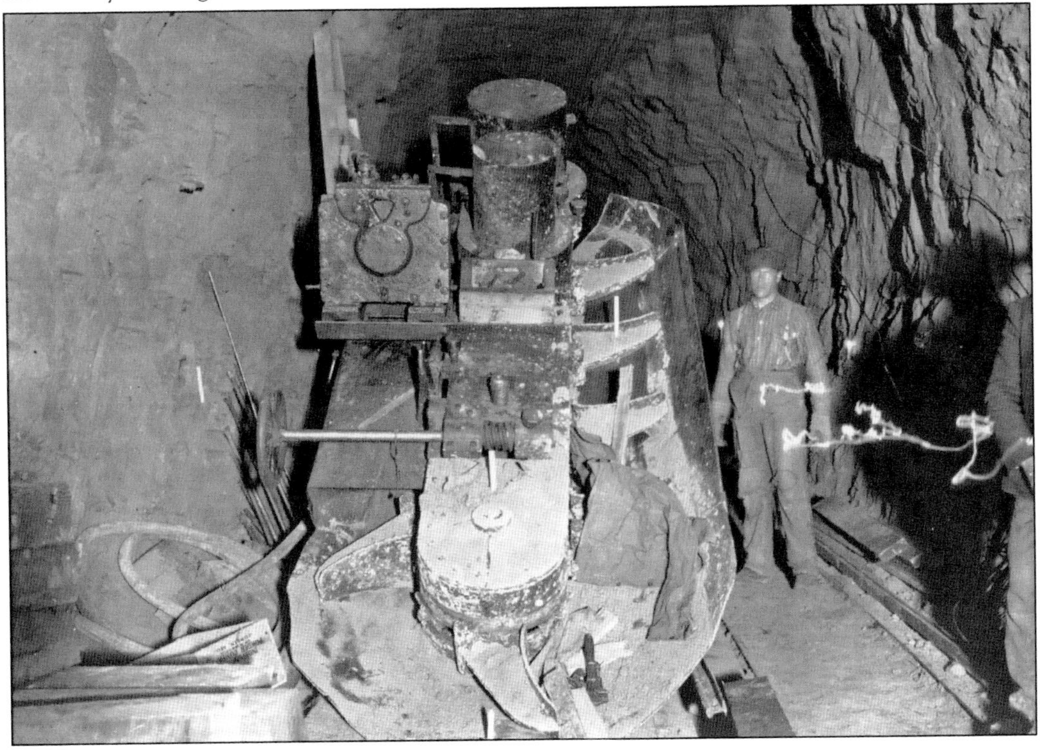

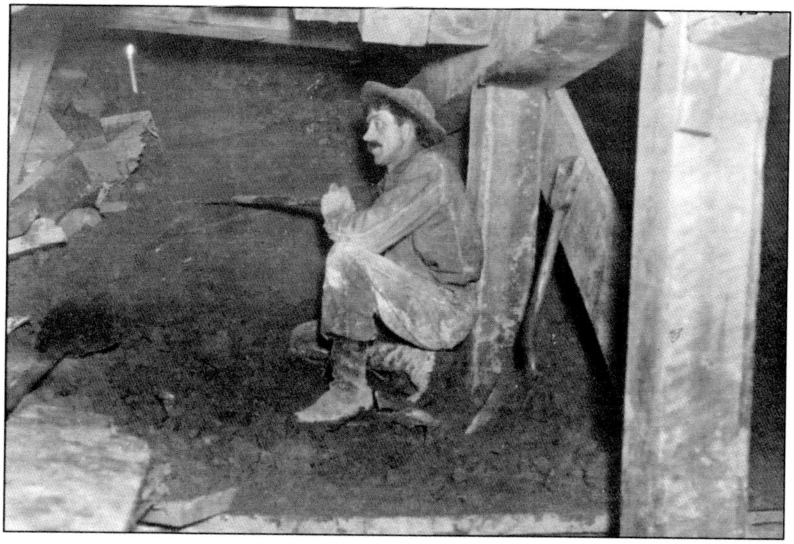

Collapsed earth remains from an accident that occurred on September 25, 1906. Tunneling through the soft dirt clearly posed a great danger of cave-ins. Note the large wooden beams used to support the tunnel. Surprisingly no workers lost their lives constructing the tunnel or Corbett Dam. (SIDA.)

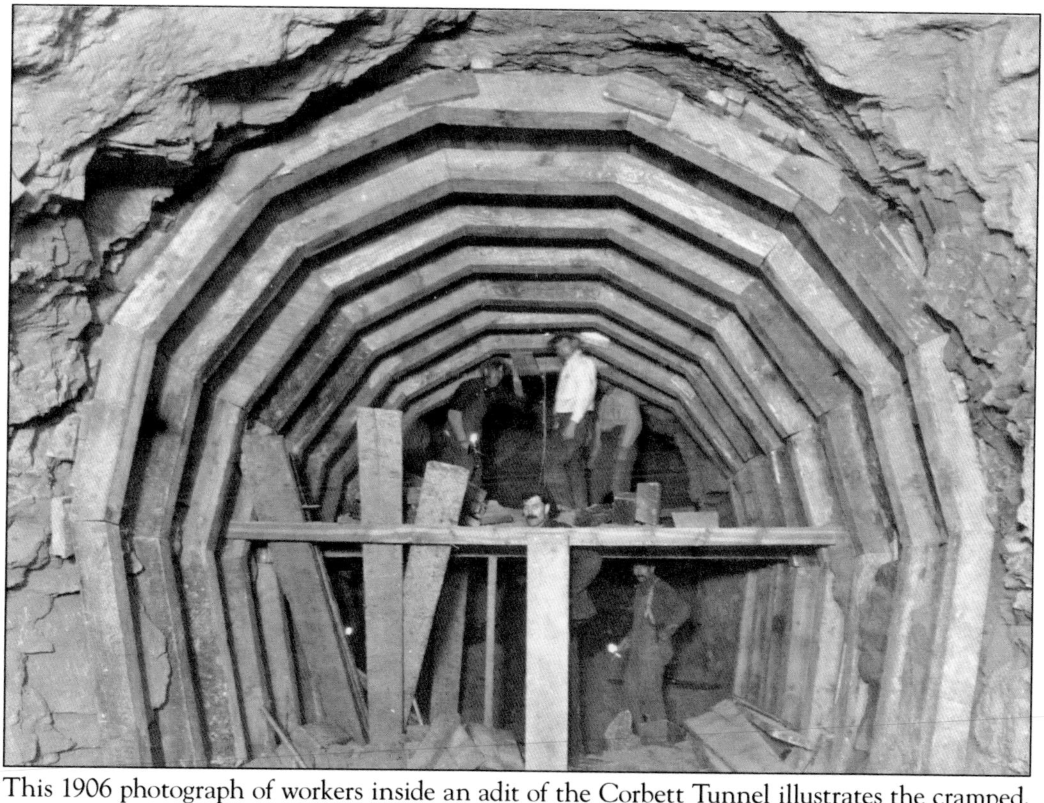

This 1906 photograph of workers inside an adit of the Corbett Tunnel illustrates the cramped, dark working conditions, as well as the extensive timbering system used to support the tunnel. (SIDA.)

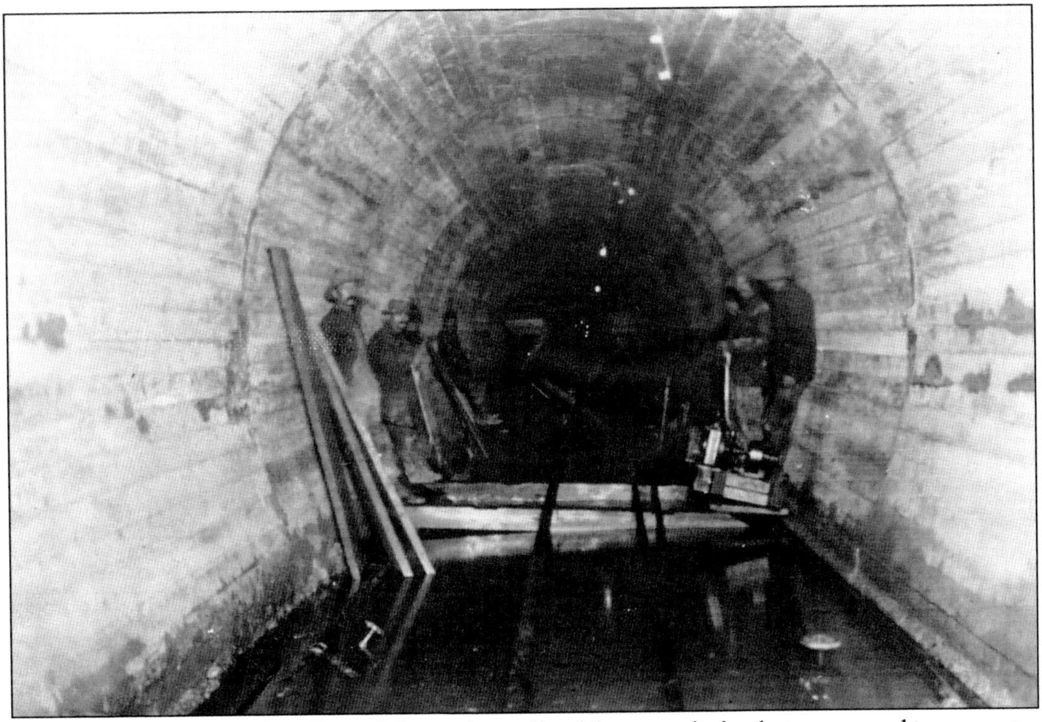

This photograph of Corbett Tunnel shows the walls of the tunnel after being covered in concrete. The caption of this image noted the tunnel flooded one week before. Notice the standing water on the floor. (SIDA.)

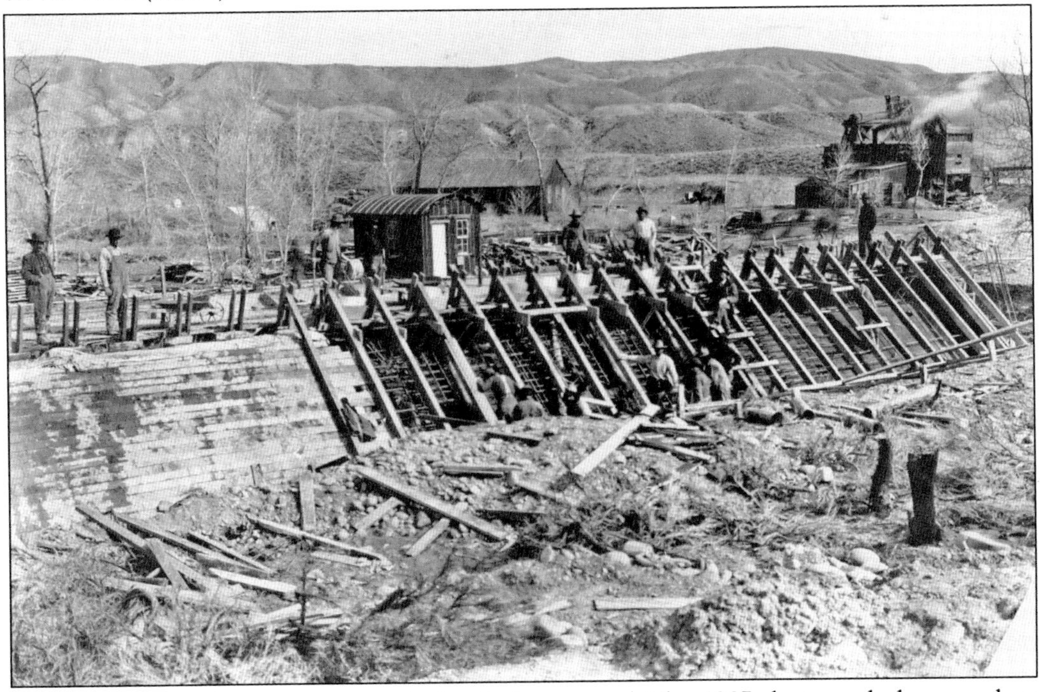

The Corbett Dam diverts water into the 3-mile-long tunnel. This 1907 photograph shows workers constructing the weir of the dam. (SIDA.)

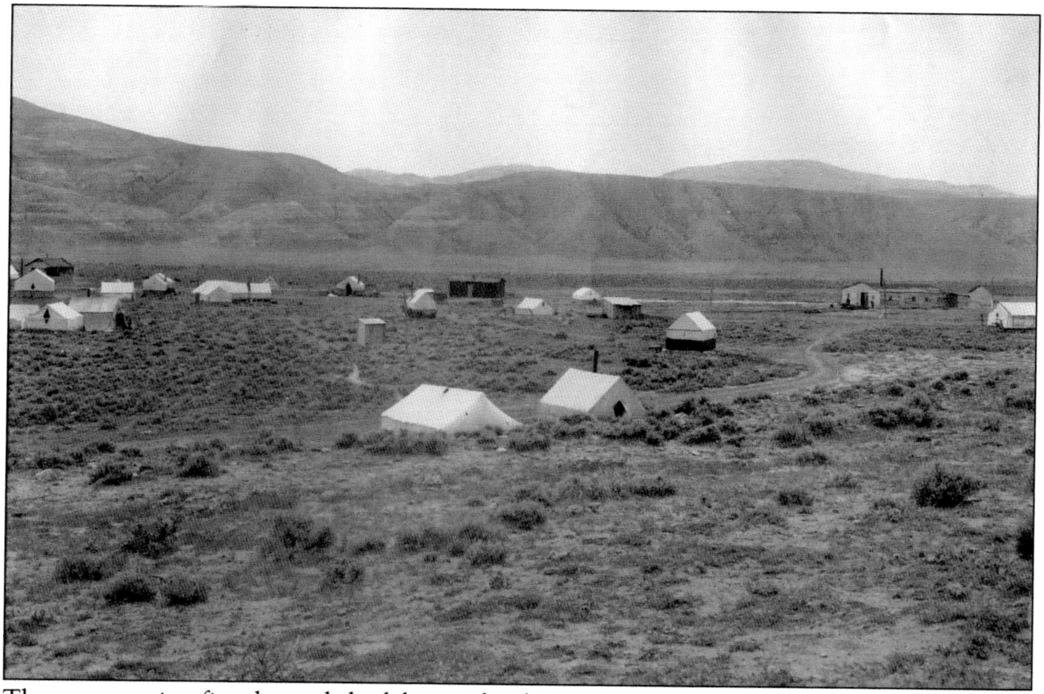

The construction firm housed the laborers for the Corbett Dam and Tunnel in tents. Workers were segregated by their ethnicity and marital status. The cluster of tents pictured above is the bachelor's camp. The photograph below depicts the Italian quarter of the construction camp. All workers adhered to strict rules, such as not spitting on the floors of any building in the camp. (Both SIDA.)

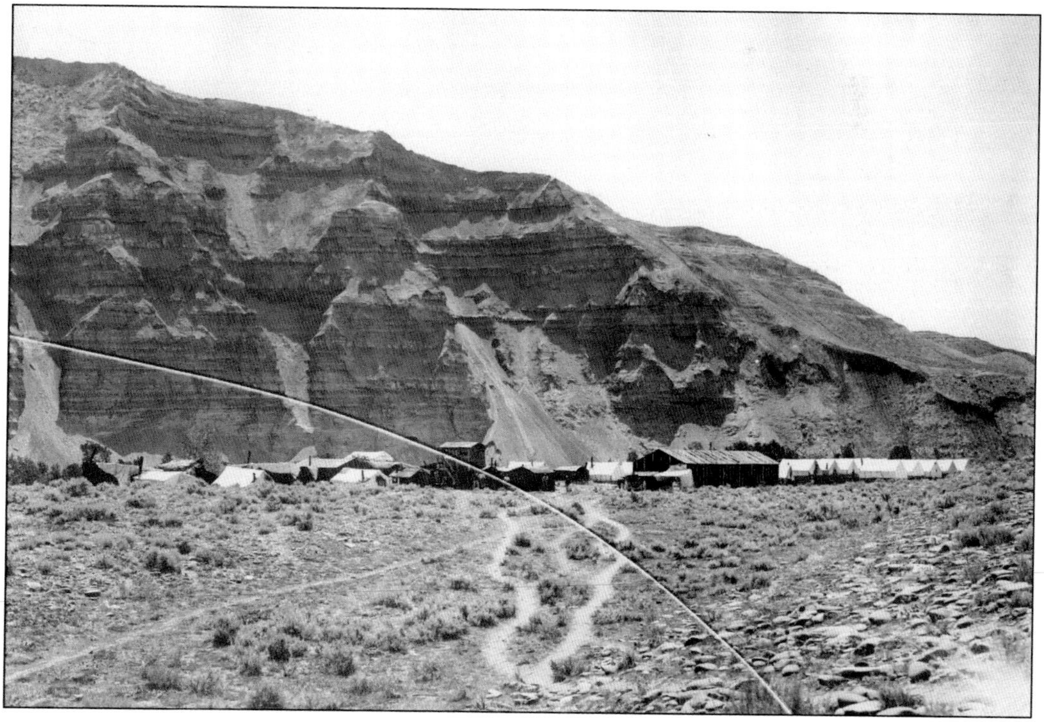

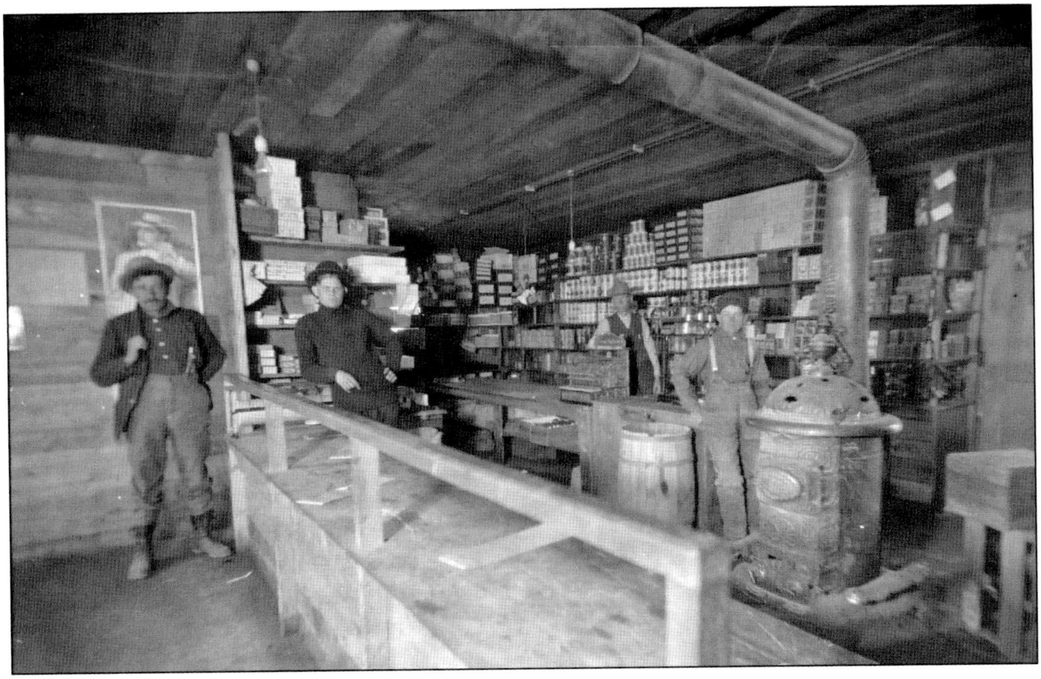

Due to the isolation of the Corbett Dam site, workers relied on the commissary for groceries, clothing, and other supplies. These photographs taken in 1907 illustrate the wide selection offered by the commissary. Note the advertisement of the well-dressed man hanging on the wall in the above photograph. This image seems out of place when compared to the photograph below of two men standing behind a table stacked high with pairs of work pants. (Both SIDA.)

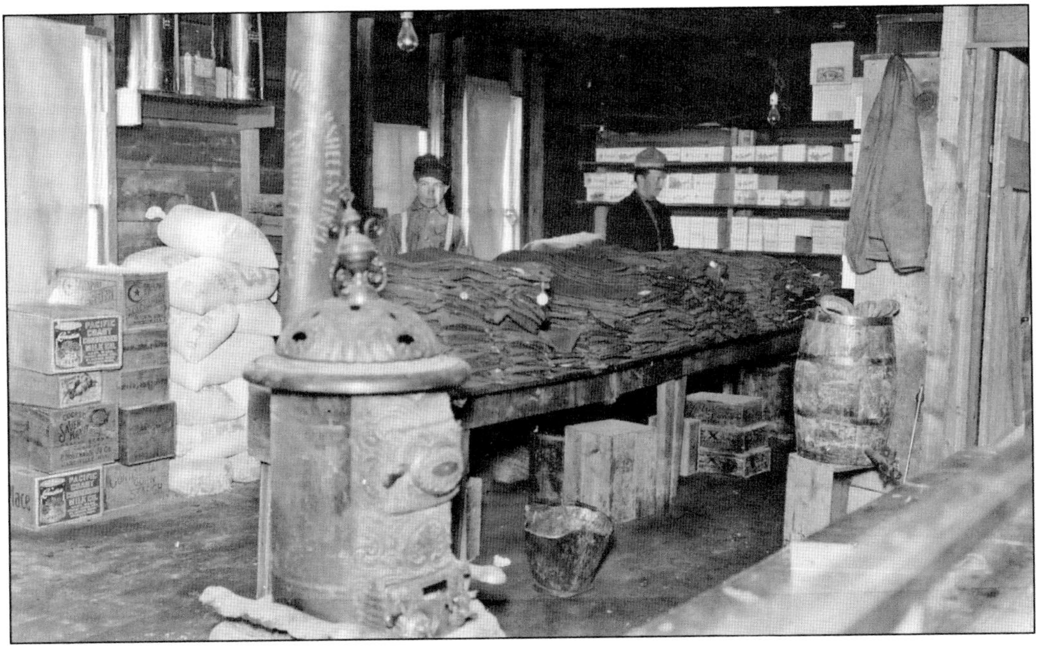

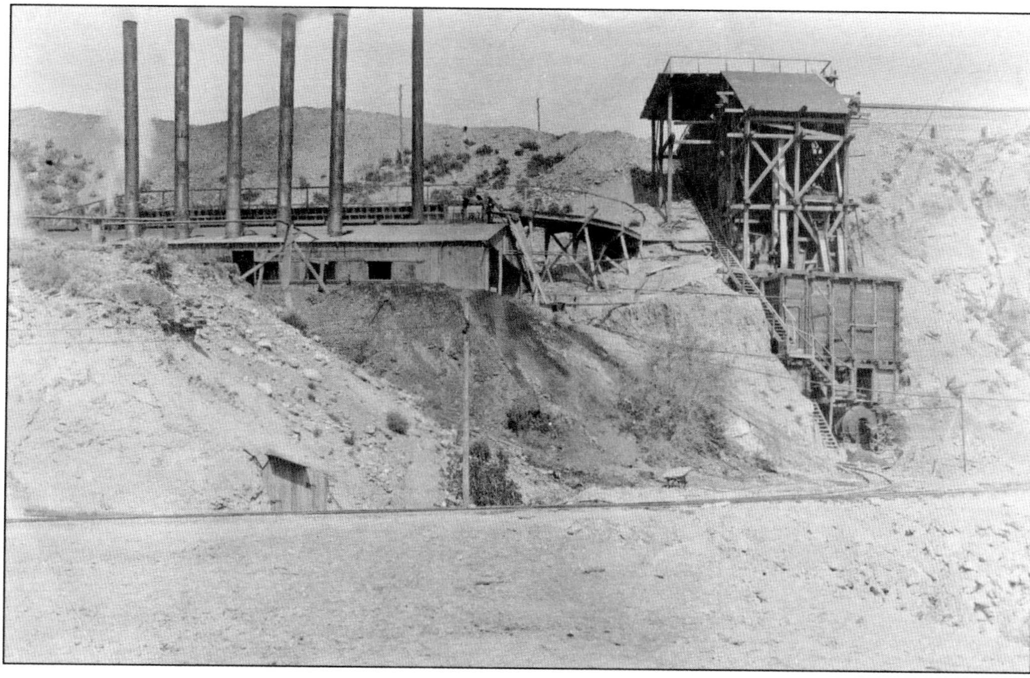

To complete the Corbett Dam and Tunnel, a vast amount of concrete was needed. The photograph above shows the concrete plant near adit number one. Note the long staircase ranging from the track to the top of the plant. The photograph below shows the steam engines within the power plant. (Both SIDA.)

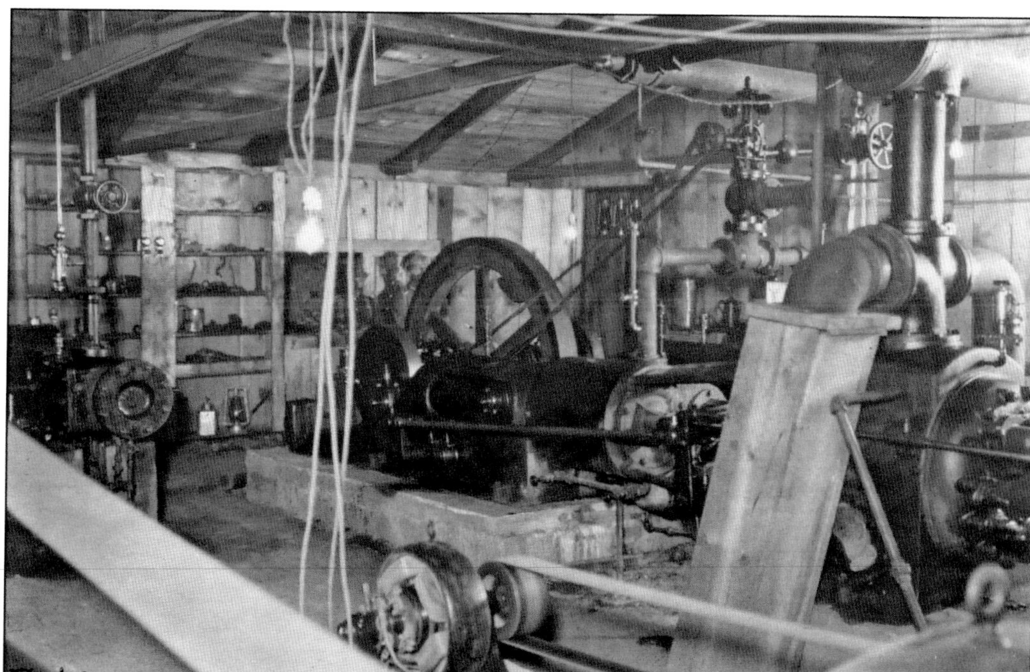

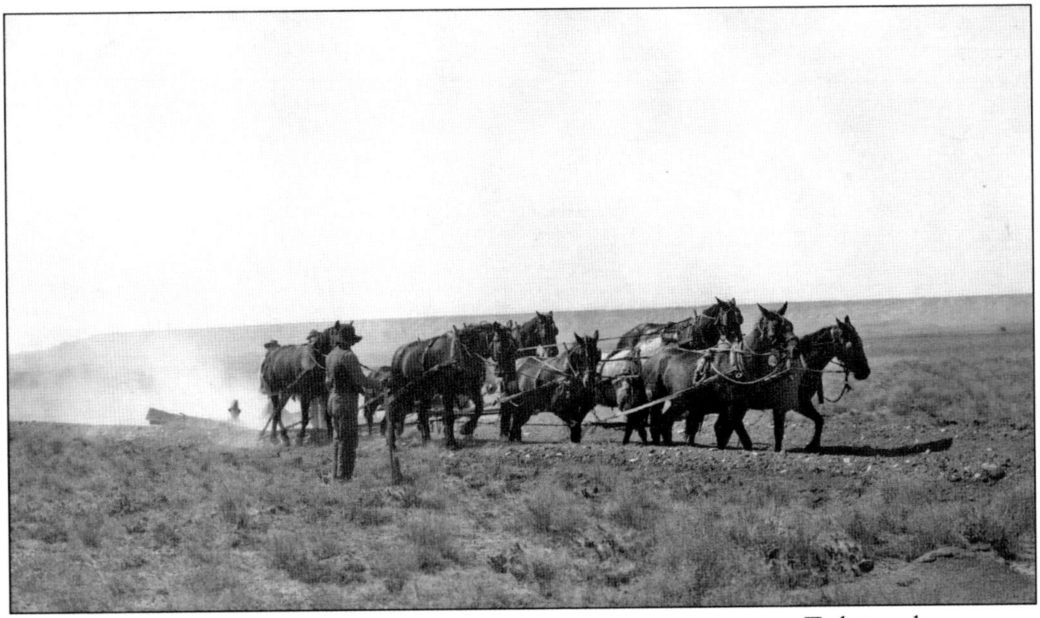

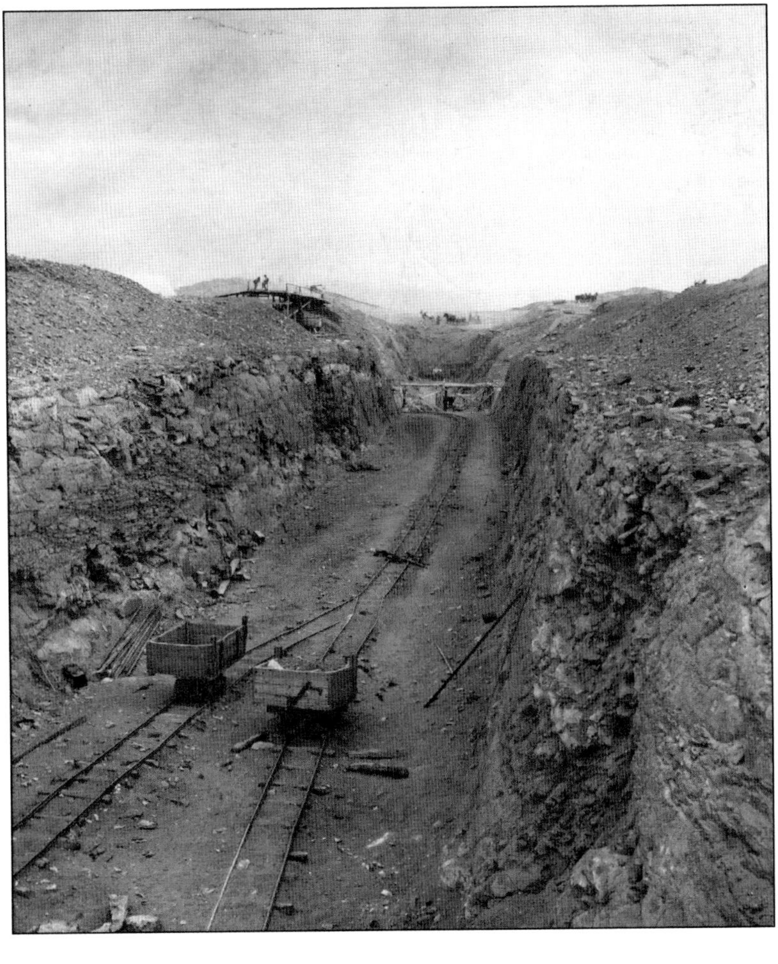

To bring the water from the end of the Corbett Tunnel to the lands of the Garland Division, a canal needed to be dug with manpower and horsepower. The above photograph captures a ditching machine in action. At left, workers dig away at a cut for the canal. (Both SIDA.)

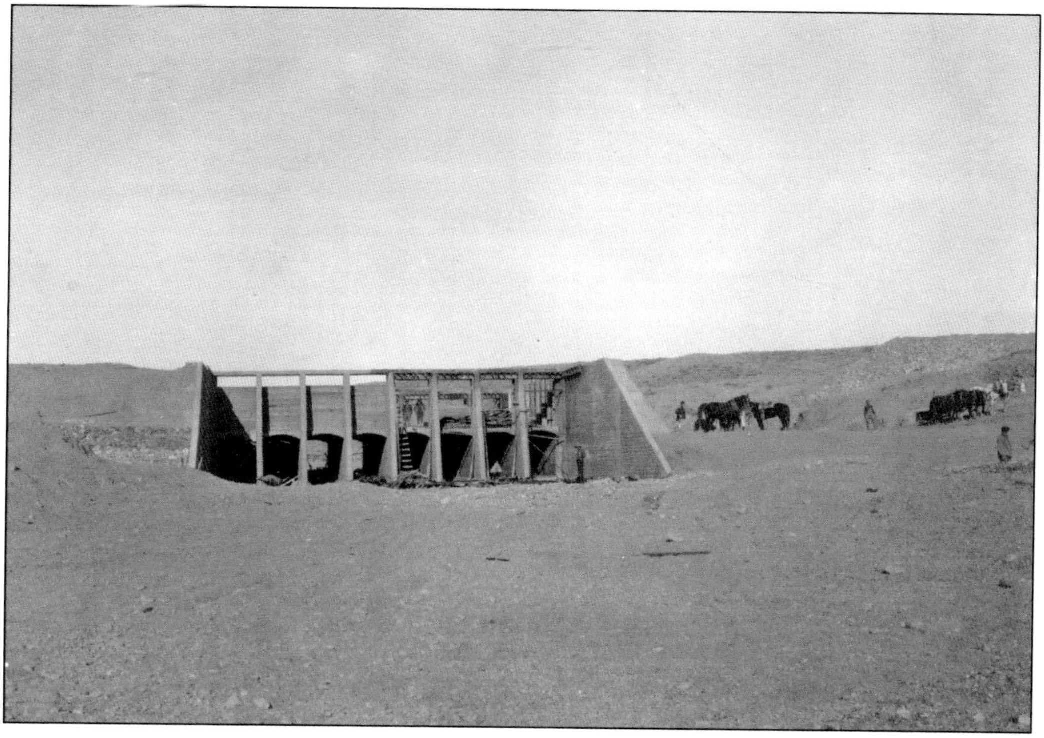

To complete the canal, aqueducts to cross streams needed to be constructed. The above image shows Eaglenest Crossing under construction in 1908, which brought the canal over Eaglenest Creek. A smaller camp housed the workers and engineers of this canal. The photograph below shows the engineer's office building in 1907. (Both SIDA.)

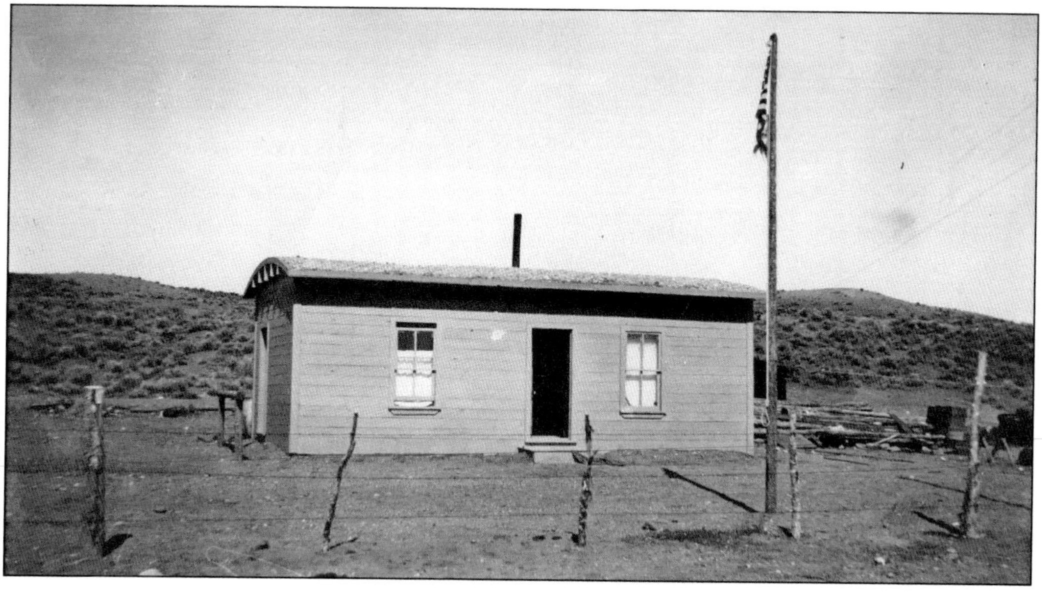

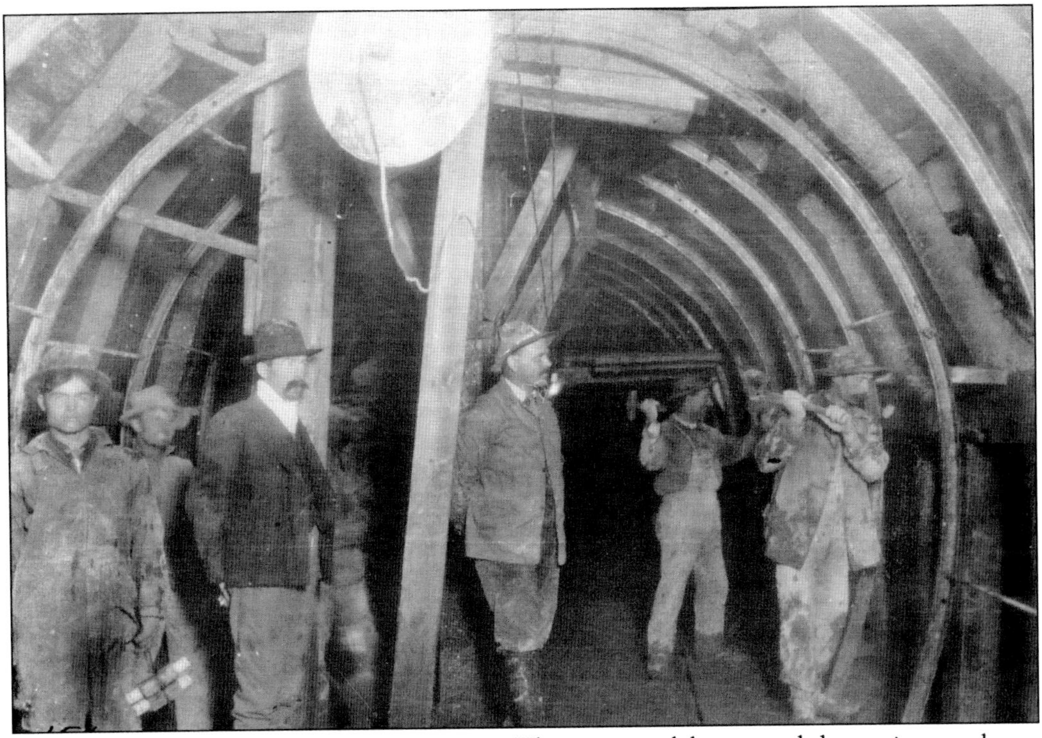

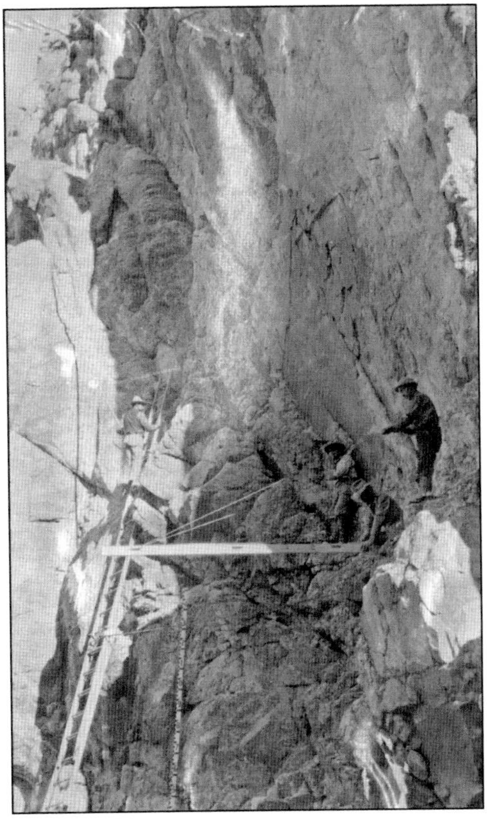

The common laborers and the engineers who worked on the Shoshone Project were the true unsung heroes of the day. The willingness of the men to work in cramped, dirty conditions, as demonstrated in the above image, ensured water would be diverted to the arid landscape. The willingness of the project's engineers to place themselves in dangerous situations, as pictured at left, allowed them to successfully oversee an amazing feat of engineering. (Both SIDA.)

After the first construction company defaulted, the second contracting firm finished the Corbett Dam in 1908. The cost of the Corbett Dam and Corbett Tunnel totaled $97,467. On April 27, 1908, water was turned into the tunnel and delivered to the Garland Division. Eager homesteaders could now farm the arid lands. (SIDA.)

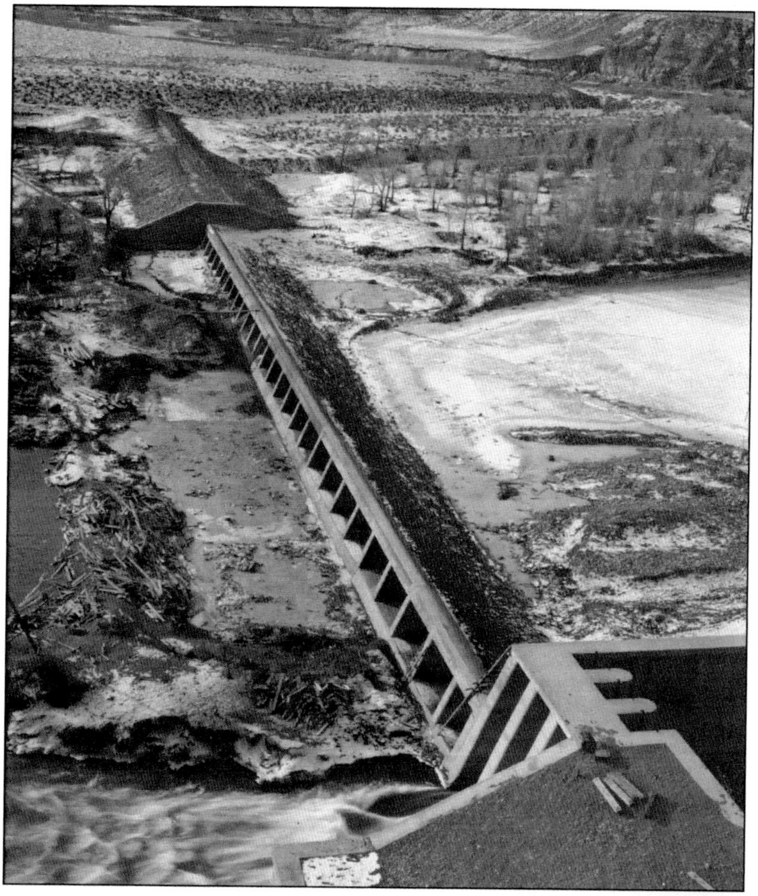

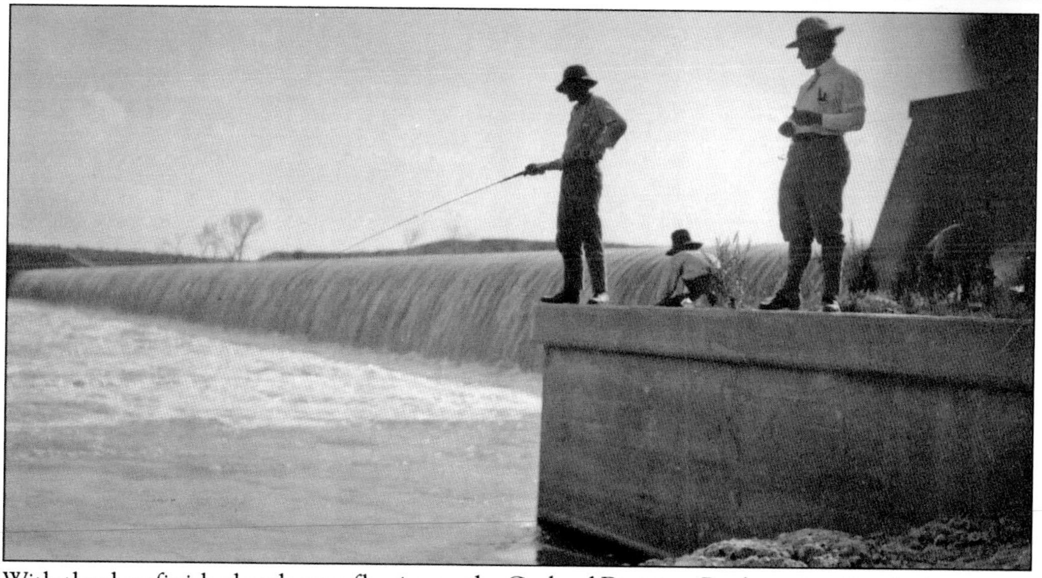

With the dam finished and water flowing to the Garland Division, Reclamation Service inspectors found time to fish. This photograph shows three Reclamation Service employees trying their luck at fishing from the Corbett Dam. (SIDA.)

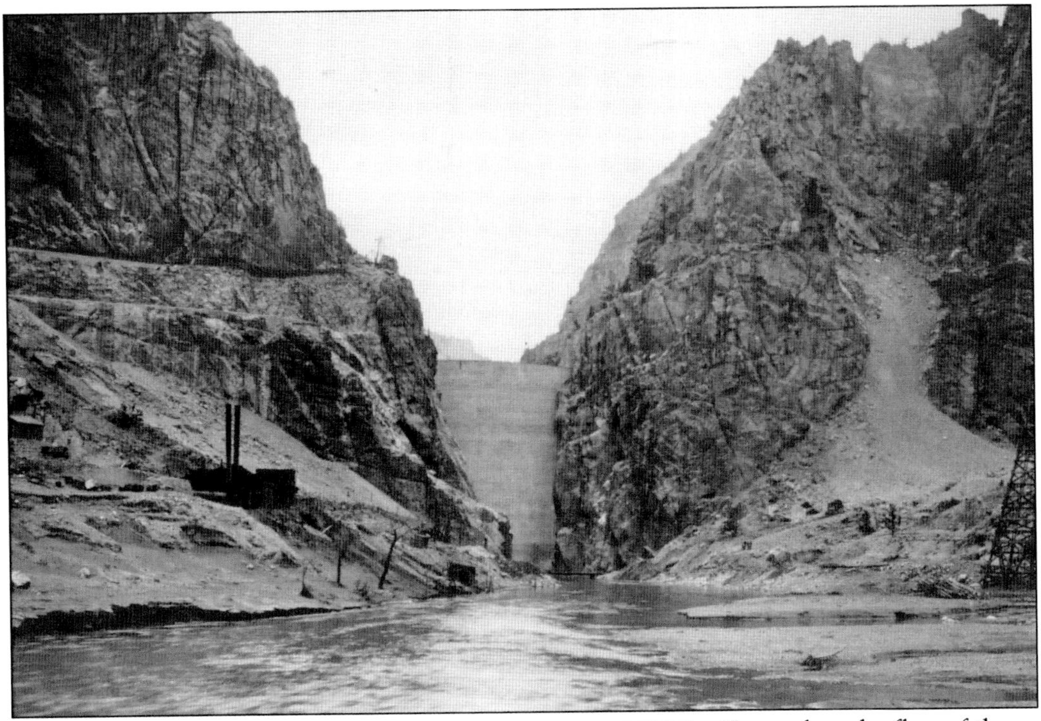

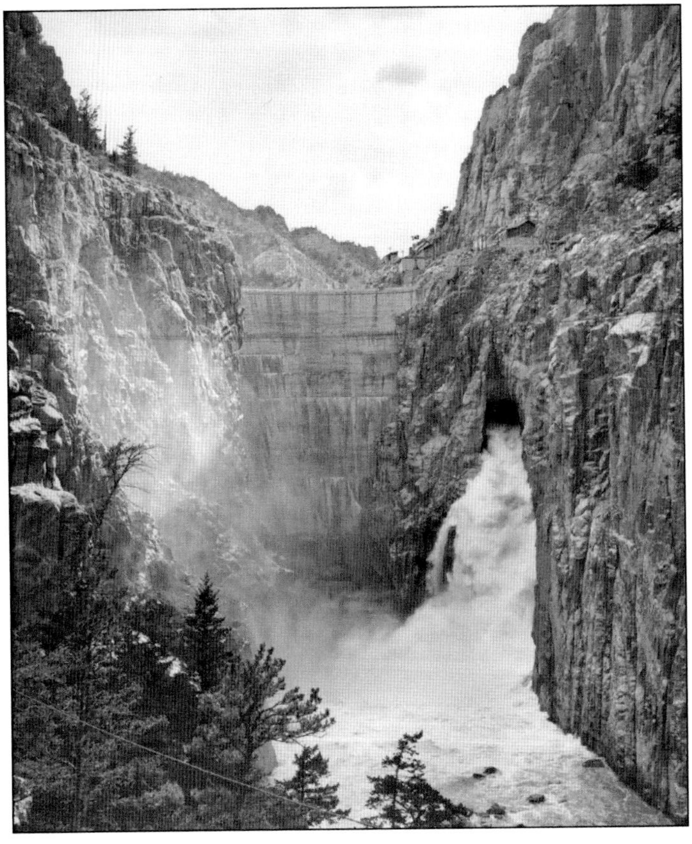

To regulate the flow of the Shoshone River and to store water for use downstream, the Reclamation Service began working on the Shoshone Dam in 1905. The dam was completed on January 15, 1910, at a total cost of $929,658. Three contracting firms went bankrupt constructing the dam, and seven workers lost their lives. The above photograph shows the dam looking downstream before the reservoir filled with water. The photograph at left shows the completed dam looking upstream with water flowing from the other side of the dam through the spillway. In 1946, the Shoshone Dam was renamed Buffalo Bill Dam. (Above, SIDA; at left, PCA.)

Three

Homesteaders Arrive and Powell Is Born

On April 27, 1908, water flowed from the Shoshone River through the Corbett Tunnel into the Garland Canal for the first time. The Reclamation Service offered the first homestead entries to potential settlers. Mostly individuals from professional occupations such as lawyers, doctors, photographers, and teachers composed the first group of settlers moving into the Garland Division. The Burlington and Missouri River Railroad built a railroad line from Toluca, Montana, to Cody, Wyoming, in 1901, allowing the homesteaders to arrive by train. Even with rail service to the growing division and a ready supply of water to irrigate crops, homesteading the Powell flat still proved to be a difficult process. Building a new home in a treeless and desolate landscape, in addition to learning the fine art of irrigating crops, challenged many of these modern homesteaders. Despite these obstacles, many homesteaders established successful farms; some continued to be farmed for many generations by the same family. Many assumed the communities of Garland, 5 miles east of Powell, and Ralston, 5 miles west of Powell, would now boom due to the increased numbers of settlers; however, Camp Colter soon became the town of Powell, quickly deflating any hopes of an improved economy or increased population for Garland and Ralston.

Established in 1907, Camp Colter provided housing to Reclamation Service employees and the railroad soon added a siding for the camp. Due to its central location within the Garland Division, businessmen, settlers, and the Reclamation Service believed it to be a good site for a town. Buffalo Bill Cody and the Lincoln Land Company, under the auspices of the Burlington and Missouri River Railroad, owned property in Garland and Ralston. Both pulled a number of political strings attempting to keep Camp Colter from becoming a town. Buffalo Bill tried to enlist Theodore Roosevelt's support in his efforts to squelch Powell; however, by that time Roosevelt had tired of Buffalo Bill's numerous political requests and did not intervene. In 1908, a post office was established but due to another railroad siding with the name Colter, the name Powell, in honor of John Wesley Powell, was substituted. On May 25, 1909, the Reclamation Service sold town lots, and by May 10, 1910, Powell was officially incorporated as a town by the State of Wyoming.

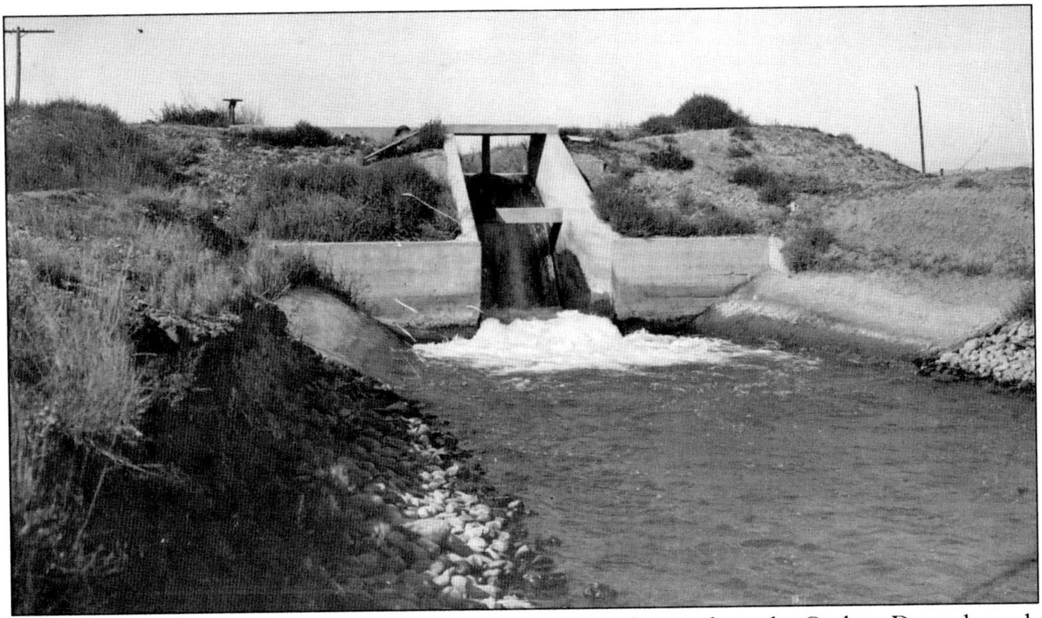

On April 27, 1908, the Reclamation Service turned diverted water from the Corbett Dam, through the Corbett Tunnel, and into the Garland Canal. This water proved to be the lifeblood of the future community of Powell. With abundant water, homesteaders transformed the arid sagebrush flats into irrigated farm plots that produced various crops during Wyoming's short growing season. With the success of the Garland Division, the Reclamation Service focused on opening new divisions surrounding the Powell area. The Frannie-Deaver Division opened to homesteaders in 1917; the Willwood Division opened in 1927; and the last division, the Heart Mountain Division, opened for homesteading in 1946 shortly after the end of World War II. (Both SIDA.)

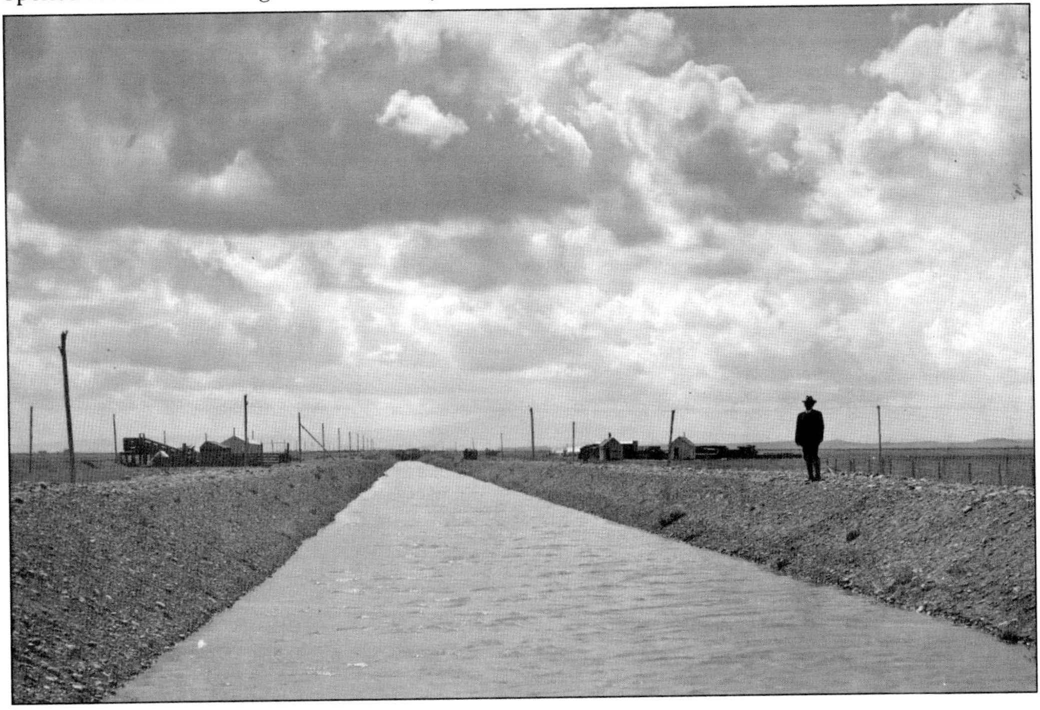

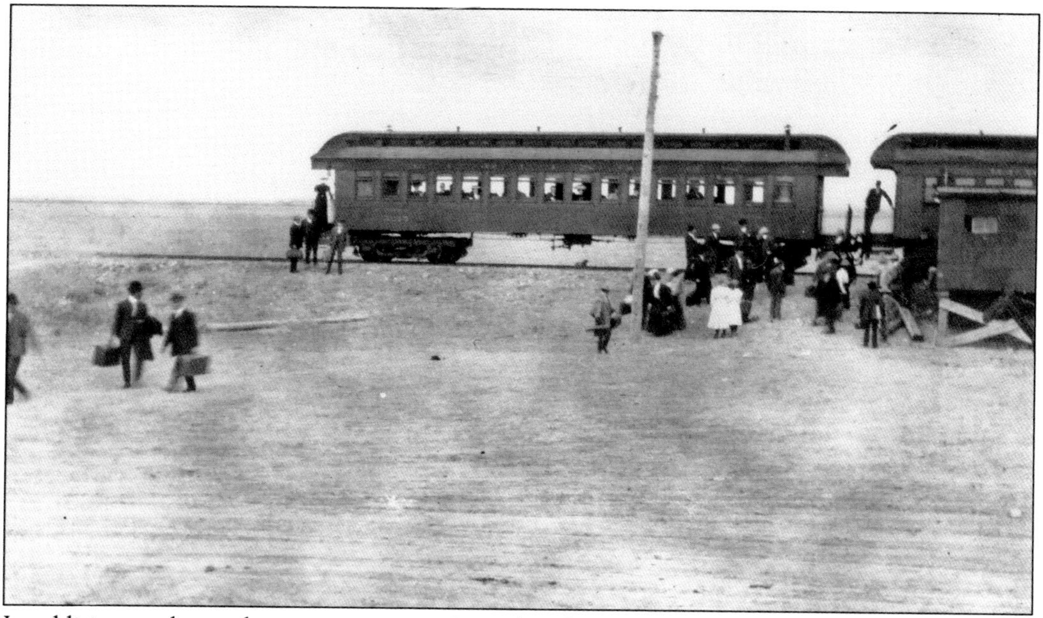

In addition to the ready access to water, the railroad assisted settlers in establishing their farms and businesses. Most homesteaders of the Garland Division arrived to their new home by train. The railroad connection not only brought new families to the area, it also provided goods and services from distant regions. The railroad hauled lumber, hardware, canned goods, and other groceries to homesteaders. After harvesting their crops, settlers could also ship their harvest to distant markets by rail. The image above captures settlers disembarking from the train. Below a train moves past a group of men building a home. (Both SIDA.)

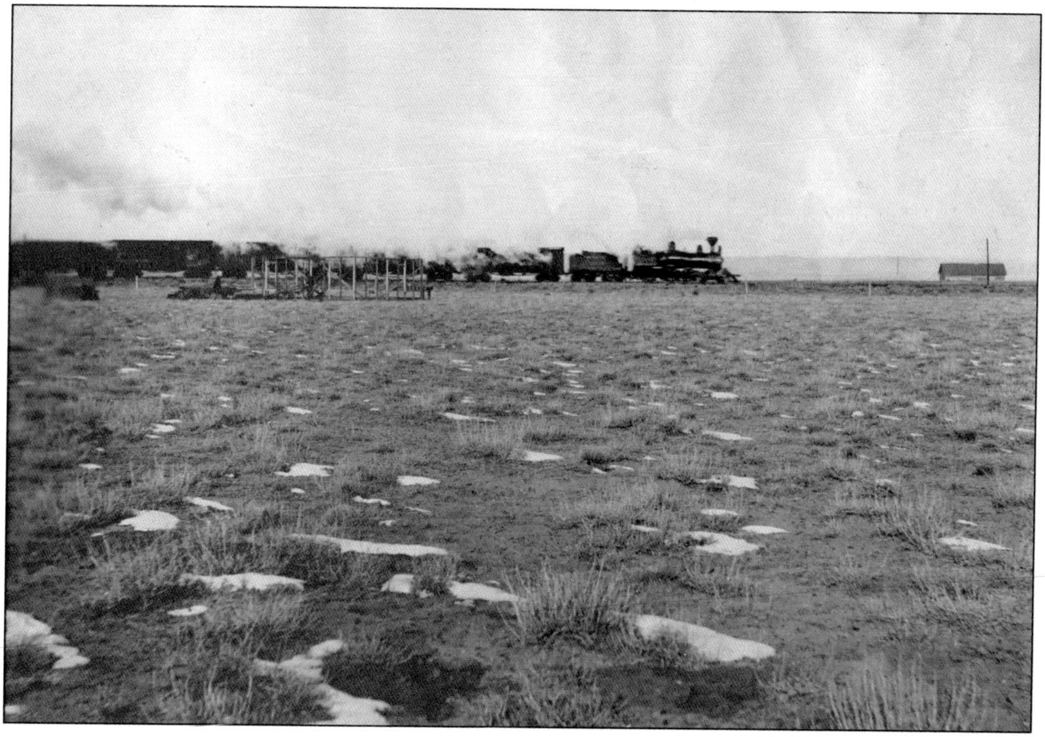

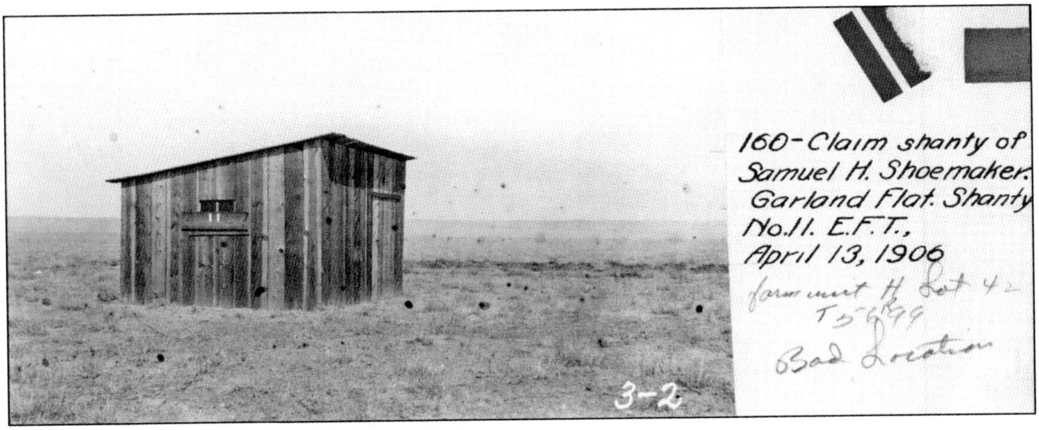

The Reclamation Service allowed homesteaders to apply for land entries in 1907, before the completion of the Corbett Project. Depicted in these two images are two claim shacks built in 1906 by early claimants. Although there appears to be little difference in these two shacks, a Reclamation Service official wrote on the side of the above photograph that this shack, built by Samuel Shoemaker, was in a "bad location." The same official noted on the photograph below that the shack built by William Shoemaker was located on "good" land. (Both SIDA.)

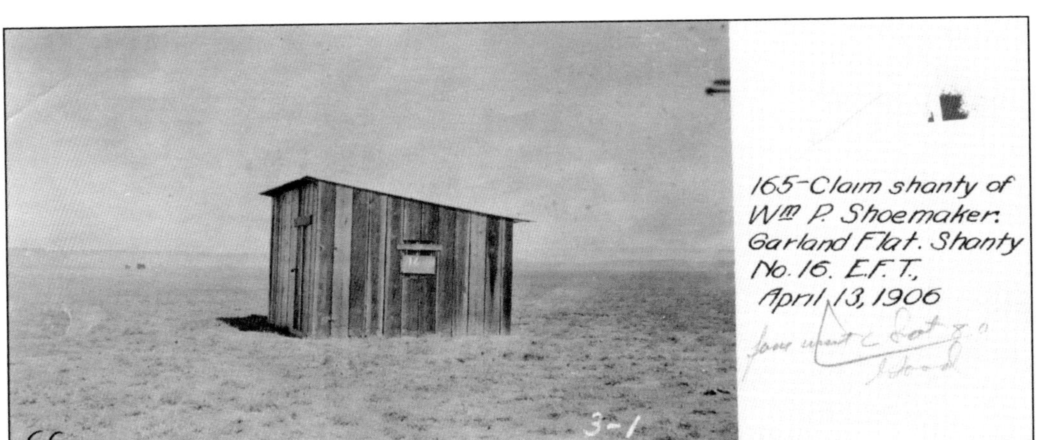

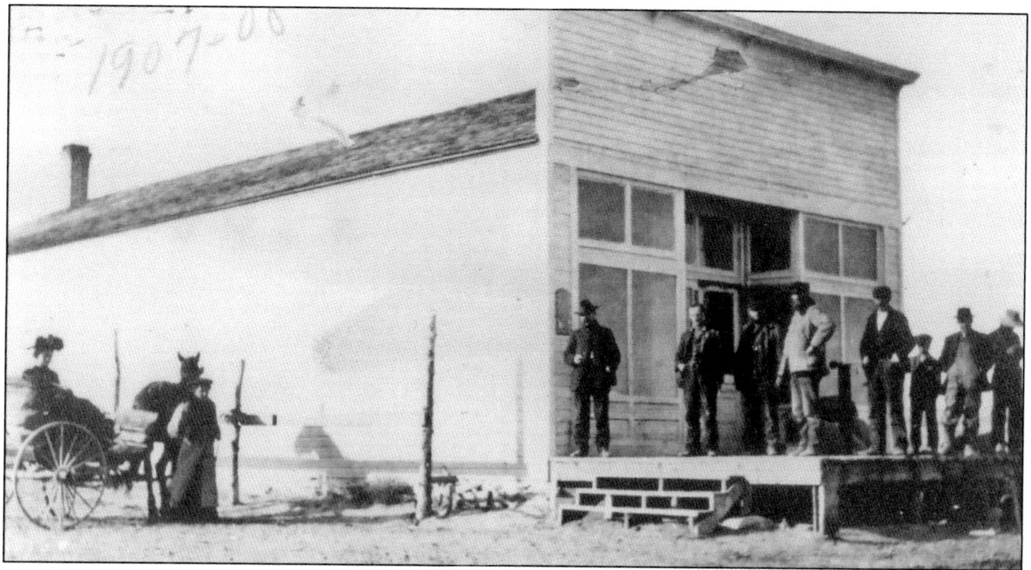

The settlement of Ralston, named after a local saloon keeper and located 5 miles west of Powell, sprung up along the tracks of the Burlington and Missouri River Railroad in 1901. Buffalo Bill Cody hoped Ralston would boom as a result of reclamation; thus allowing him to make some money from selling town lots that he owned to potential businesses. Unfortunately for Buffalo Bill and the residents of Ralston, the establishment of Powell greatly curtailed Ralston's future economic growth. This photograph shows a group gathering at A.P. Libby's store in Ralston. (PCA.)

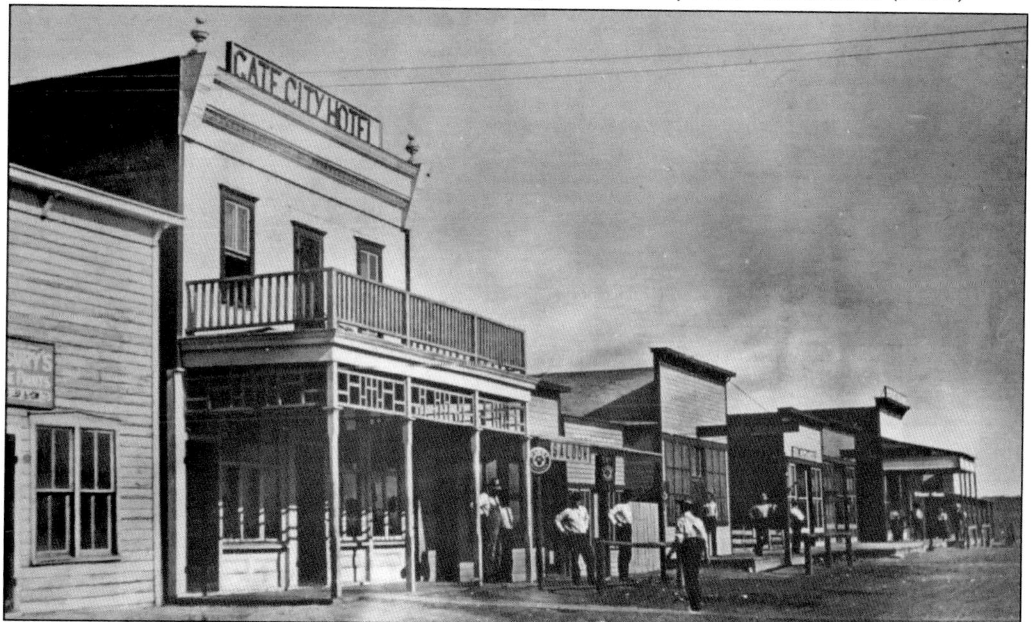

The settlement of Garland, possibly named after the Garland brothers who operated a freighting firm in the community, developed along the railroad 5 miles east of Powell. At its height, Garland supported 300 residents and offered a bank, two hotels, and a handful of saloons. Due to the Reclamation Service's policy of not allowing a saloon near one of their construction camps, temperance-minded businessmen and settlers preferred to conduct business in the more sober setting offered in Powell. Like Ralston, Garland's economic prosperity collapsed with the establishment of Powell. (PCA.)

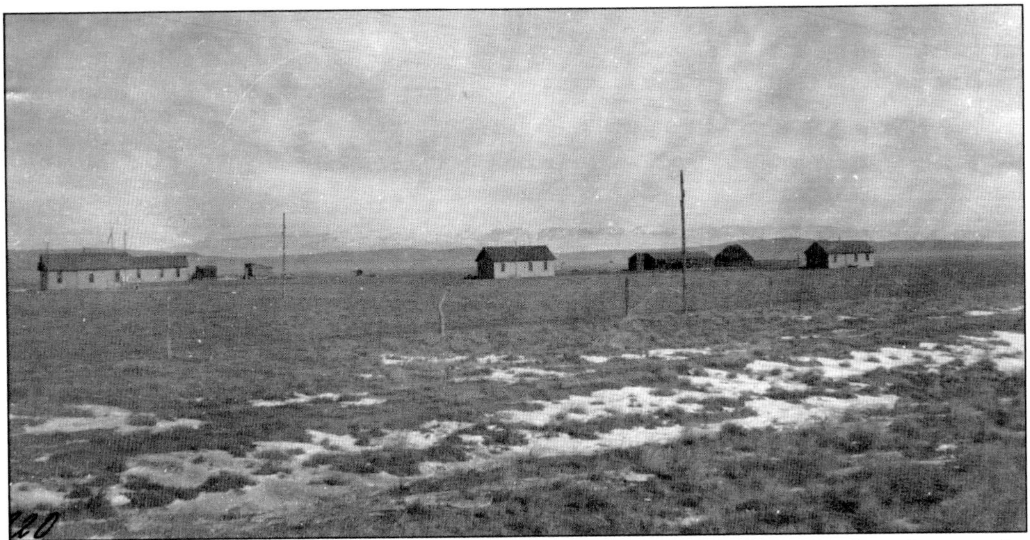

The Reclamation Service established Camp Colter in May 1906 to house workers digging the canal and ditches necessary to open the Garland Division. Camp Colter started as a "tent city" but soon acquired a sense of permanence as the Reclamation Service built a handful of wooden structures. Camp Colter also housed the Reclamation Service's Shoshone Project headquarters building, from which settlers and businessmen would vie for homesteads and town lots. When the Reclamation Service asked to establish a post office in Camp Colter, officials dropped the name of Colter, a name already used by the Burlington Railroad for another siding. They decided on the name Powell to honor John Wesley Powell. Note that the same bison skull appears in the photograph on page 20. (Both SIDA.)

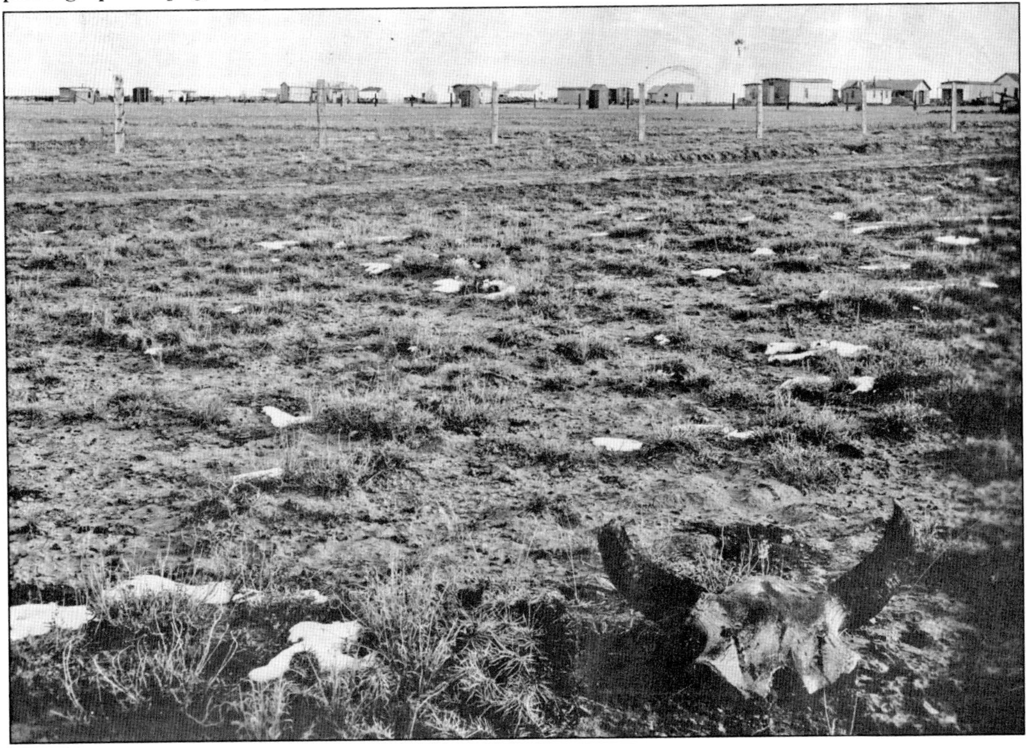

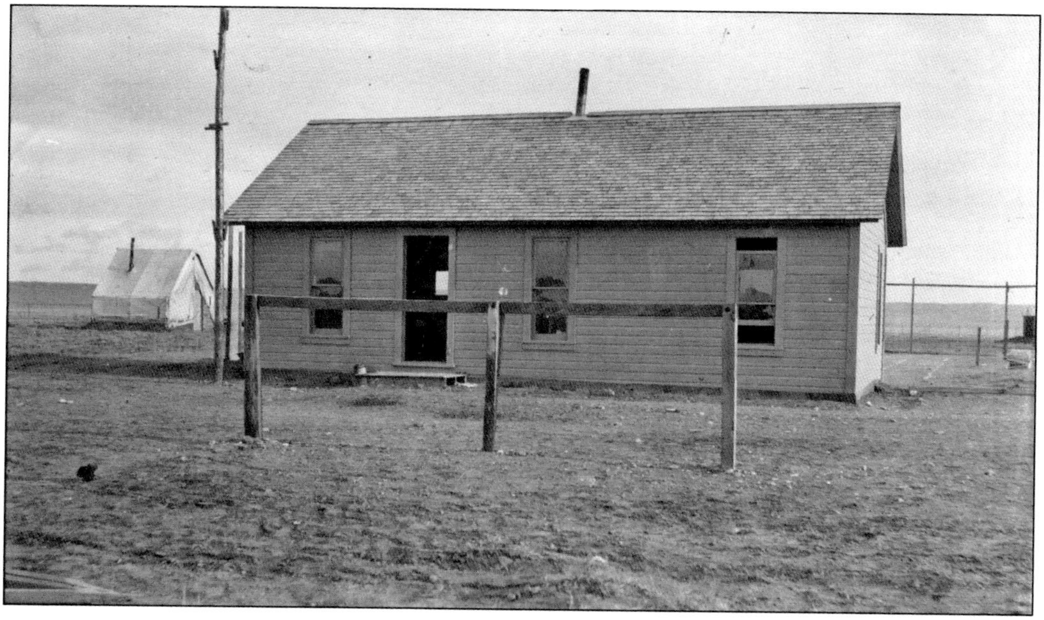

Powell emerged during the Progressive Era. Progressives believed that ideal communities could be developed through scientifically managed programs implemented by professional government agencies. Not only would the Reclamation Service engineers develop an advanced reclamation project with scientifically engineered dams and canals, they would also engineer the settlement of the new town. The above image is of the Reclamation Service engineer's office in Camp Colter. The image below captures the well-organized interior of the office. The presence of manuals, books, and maps indicate the scientific approach the Reclamation Service used to settle the Garland Division and to establish the future town of Powell. (Both SIDA.)

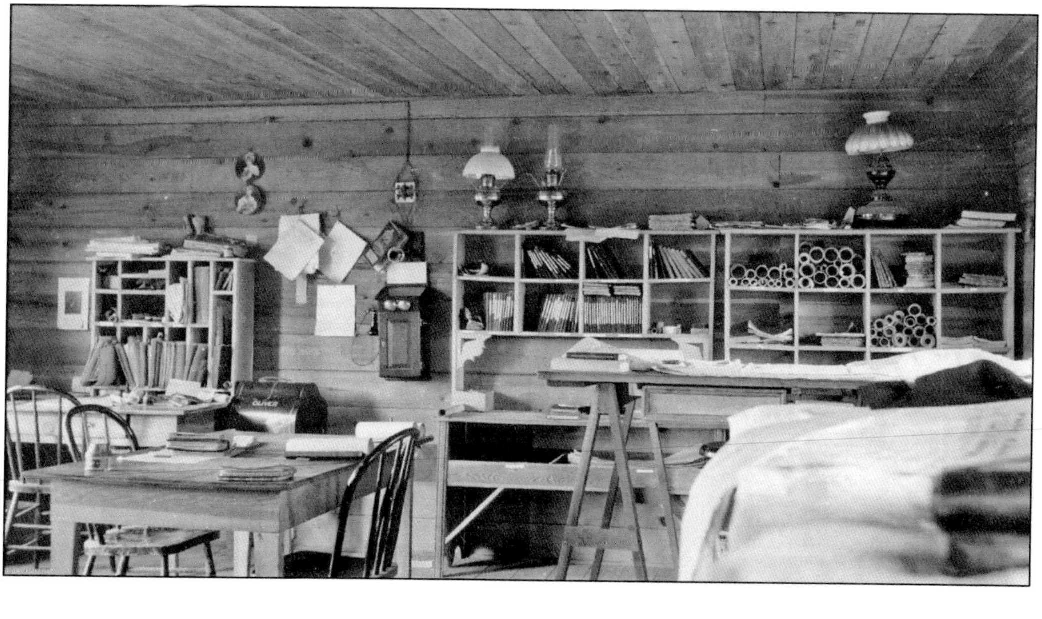

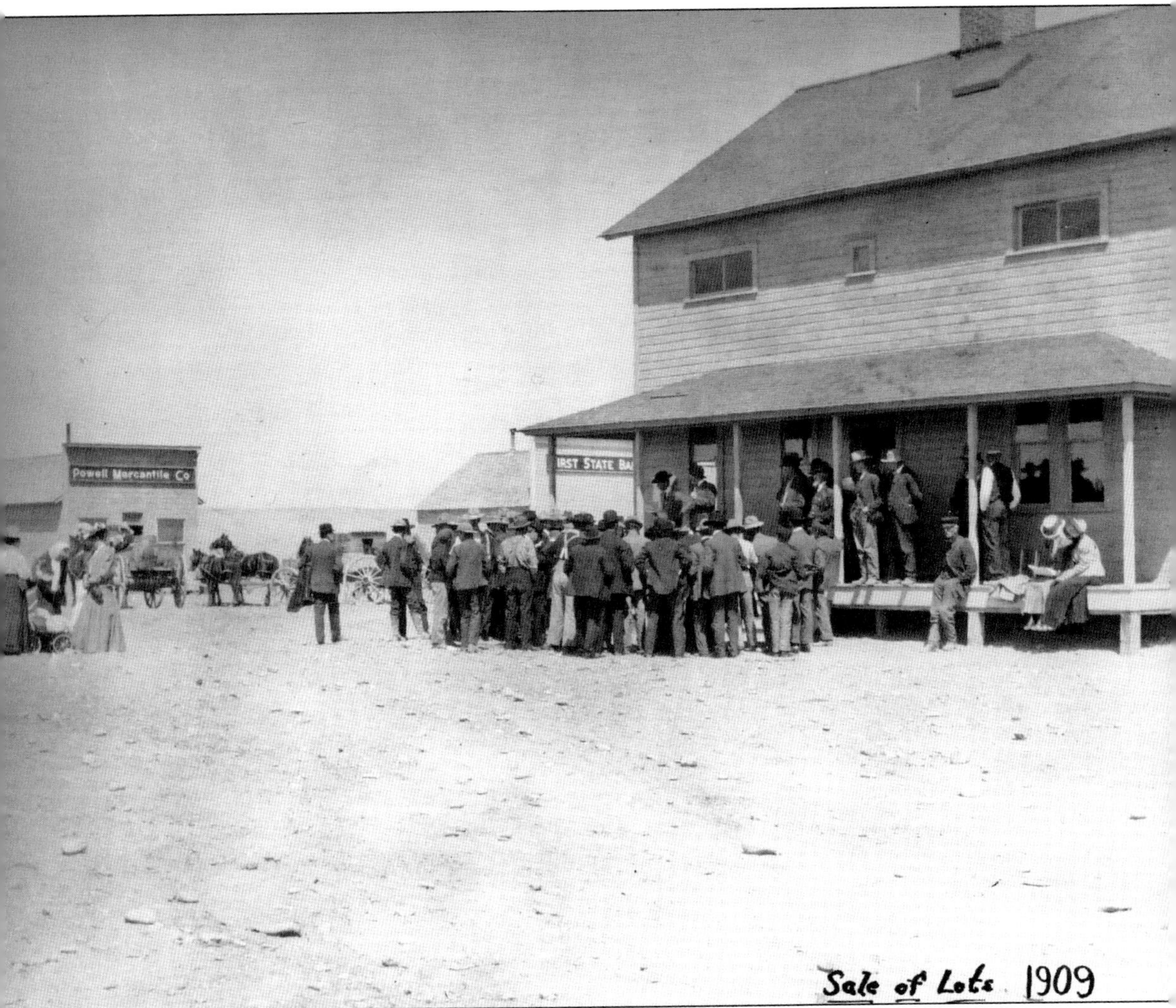

Sometimes the Reclamation Service's well-organized plans did not mature. Originally the Reclamation Service planned for Clark Street, the widest of all of Powell's streets, to be the business district; however, prospective businessmen selected Bent Street to obtain larger plots at a less expensive price. A number of businessmen are pictured here gathering for the sale of town lots in front of the newly constructed two-story Reclamation Service headquarters. The sale of town lots on May 25, 1909, is considered to be the date that Powell began and is the date that Powell marks as its founding. In the background, the Powell Mercantile and the First State Bank are visible along Clark Street. These businesses would later relocate to Bent Street. (SIDA.)

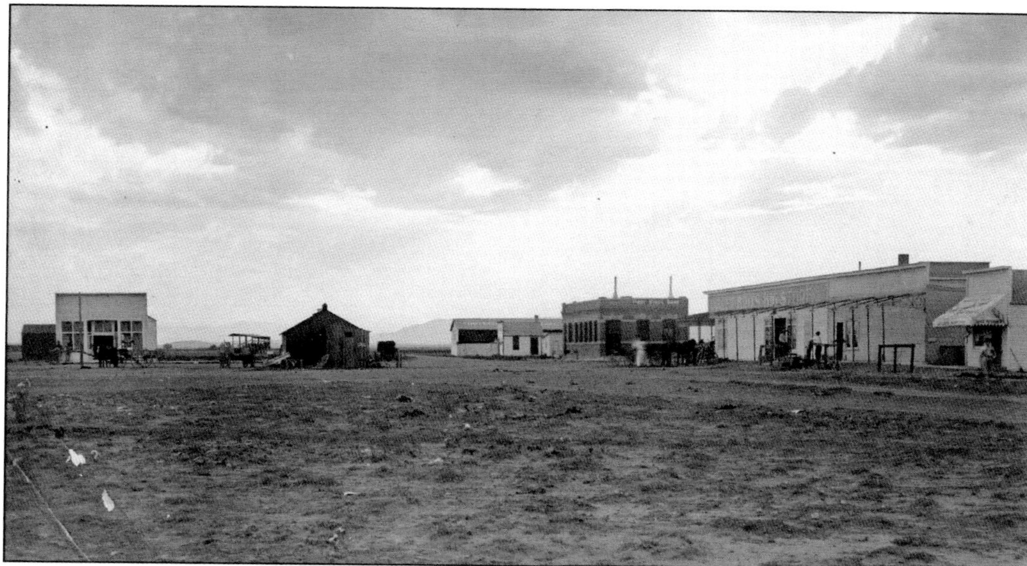

After ignoring the Reclamation Service's desire to open Clark Street as Powell's business district, a handful of businessmen set up various establishments on Bent Street. The photograph above shows Powell's Bent Street, looking west from Second Street. The businesses, from left to right, are as follows: Dr. J. D. Lewellen's Drug Store, Sam Richard's blacksmith shop, the Templeton Lumber Company yard and office, the First State Bank, Pratt Brothers Big Store, and Lehaman's Tailor Shop. The image below, looking south, depicts the intersection of Bent and Second Streets in the winter of 1909–1910. The stores in the top half of the photograph are, from left to right, the First State Bank, a hardware store, two homes, the basement of the soon-to-be-built Presbyterian church, a harness shop, and Pratt Brothers Big Store. The stores in the bottom half of the photograph are, from left to right, a lunch counter/confectionery, the *Powell Tribune*, Lewellen's Drug Store, the post office, A. P. Libby's General Merchandise, and the Powell Mercantile Company. (Both HM.)

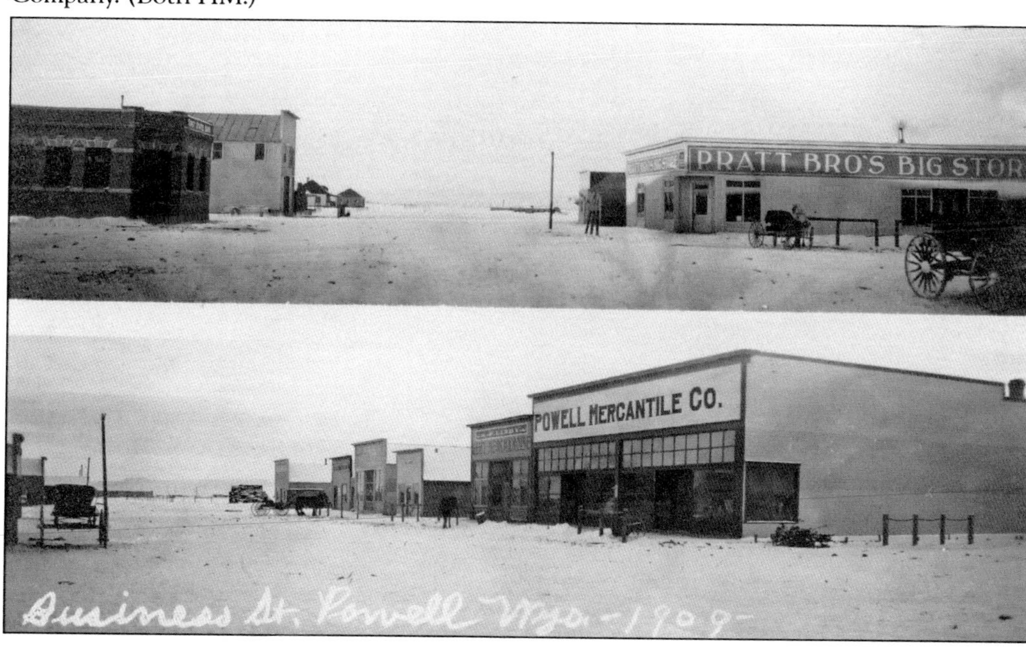

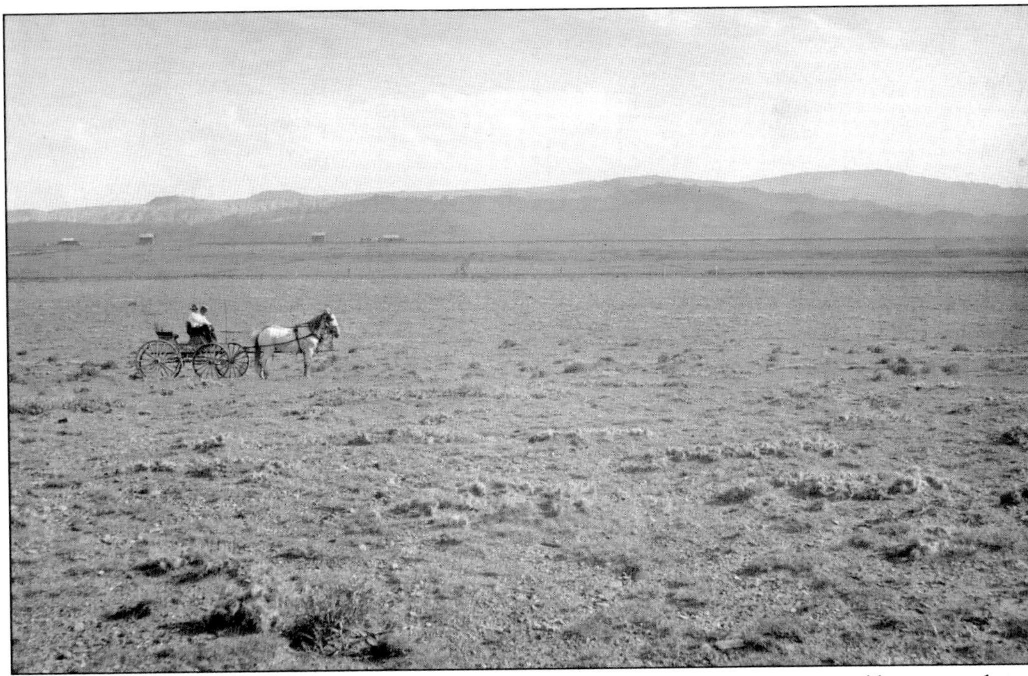

The Reclamation Service assisted homesteaders by escorting them out to potential homestead sites in what was derisively called "sucker wagons." The image above depicts potential settlers being shown the land from one of these wagons. When a homesteader filed on a claim, they needed to build a home and clear the land. The Reclamation Service continued to assist homesteaders with instruction on how to irrigate the land properly. The image below depicts the government plot of land used to illustrate the proper irrigating techniques. Even with this training, many homesteaders found irrigating their land to be a great challenge. A number of well-dressed Reclamation Service officials observe the irrigation of the government plot. (Both SIDA.)

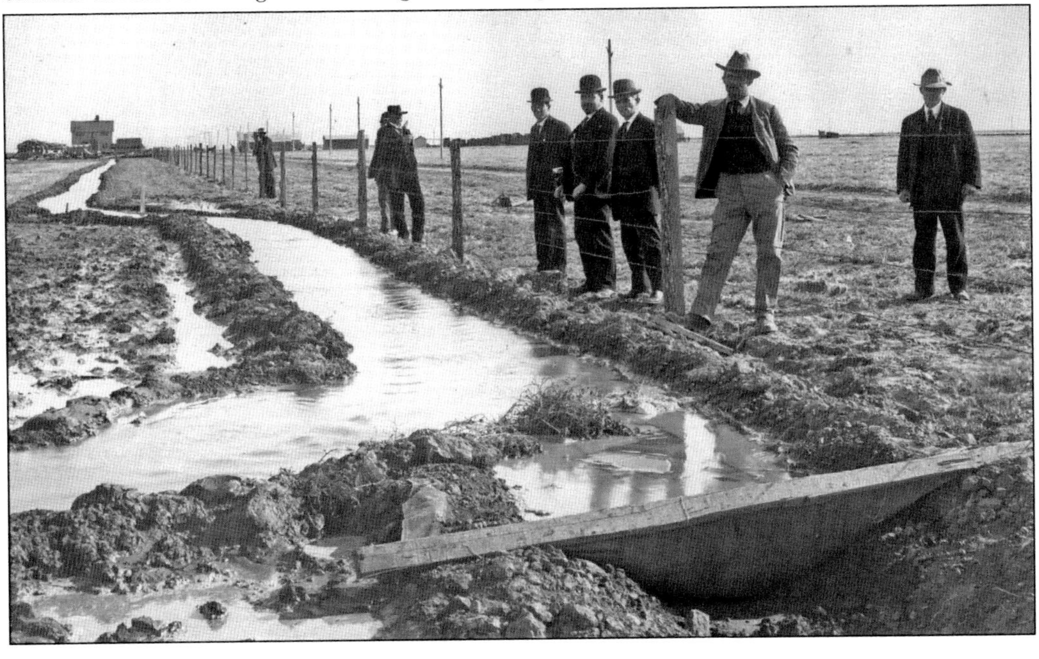

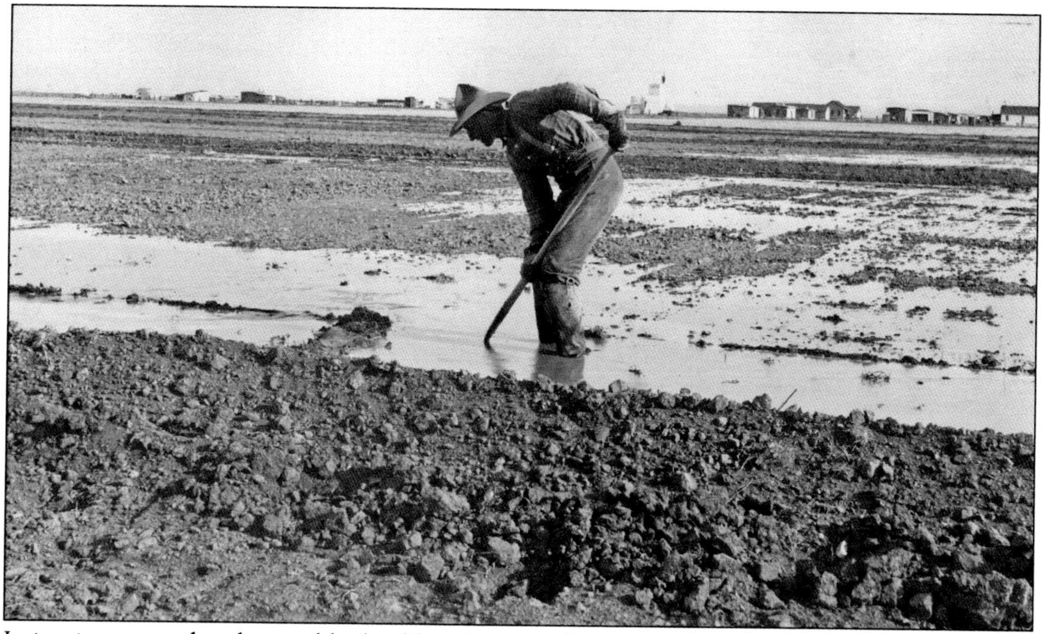

Irrigating proved to be muddy, backbreaking work, as seen here. It took some time before homesteaders perfected the art of irrigation. Many farmers turned water onto their land only to have it go everywhere except where they wanted it to go. Also, many homesteaders used too much water, which caused bogging and, in some cases, caused alkali to rise to the surface making the land infertile. (SIDA.)

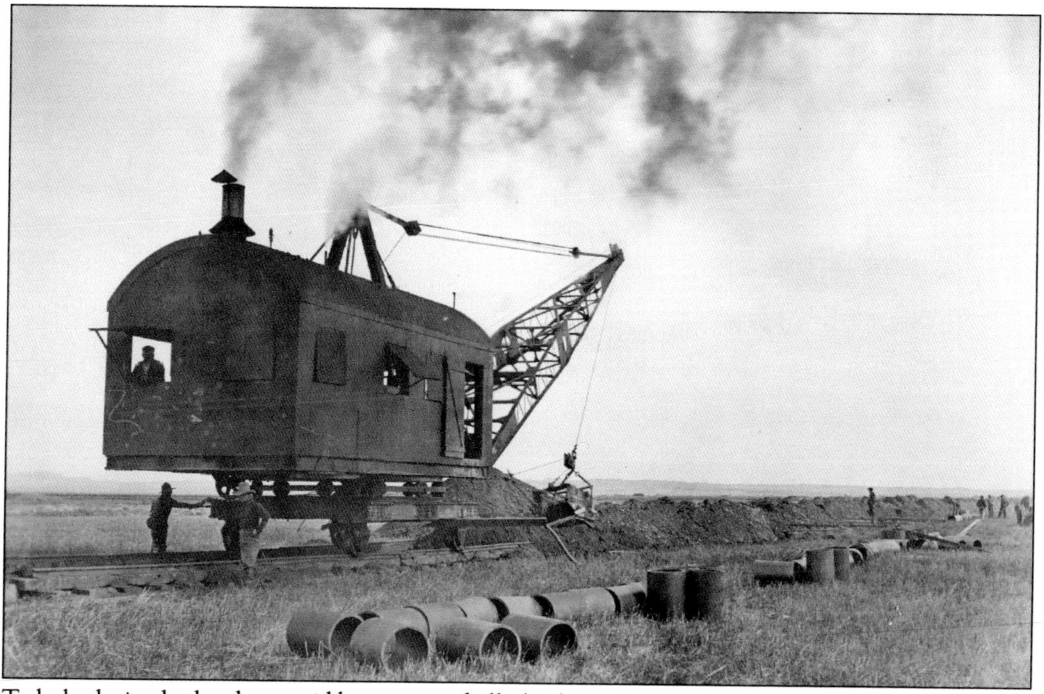

To help drain the land to avoid bogging and alkali, the Reclamation Service established a system of clay drainpipes to assist in draining the land. Using shovels and a dragline, nicknamed the Vulcan, pictured here, crews dig a trench for the clay pipe lying on the ground. (SIDA.)

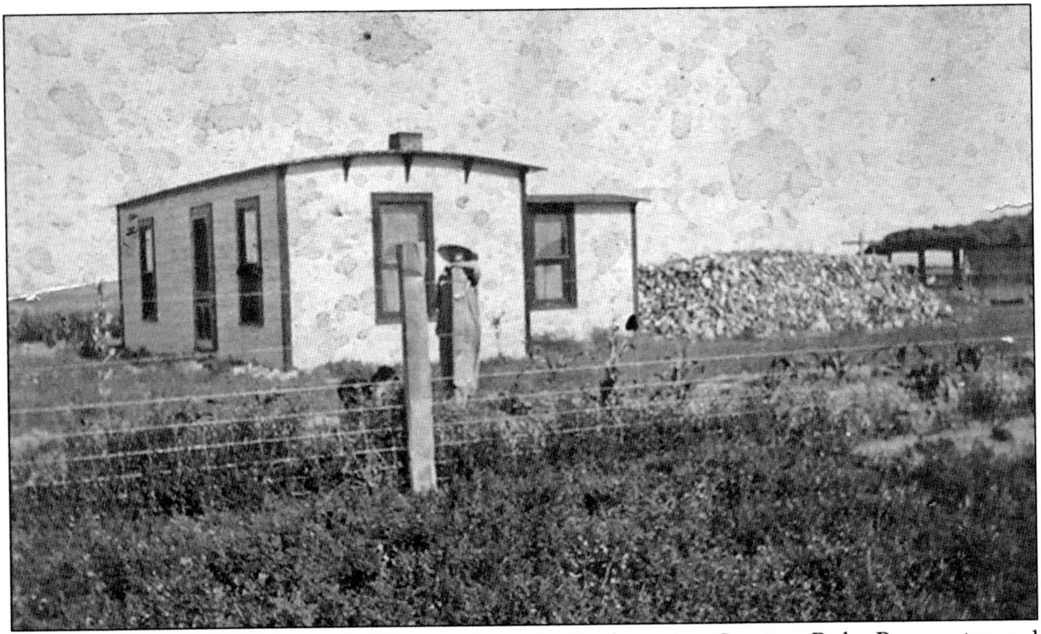

Sometimes homesteaders acquired houses from the Reclamation Service. Ruby Bever, pictured here with her dog, stands in front of the Bever homestead house. The house is known as a "boxcar top" house. A number of these boxcar top houses were situated around the Garland Division. The Bevers, originally from Indiana, soon planted trees around their homestead to remind them of their former homes. (Author's collection.)

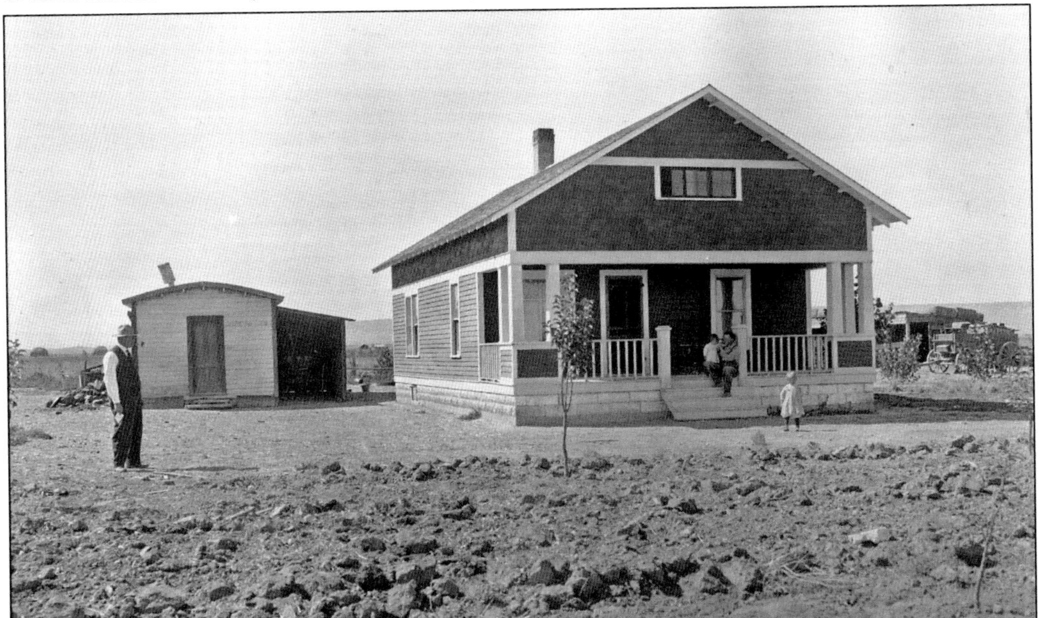

Small dwellings housed families in the first few years of the homestead process. When the family could finally afford a new home, usually the old homestead houses served other purposes. Pictured here is the Cherry family homestead. The Cherry family homesteaded in 1909 and lived in the boxcar top house until 1914, when they completed their new home. (SIDA.)

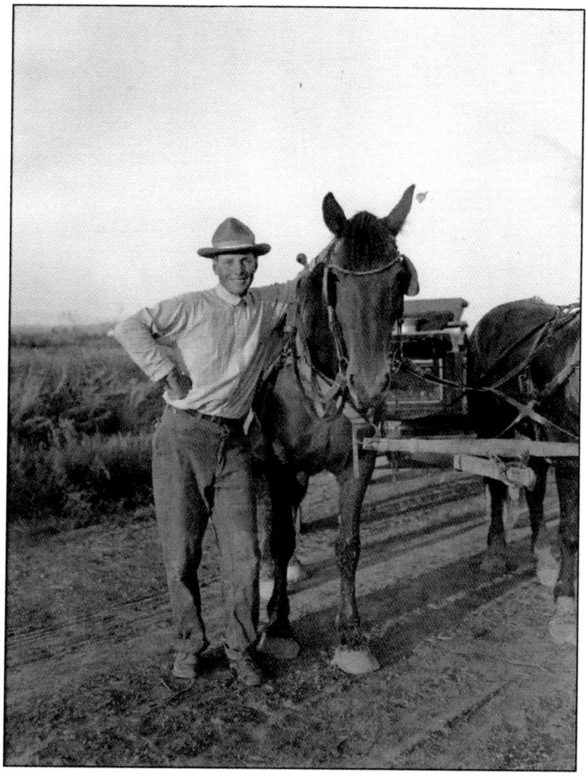

The majority of the Garland Division homesteaders were young people with professional backgrounds. Pictured at right is Kris Fesenbek, a project settler, with his horses and wagon on December 15, 1908. The photograph below depicts a happy Monte Fesenbek, Kris's wife, on a mowing machine, cutting wheat on the family homestead in 1910. (Both SIDA.)

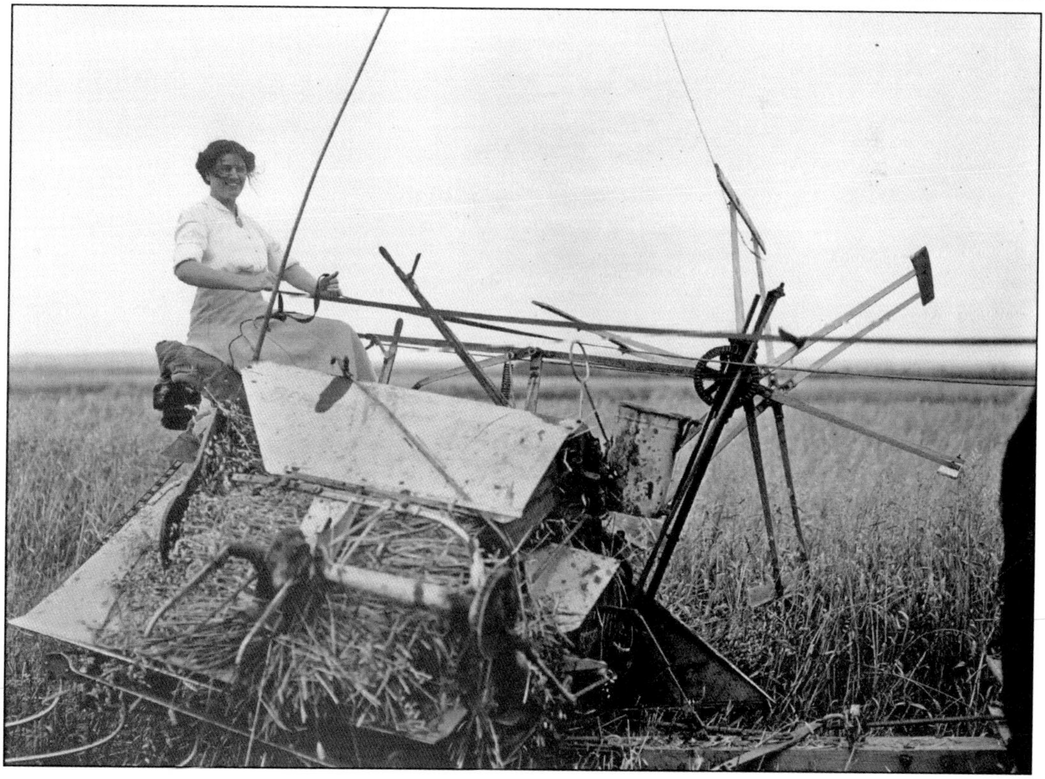

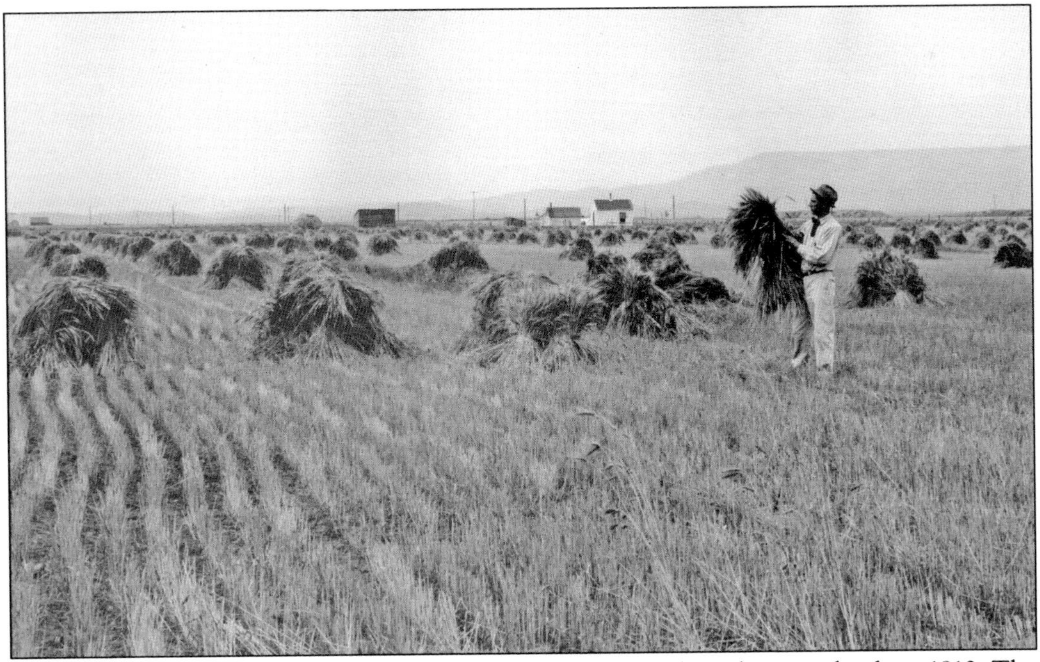

This photograph shows Mr. William G. Mudgett inspecting his wheat in shock in 1910. The success of the Garland Division encouraged the Reclamation Service to move forward on the Frannie-Deaver Division, located northeast of the Garland Division. Unfortunately, the lands in the new division did not prove to be as fertile as in the Garland Division due to alkali, and the drop in agricultural prices after World War I caused additional problems for the homesteaders on the Frannie-Deavor Division. (SIDA.)

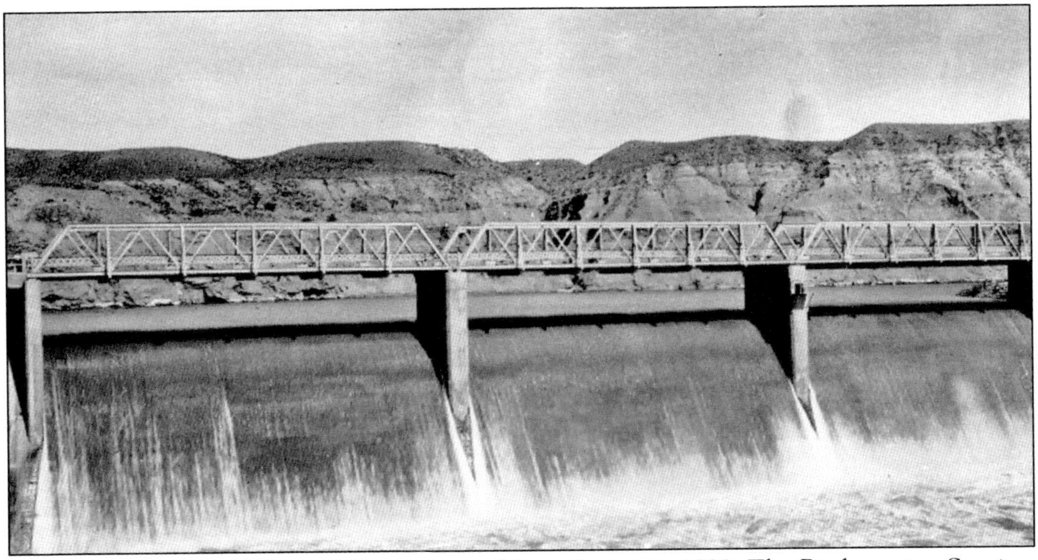

Construction of the Willwood Dam, pictured here, began in 1920. The Reclamation Service, renamed the Bureau of Reclamation in 1923, planned to irrigate over 11,000 acres in the Willwood Division, located south of the Garland Division, on the other side of the Shoshone River. Settlement for this division opened on June 10, 1927. The structure on top of the Willwood Dam is a bridge for auto traffic to cross the river. (SIDA.)

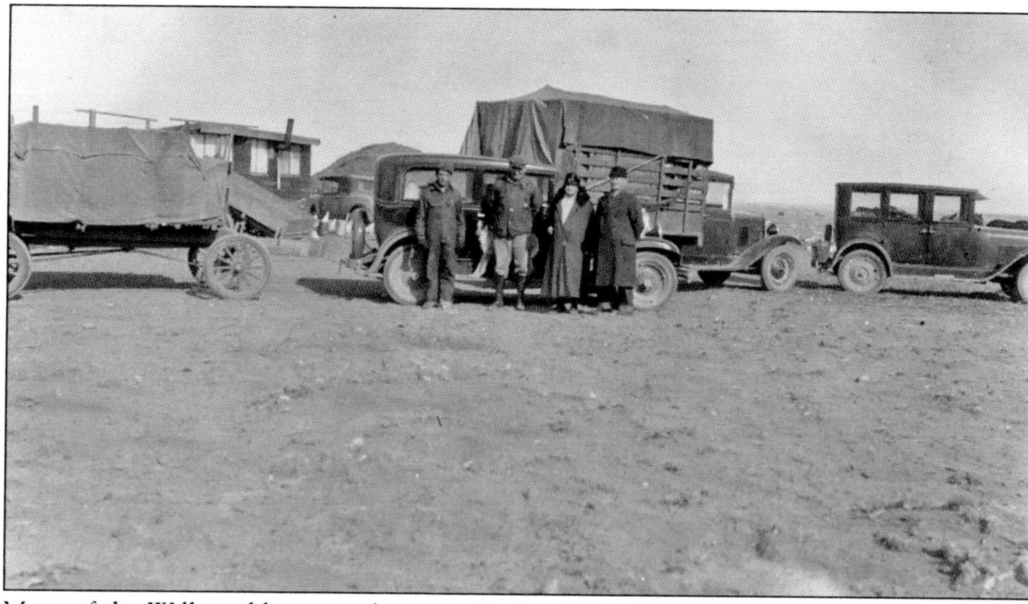

Many of the Willwood homesteaders were displaced from the Garland Division by poor land. Other homesteaders drove long distances to homestead on the Willwood. Pictured here in no particular order are Willwood homesteaders Mr. and Mrs. Richard Vogel, Richard Sievers, and the Vogels' son Mielan, having just arrived from Albert City, Iowa. (SIDA.)

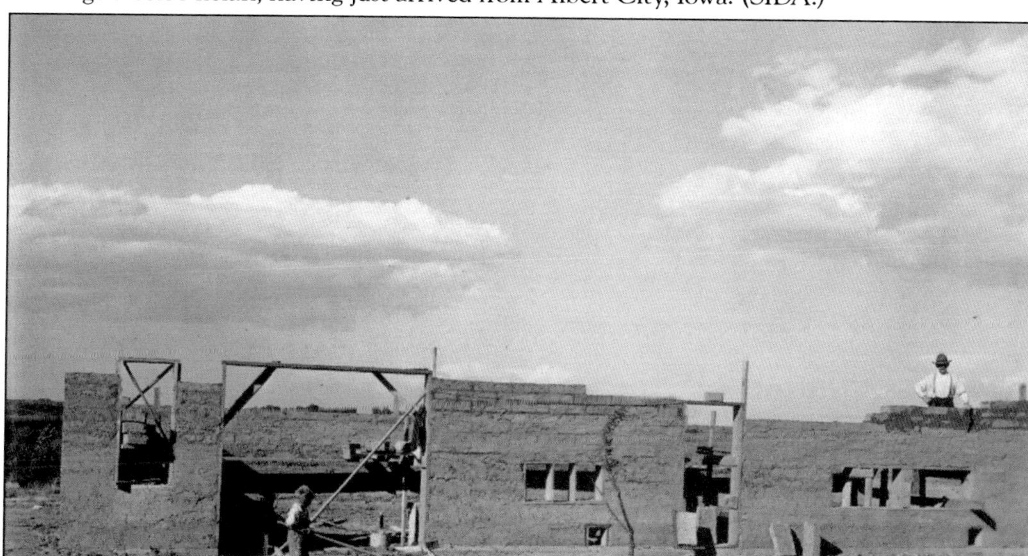

Homesteaders on the Shoshone Project used a variety of resources to construct outbuildings for their farms. Sometimes readily available natural resources provided a less costly alternative to other building supplies. Here Willwood settler Mars Christofferson, pictured with one of his children, builds an adobe chicken house in 1930. (SIDA.)

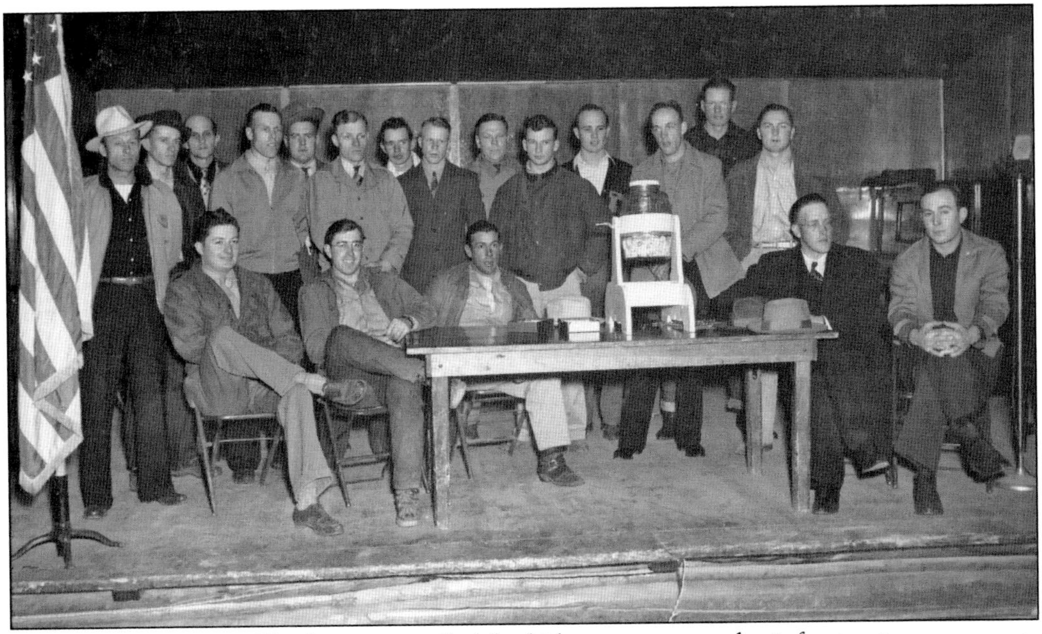

In 1939, the Bureau of Reclamation called for bids to construct the infrastructure necessary to irrigate the Heart Mountain Division, located west of the Garland Division. World War II threatened the completion of the project. Fortunately for future homesteaders, Japanese interned at the Heart Mountain Relocation Center finished the project. The Heart Mountain Division called for applications in 1946, and the recipients of the first land drawing are pictured here in Powell on February 4, 1947. From left to right are (first row, seated) Robert Bishop, Clyde Dugger, Roy Myers, Paul Scheuneman, and Harry T. Ketchum; (second row) Harvey Latham, Warren Johnson, Dean Baker, Albert Johnson, Richard Kester, Dale Good, William Ross, and Glenn Mangus; (third row) Wesley Hedrick, W. C. Weymiller, H. L. Downer, Fred Giles, Herbert Gillett, and Leslie Bovee. (PCA.)

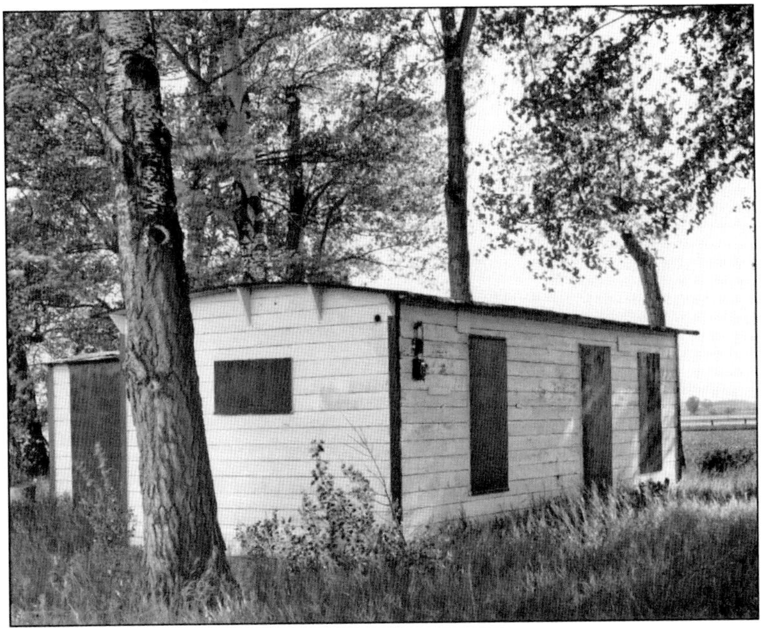

The Bever homestead, pictured on page 48 as well, stands abandoned. In 2006, the Homesteader Museum acquired the boxcar top house and moved it to the museum grounds in Powell. This image is of the structure shortly before that move. Today the Bever homestead shows visitors how the homesteaders of the Garland Division lived in the early 1900s. Note the number of trees planted by the Bever family. (PCA.)

Four

MAIN STREET

The Reclamation Service planned for the wider Clark Street to be Powell's main street; however, businessmen agreed amongst themselves to develop Bent Street as the main street to avoid paying higher prices charged for business lots. When the Reclamation Service sold town lots on May 25, 1909, Bent Street became the business district of Powell. A number of businesses sprang up in Powell to provide goods and services to homesteaders settling on the Shoshone Project. The first stores in Powell consisted of the traditional false-front wooden buildings. These wooden structures posed a problem for the development of the business district due to the occurrence of a number of destructive fires. In 1910, the Powell Mercantile erupted into flames, burning down that building and A. P. Libby's store.

On February 12, 1915, a fire began at Elder's Hardware store and burned down at least nine businesses. Town residents attempted to stop the fire by setting off dynamite charges, but the explosions only caused more damage by shattering a number of windows. In December 1915, the town organized a volunteer fire department and a new alarm bell ensured the volunteers could be called when another fire erupted. When not fighting fires, the firefighters wetted down the dry dirt streets to curtail dust. After a few years, wooden structures on Bent Street were replaced by brick structures, and sidewalks and oiled roads curtailed the dust. Through the first half of the 20th century, Bent Street housed a number of buildings from Colter Avenue, later misspelled as Coulter when Powell posted its first street signs in 1941, to Third Street. Over the last 100 years, a number of businesses came and went, producing an interesting cross-section of Powell's main street.

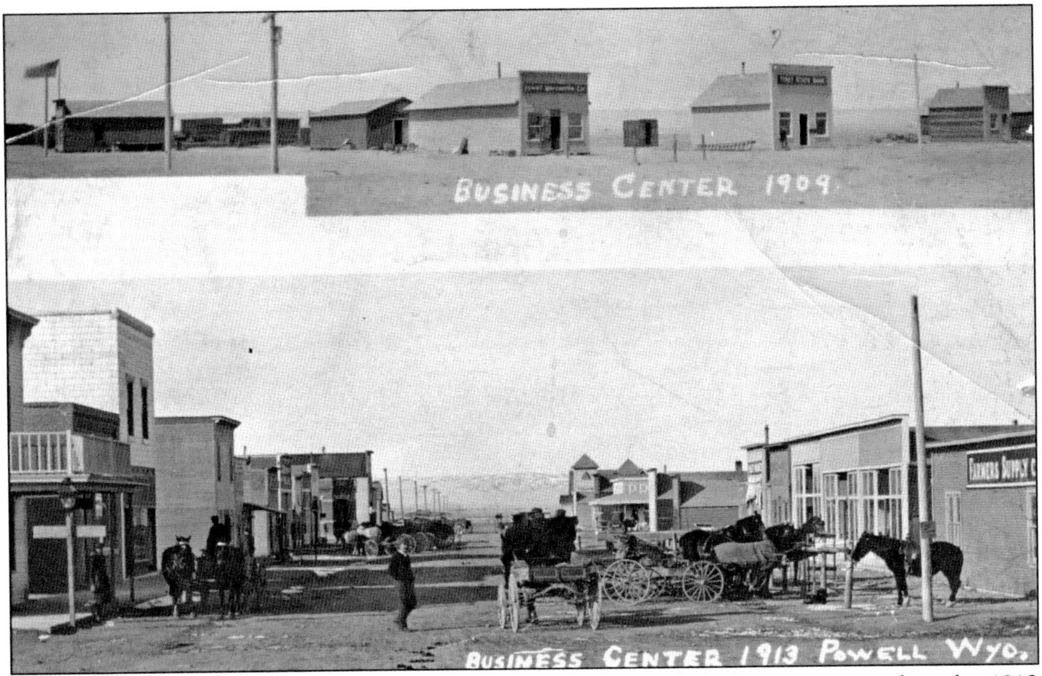

This photograph depicts Powell's 1909 business district on Clark Street compared to the 1913 business district on Bent Street. The 1913 perspective demonstrates how Powell's business district expanded. Note the great number of wooden false-front structures as well as a few brick buildings, such as the First State Bank on the corner of Bent and Second Streets. (HM.)

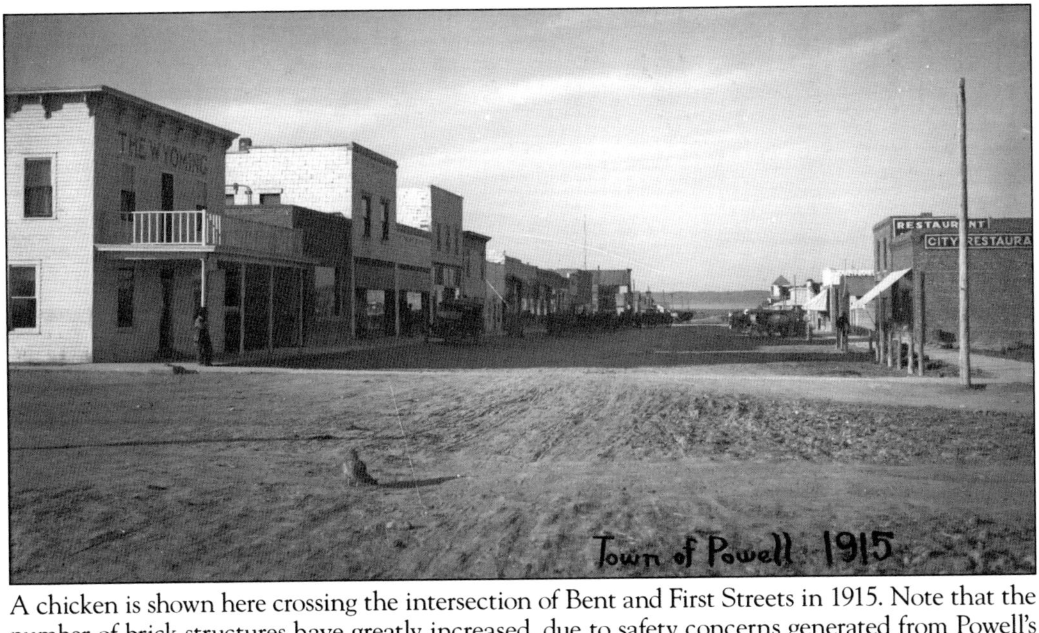

A chicken is shown here crossing the intersection of Bent and First Streets in 1915. Note that the number of brick structures have greatly increased, due to safety concerns generated from Powell's early fires. A boardwalk, absent in the photograph, now lines the east side of Bent Street. (HM.)

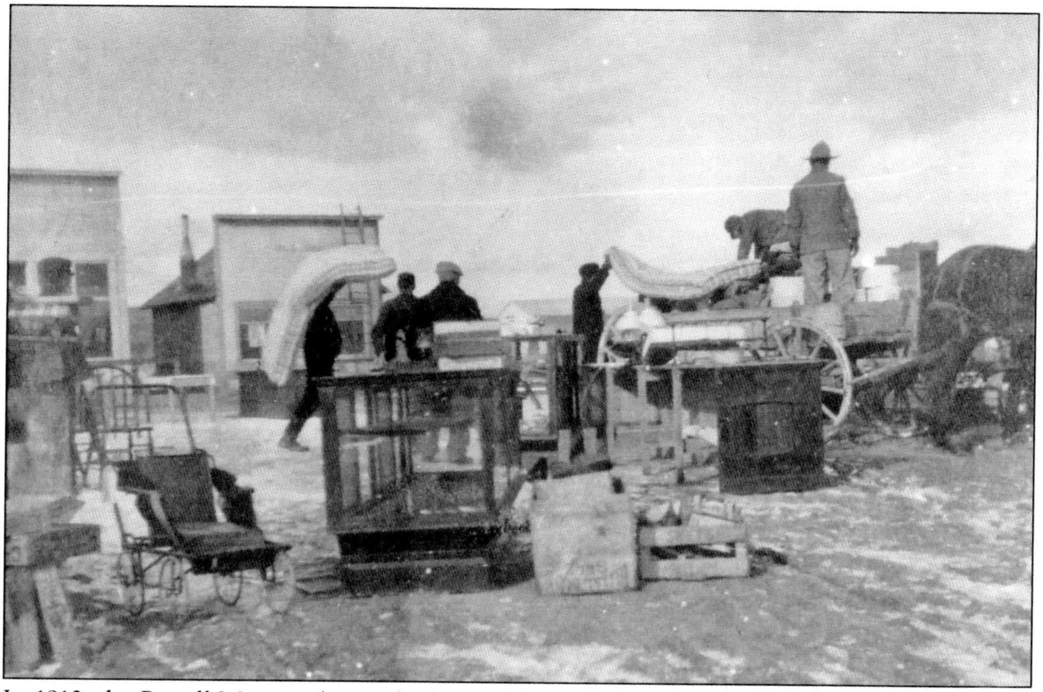

In 1910, the Powell Mercantile caught fire and burned down to the ground. A. P. Libby's store also caught fire but before the structure burned down to the ground, town residents managed to salvage most of the store's inventory. (PCA.)

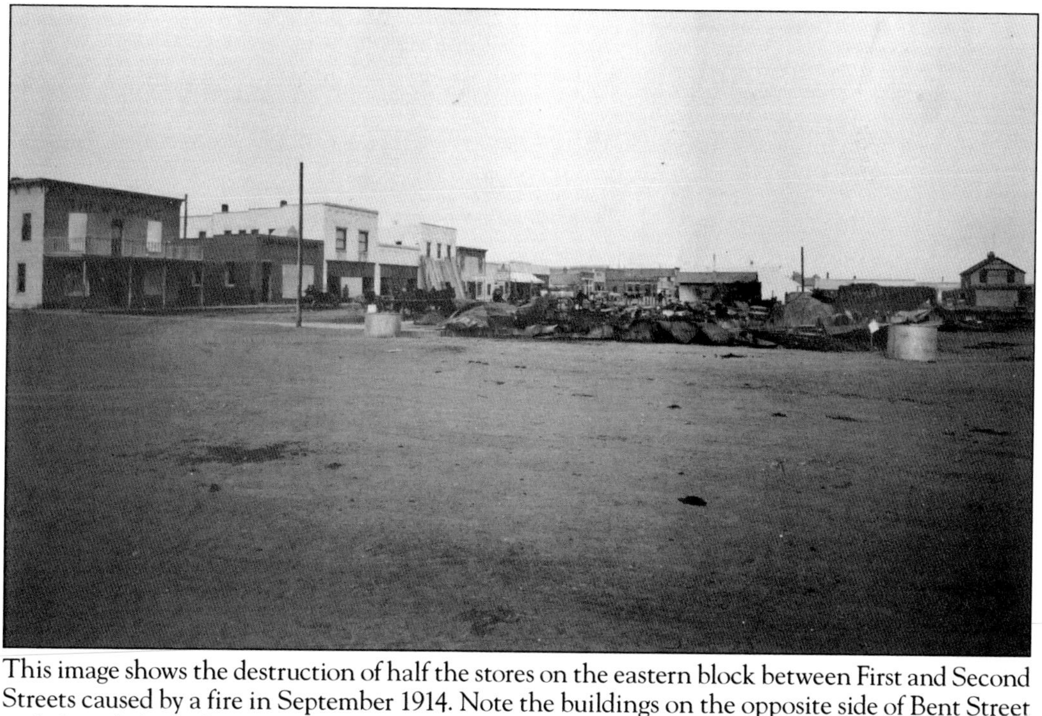

This image shows the destruction of half the stores on the eastern block between First and Second Streets caused by a fire in September 1914. Note the buildings on the opposite side of Bent Street with boarded windows. Setting off dynamite charges to smother fire was an early firefighting device, but many windows were shattered in the process. (SIDA.)

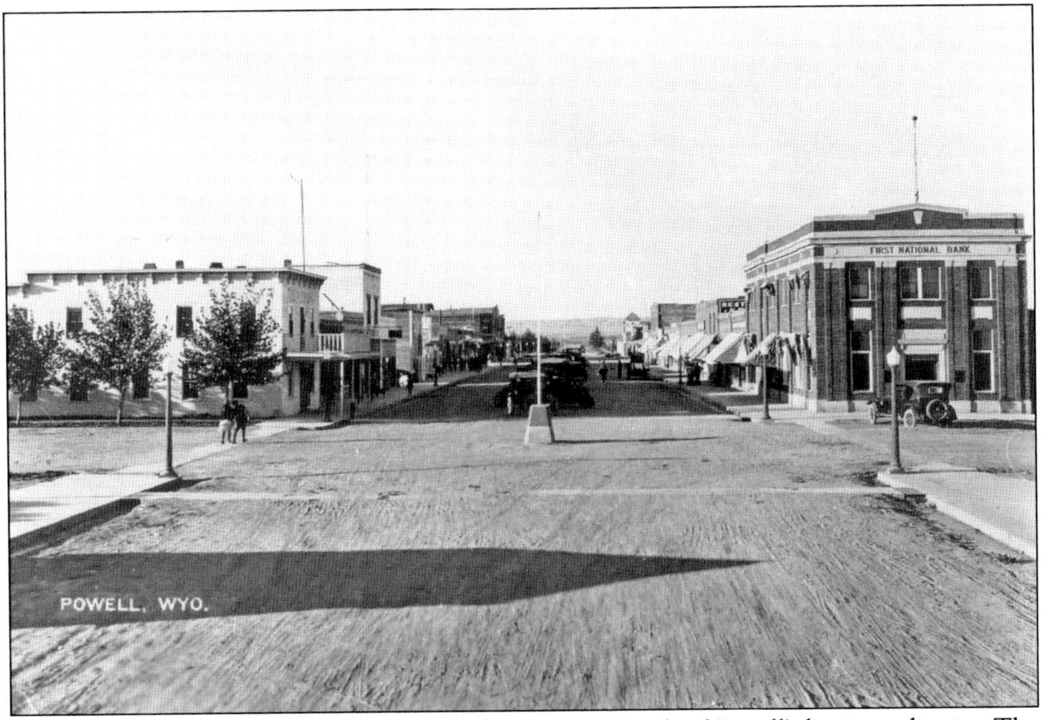

This c. 1920 photograph of Bent Street illustrates the growth of Powell's business district. The First National Bank completed its two-story brick building in 1918. Note that the sidewalks are now paved with concrete yet the road remains dirt. (HM.)

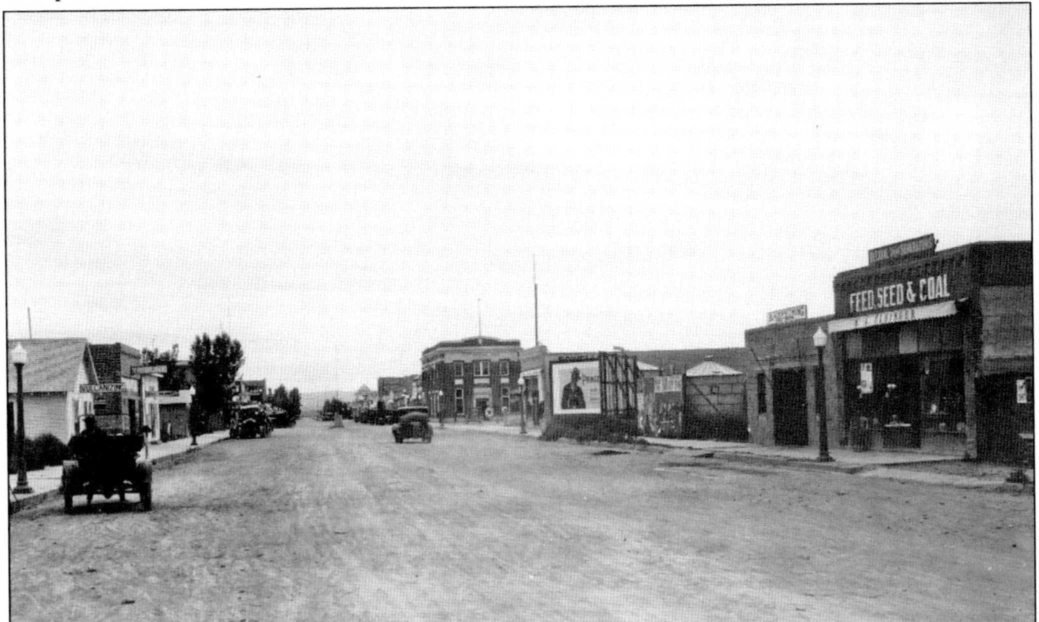

The intersection of Bent and Coulter Streets is depicted here in 1927. Note the blacksmith shop on the right side of the street that seems out of place with the number of automobiles driving down Bent Street. Also note the silos tucked behind the billboards. (SIDA.)

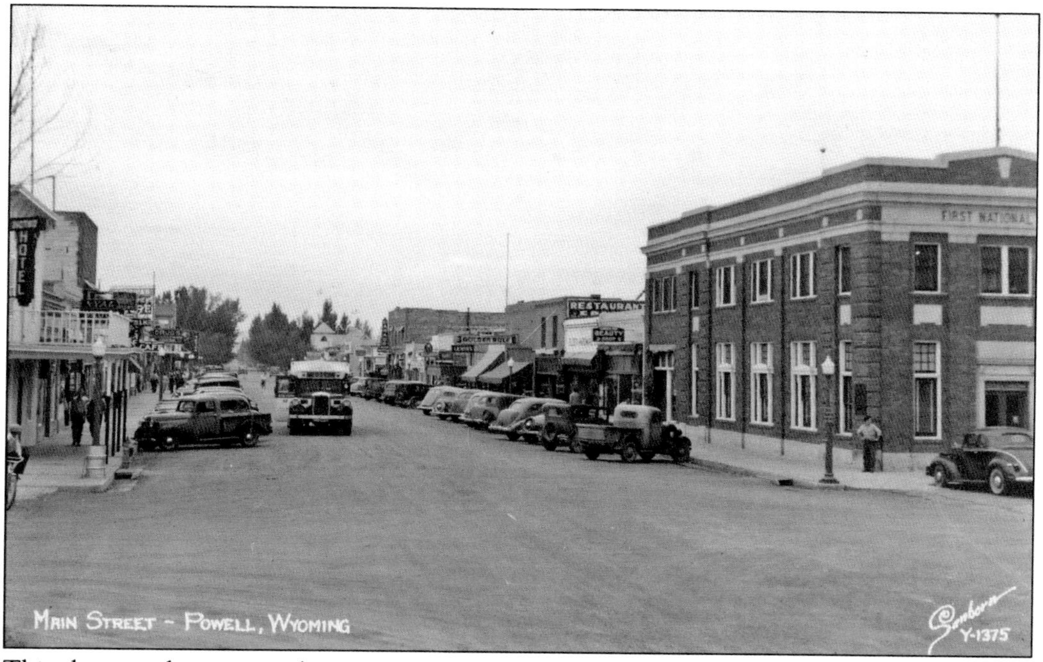

This photograph captures a bus stopping on Bent Street in 1942. Slowed by the Great Depression, Powell was rejuvenated by the economic boom of World War II and improved its downtown district. By 1947, Bent Street was paved with oil and gravel for three blocks. (HM.)

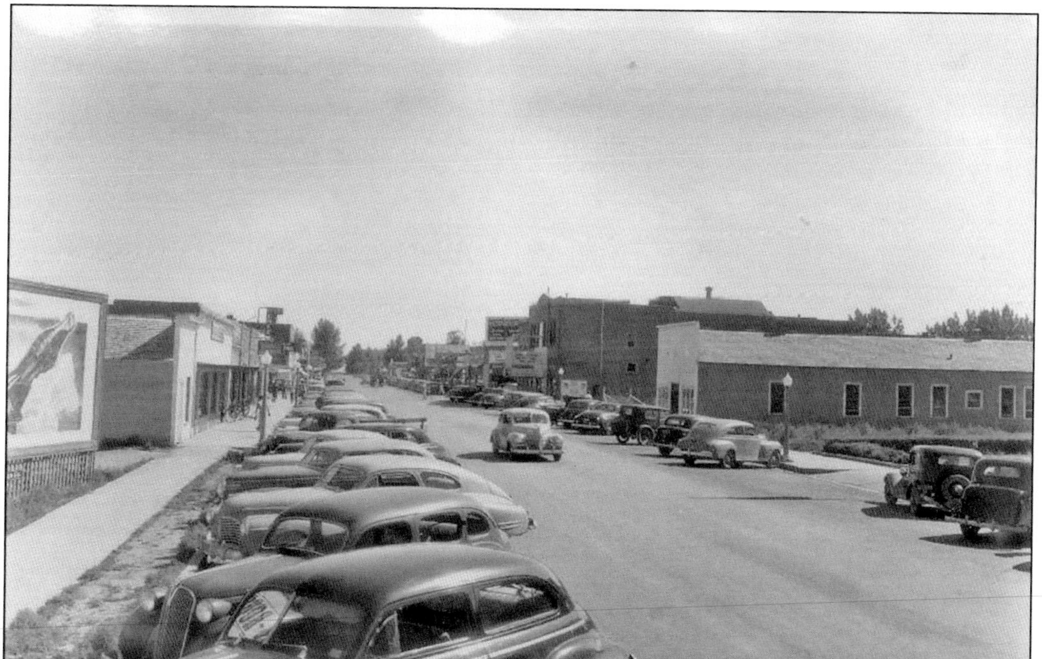

Bent Street is seen here looking south from Third Street in 1944. The two-story brick building is the movie theater. (SIDA.)

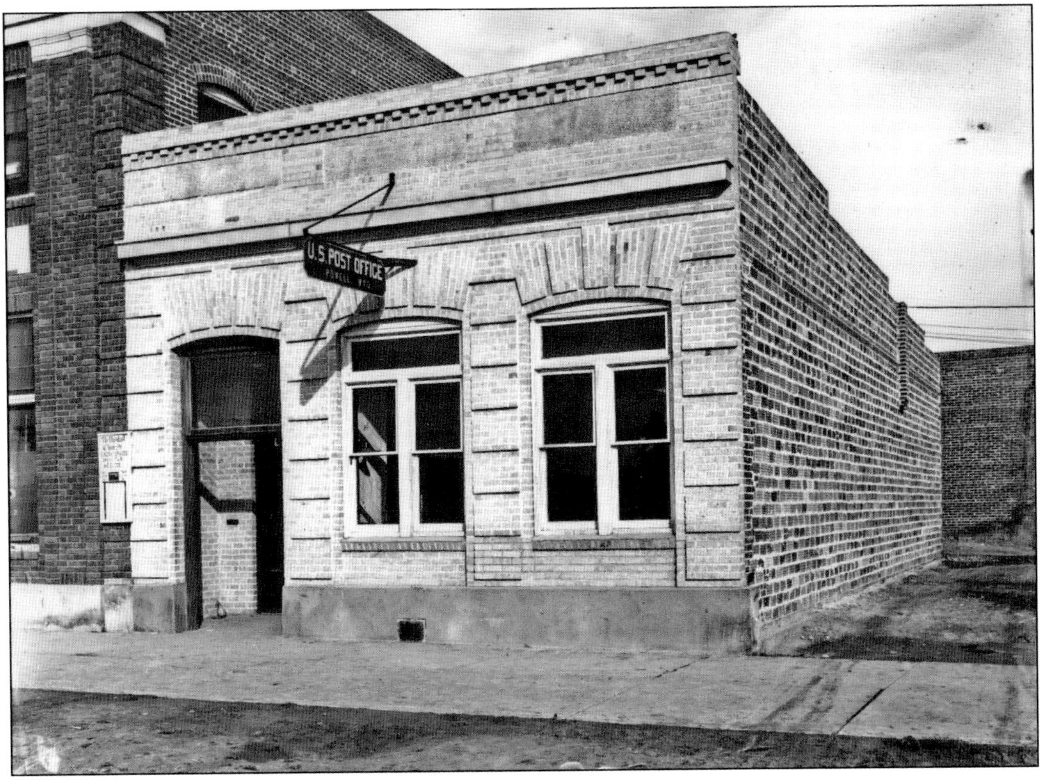

Powell's first post office was a false-front building on Bent Street (see page 45). The image above depicts Powell's post office in the 1920s. The building sat on First Street, adjoined to the First National Bank. The Works Progress Administration (WPA) completed Powell's current post office, located on the southwest corner of Bent and Third Streets, in 1937. (Both HM.)

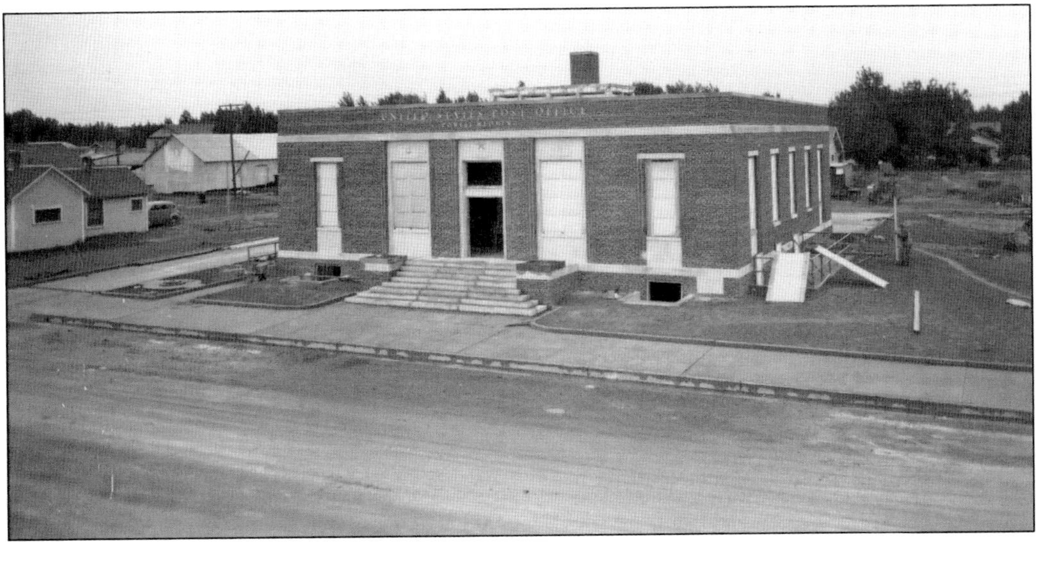

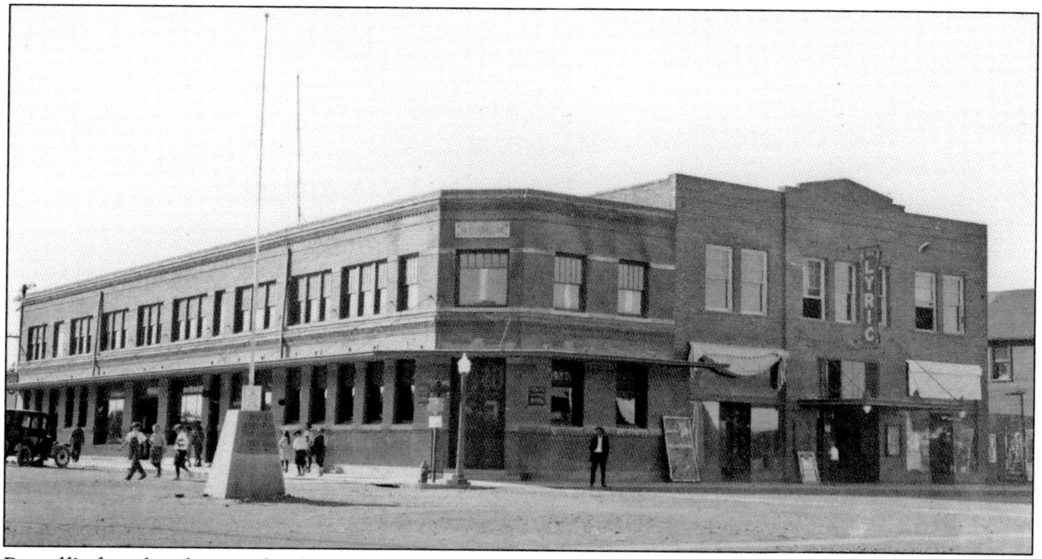

Powell's first bank was the First State Bank. Housed originally on Clark Street in a false-front building (see page 44), the bank soon constructed a brick building on the corner of Bent and Second Streets (see page 45). This one-story brick building soon expanded into a two-story structure and spread to the end of the lot, as seen here next to the Lyric Theater. The expansion of the building proved premature; the First State Bank closed in the early 1920s. The painted sign on the flagpole advertises a campground two blocks south. (HM.)

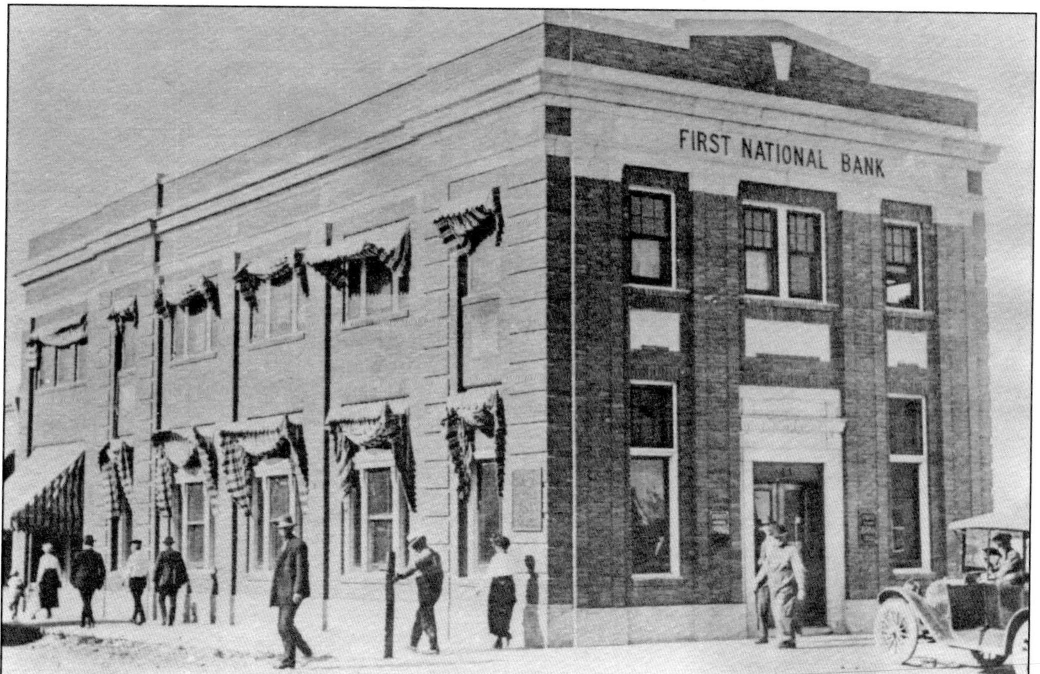

Founded in 1912 by Severt A. Nelson with a starting capital of $25,000, First National Bank weathered the ups and downs of Powell's economy into the present day. By 1917, it moved into a new $40,000 building on the corner of Bent and First Streets. First National Bank remained in this location until it moved to a newer building in the 1950s. (HM.)

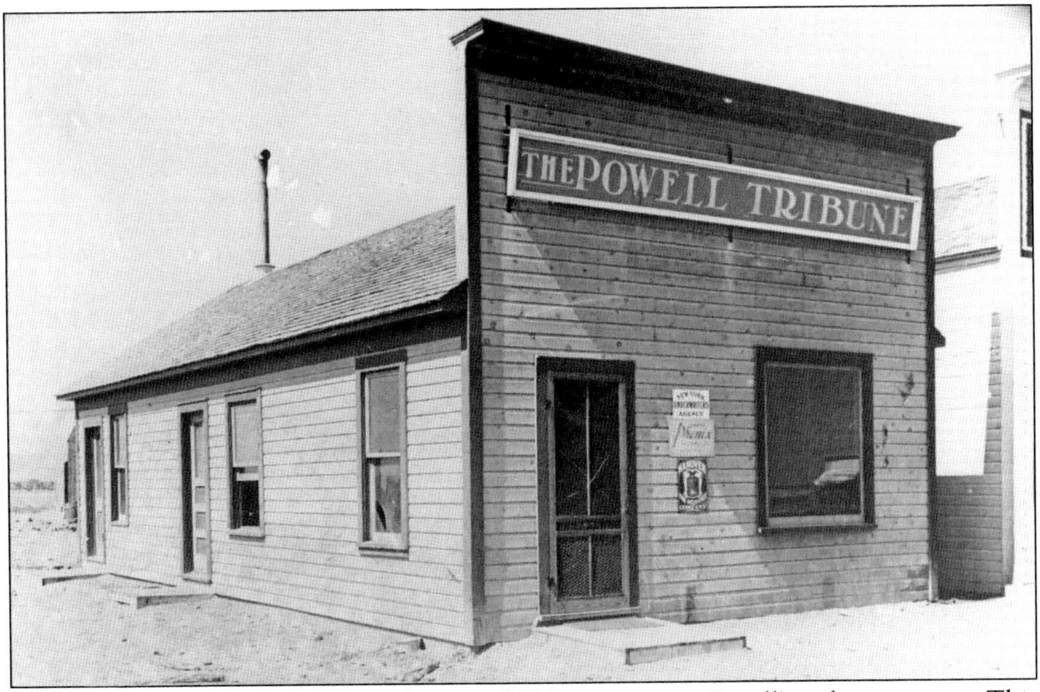

Founded by S. A. Nelson in 1909, the *Powell Tribune* remains Powell's only newspaper. This photograph depicts the first building that housed the newspaper, which was printed in Cody, Wyoming, until 1911. In 1912, Nelson sold the *Powell Tribune* to James A. Baird. Baird and his descendants worked at the newspaper for over 50 years. (HM.)

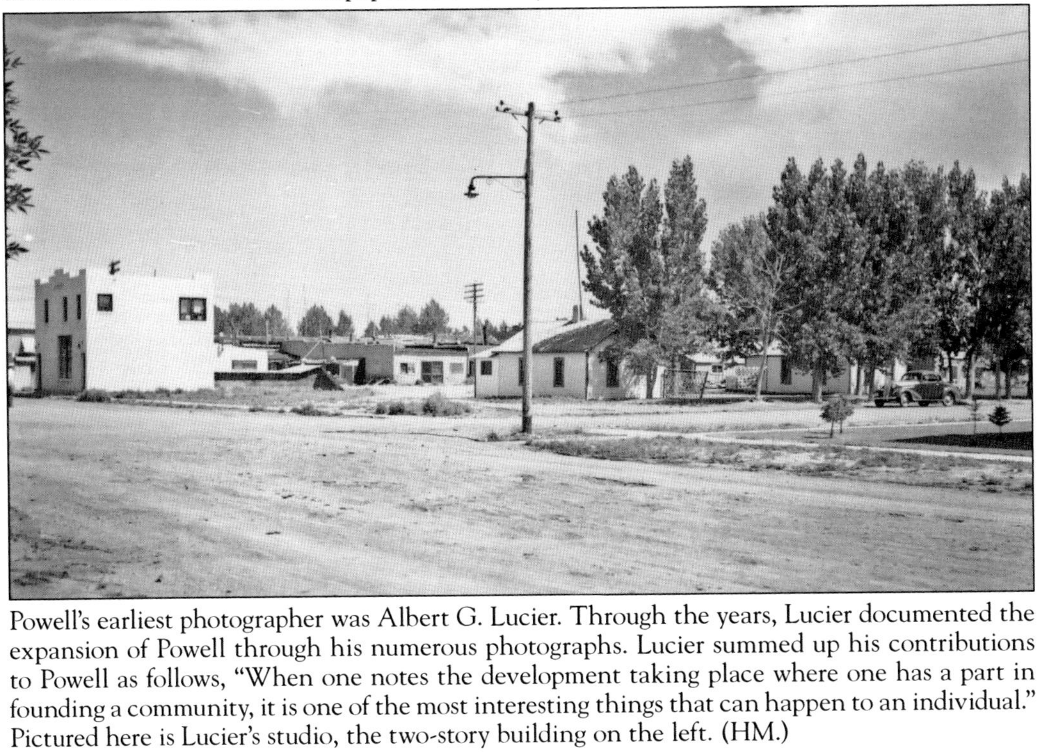

Powell's earliest photographer was Albert G. Lucier. Through the years, Lucier documented the expansion of Powell through his numerous photographs. Lucier summed up his contributions to Powell as follows, "When one notes the development taking place where one has a part in founding a community, it is one of the most interesting things that can happen to an individual." Pictured here is Lucier's studio, the two-story building on the left. (HM.)

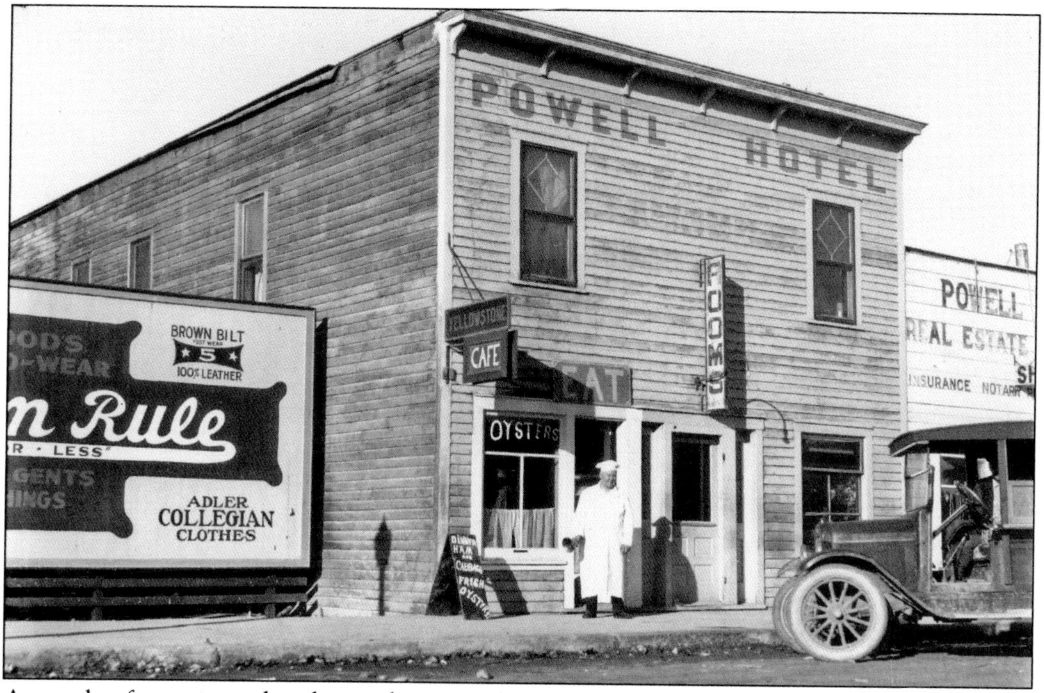

A couple of prominent hotels stood on Powell's Bent Street. The Powell Hotel, pictured here, offered meals in the Yellowstone Café. Of course, one wonders how fresh the oysters really were. The Wyoming Hotel opened in 1911 with 24 rooms and four suites (see page 54). The hotel's balcony, over its covered porch, was a prominent feature on Bent Street. (PCA.)

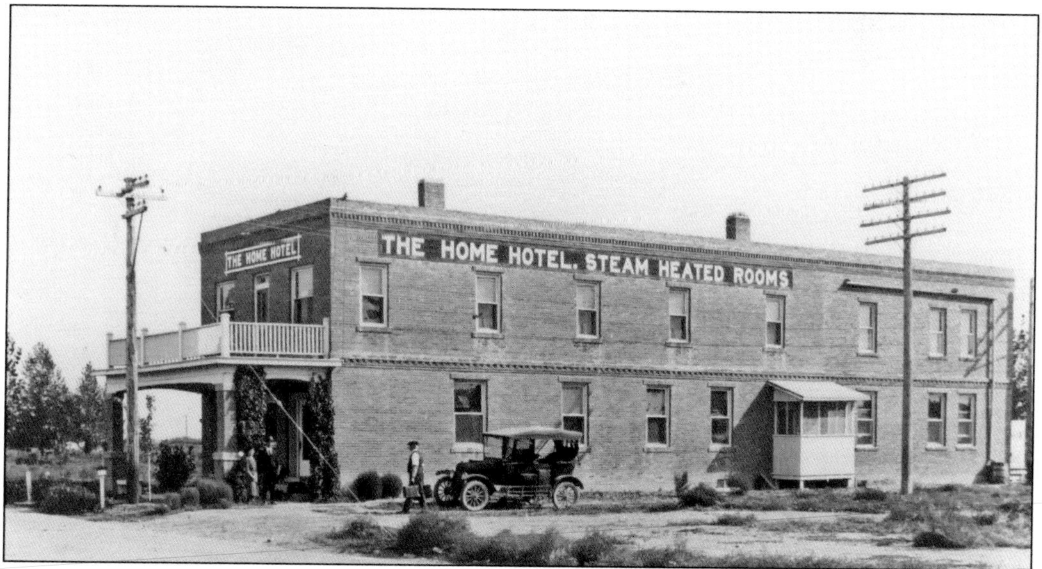

The Home Hotel, erected on First Street, expanded in the early 1920s. Its signage advertises the luxury of steam-heated rooms. The Sanborn map of Powell in 1914 indicates the Wyoming Hotel only offered stove heat and lamps for lights. (PCA.)

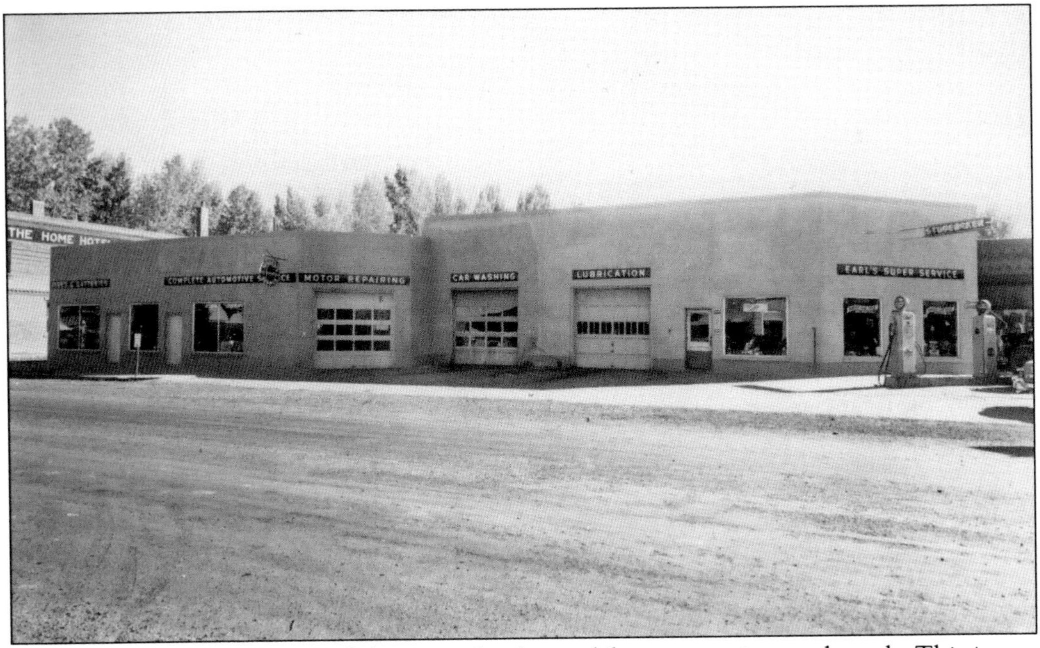

Increased ownership of automobiles created a demand for new services and goods. This image depicts Earl Learned's Texaco gas station. It was located on the southeast corner of Bent and First Streets. It was from this gas station, then operated by Otis Roulette, that Tipton Cox shot would-be bank robber Earl Durand. (FNB.)

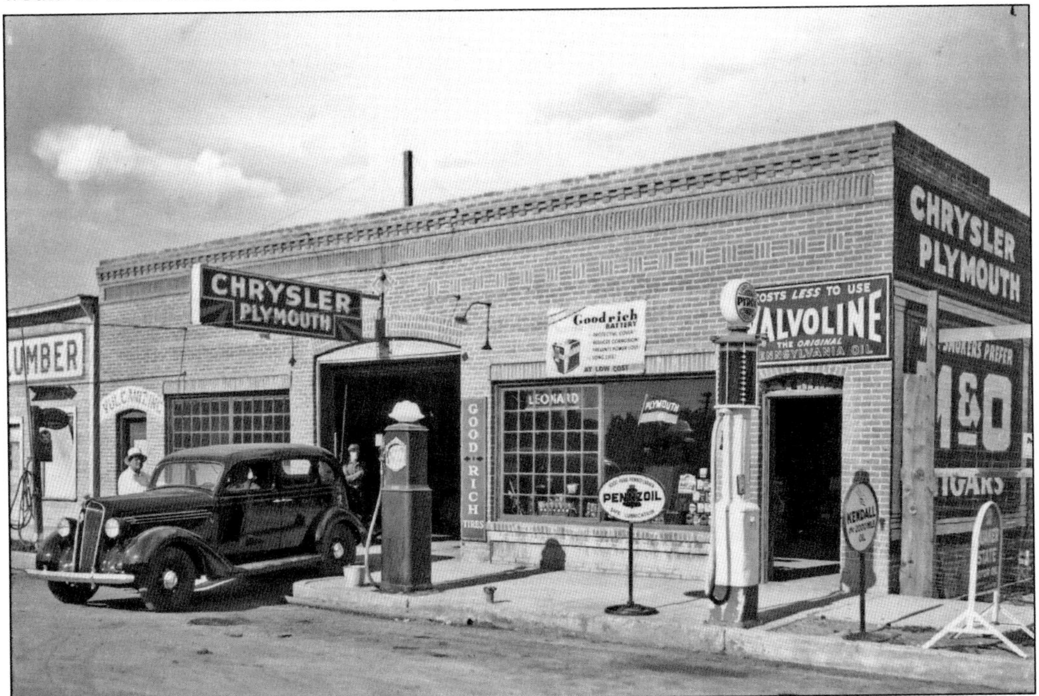

This photograph depicts Althoff Motors, located on Bent Street in between Second and Third Streets. This building was constructed around 1924. In addition to selling Chevrolet and Plymouth cars, this business also sold gasoline, oil, and tires. (PCA.)

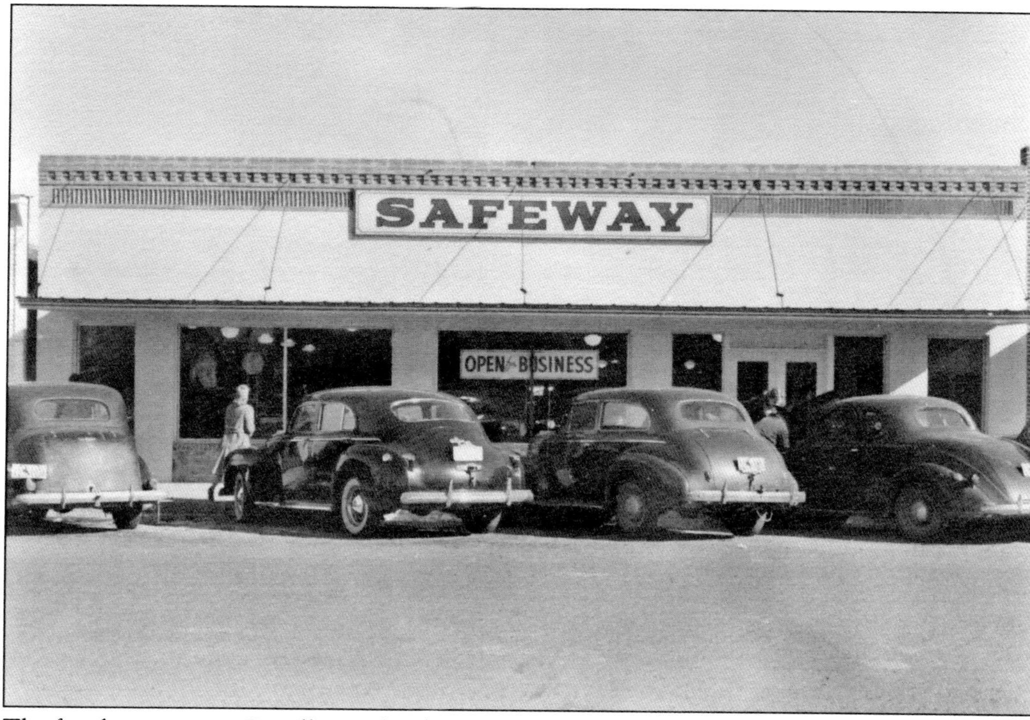

The first businesses in Powell were family-owned establishments, but in 1938 the first chain store opened in Powell, the Ben Franklin store. In 1941, Safeway opened a grocery store in the former Althoff Motors building, pictured above. In 1948, J. C. Penney opened a store on the eastern 200 block of Bent Street, pictured below. (Both HM.)

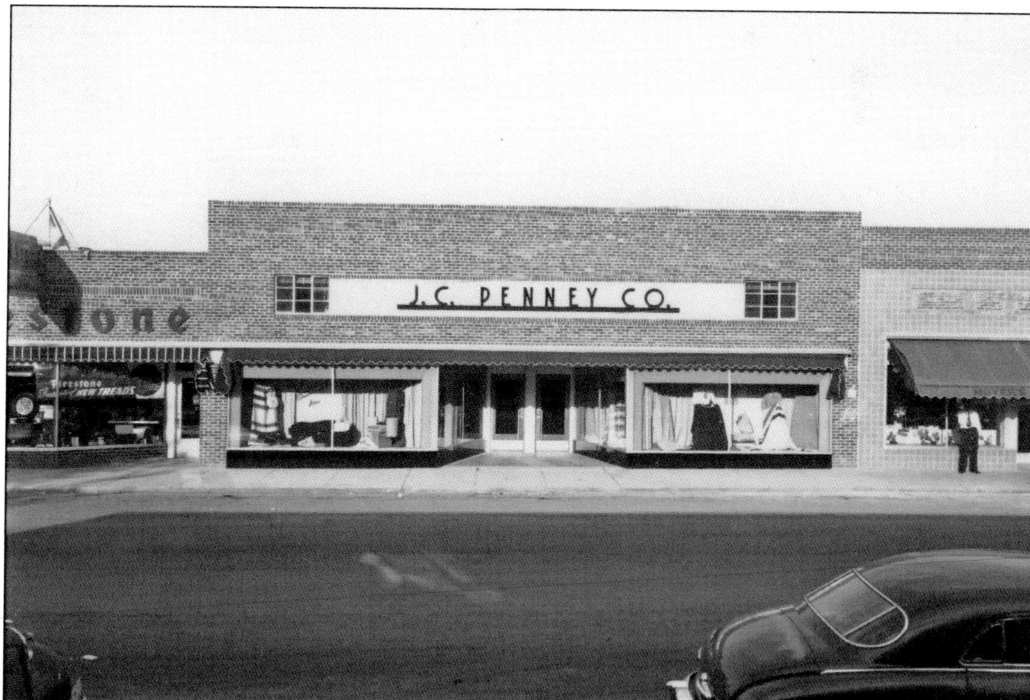

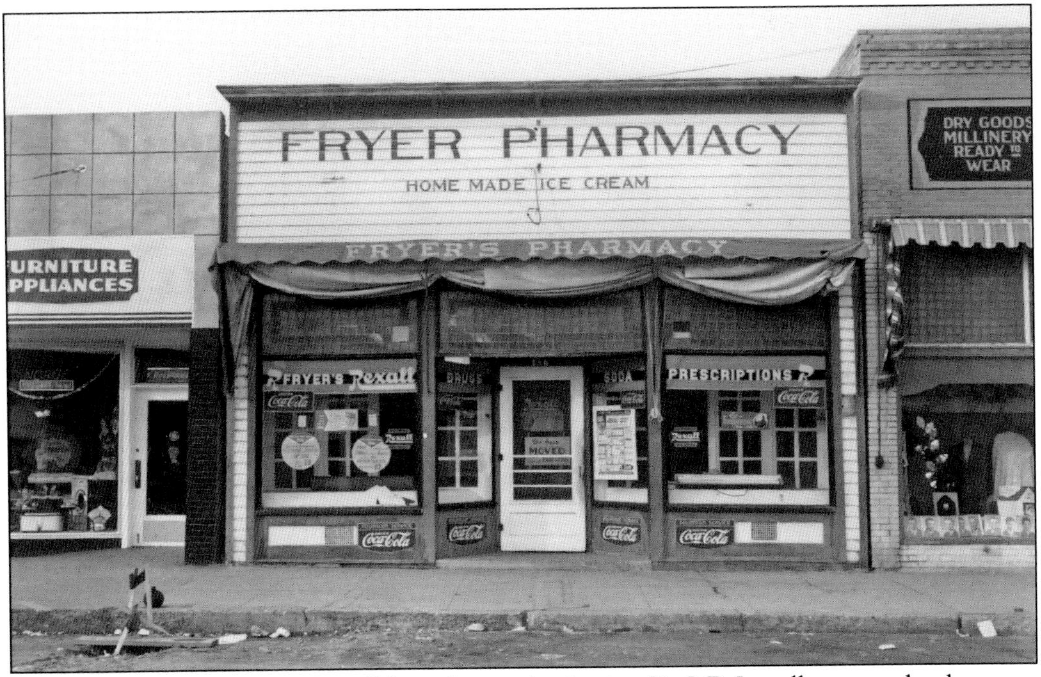

Pharmacists opened stores in Powell from the very beginning. Dr. J. D. Lewellen opened a pharmacy on Bent Street in 1909 (see page 45). Al Fryer opened Fryer's Pharmacy in 1934. (HM.)

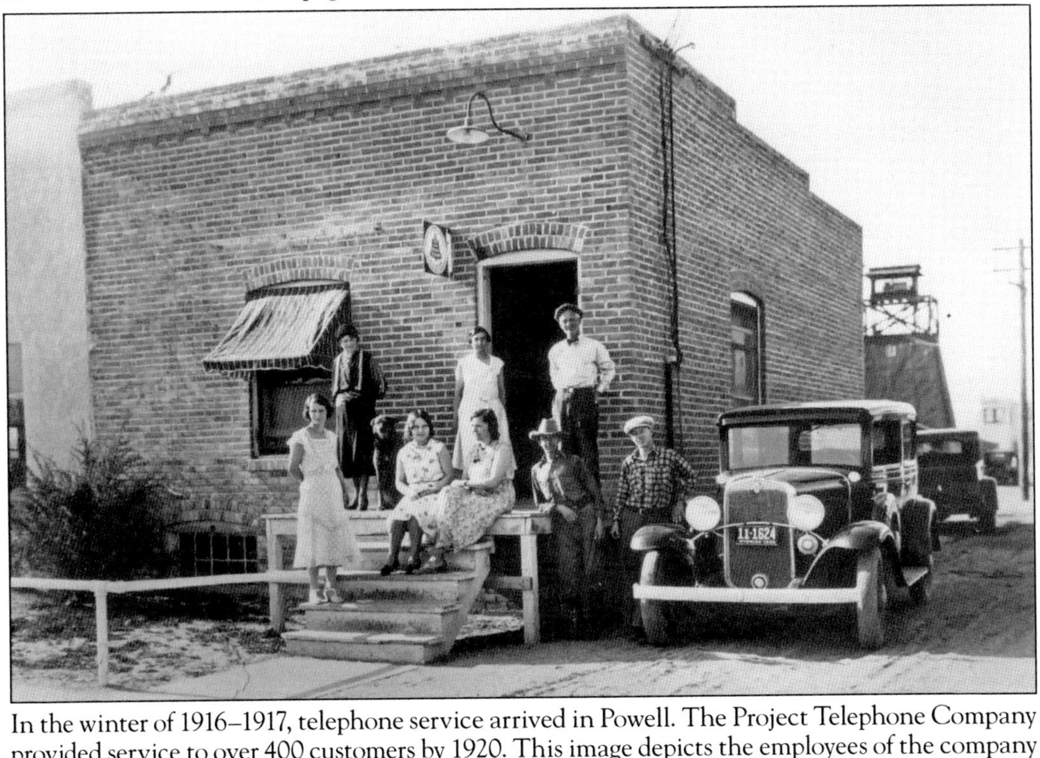

In the winter of 1916–1917, telephone service arrived in Powell. The Project Telephone Company provided service to over 400 customers by 1920. This image depicts the employees of the company sitting on the front steps of the office in the 1930s. Note the town's fire siren behind the two automobiles. (PCA.)

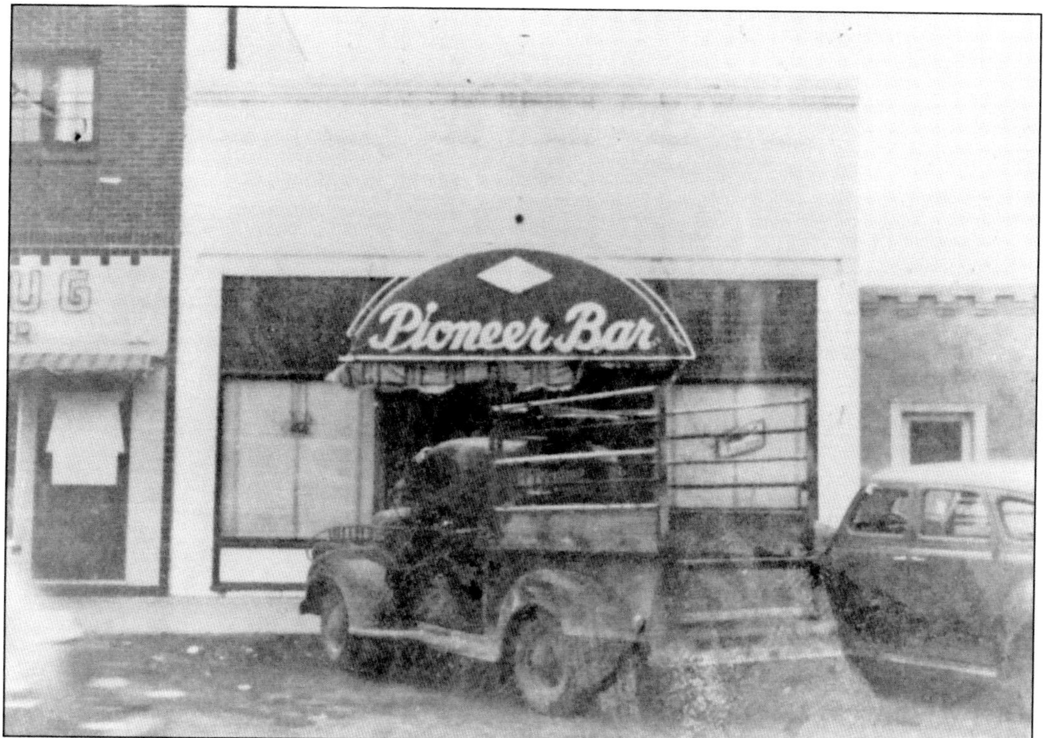

When the 18th Amendment was repealed in 1933 ending Prohibition, Powell residents allowed establishments, mainly pharmacies, to legally sell alcoholic beverages for the first time in city limits. Two of the first bars opened in Powell were the K-Bar and the Pioneer Bar, seen here with a truck parked in front. (PCA.)

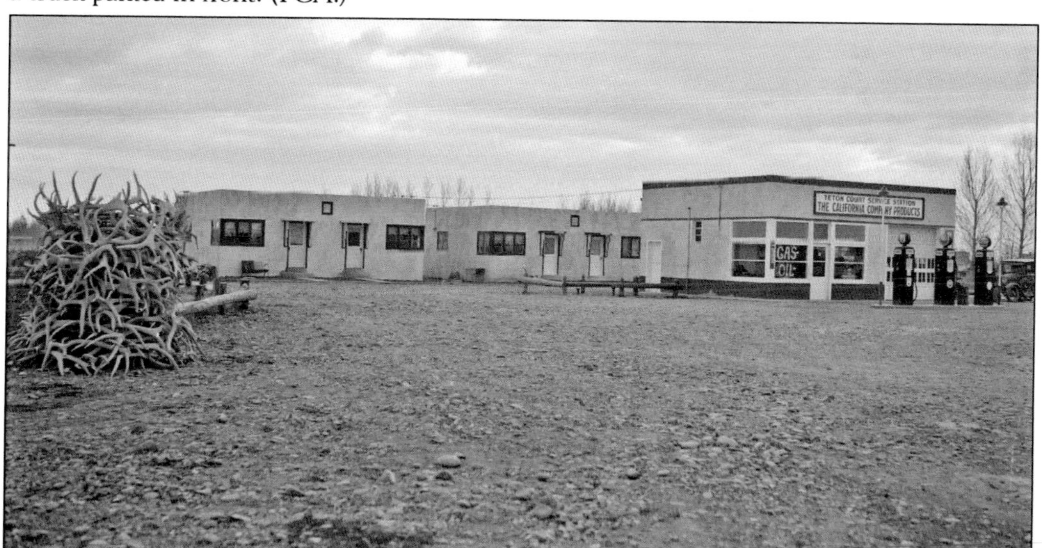

With the end of World War II, the numbers of tourists to Wyoming greatly increased. A number of travelers, en route to Yellowstone, stayed a night in Powell. Pictured here is the Teton Motor Court with gas station in the late 1940s. The pile of elk antlers gave tourists a taste of what they might see in Yellowstone. (FNB.)

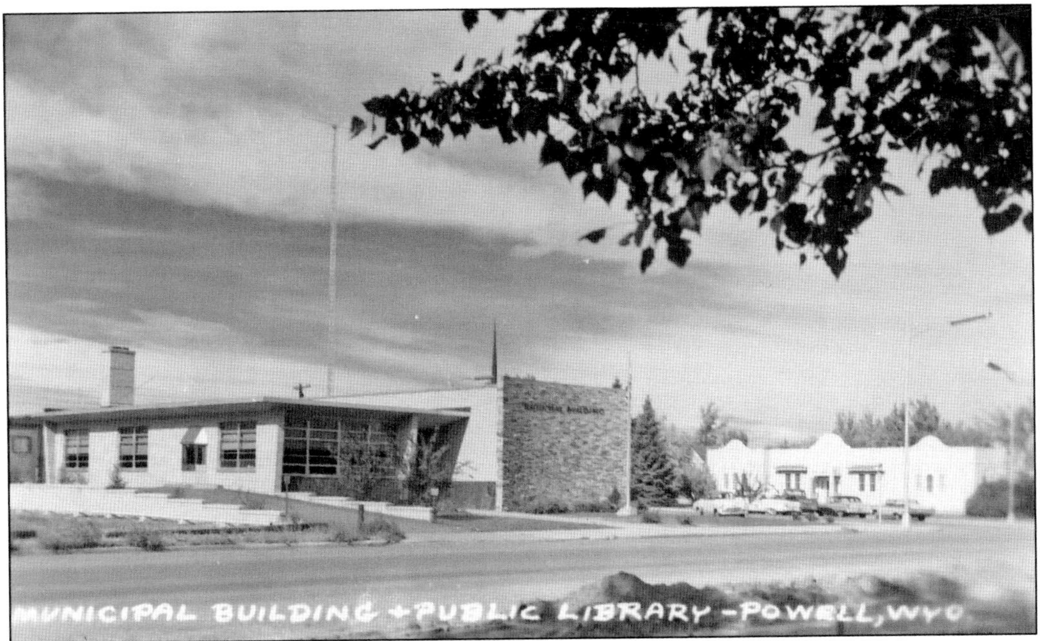

Powell's city hall originally sat on Bent Street. In the 1930s, a new facility was built between Bent and Absaroka Streets. In 1955, a new city hall, pictured here, was dedicated. The white structure on the right side of the photograph is the library, built in 1934. (HM.)

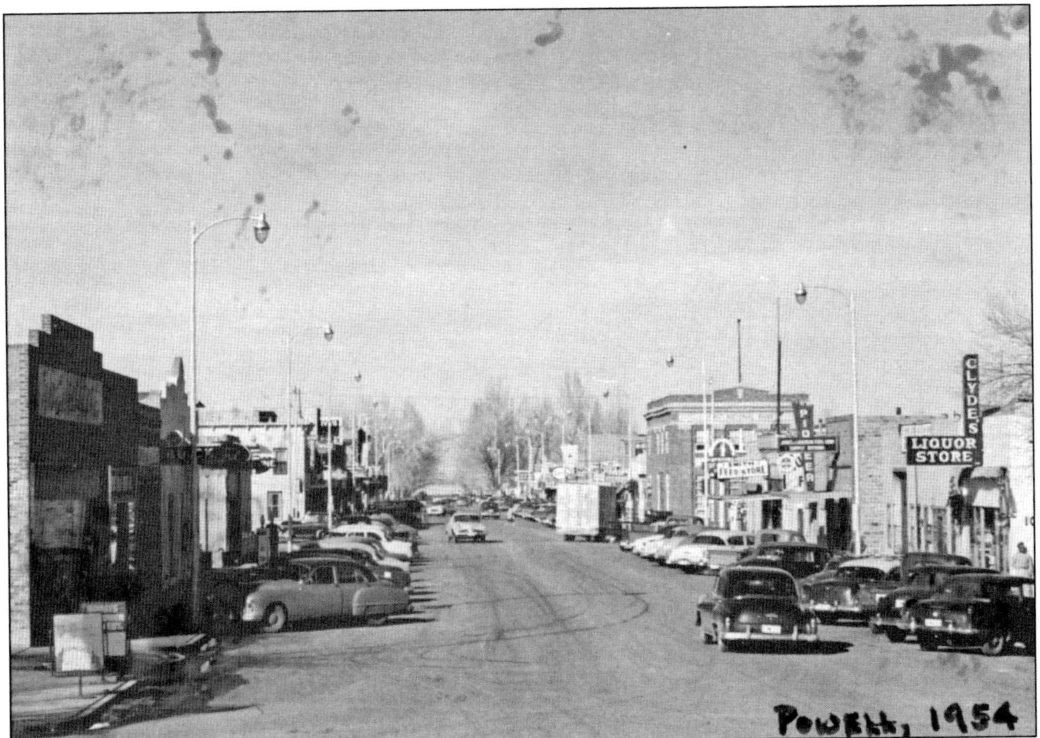

By the 1950s, Powell's business district was flourishing. This 1954 photograph of Bent Street, from Coulter Avenue, demonstrates how much Powell's main street had expanded in 45 years. (PCA.)

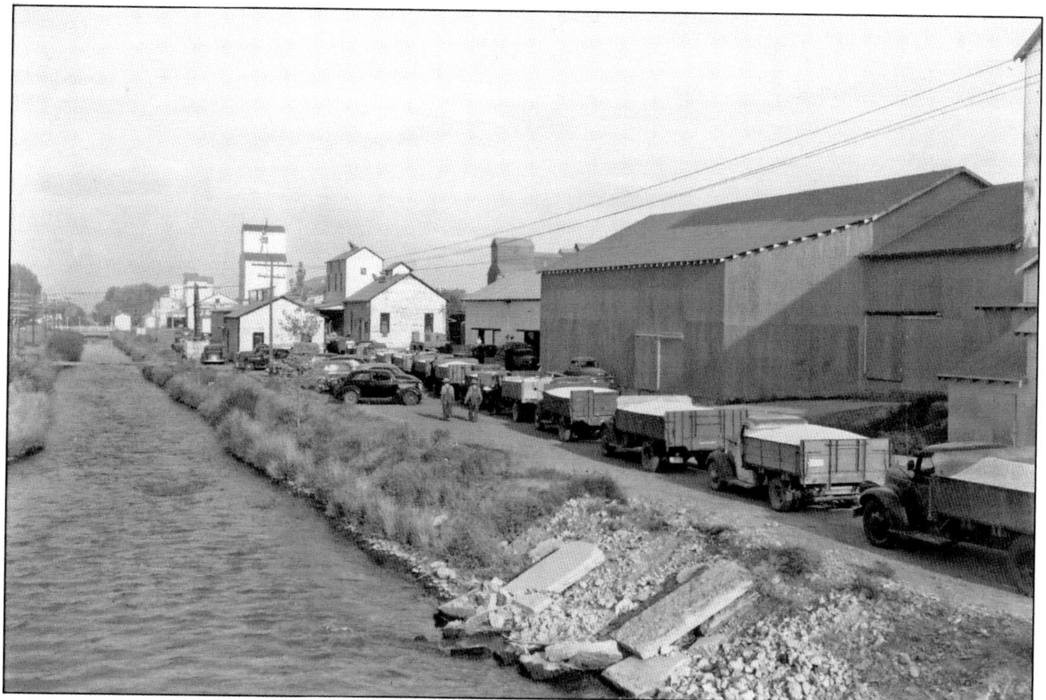

Colter Avenue, later misspelled as Coulter Avenue, is the east-west thoroughfare through town. It follows two Powell lifelines—the Garland Canal and the railroad. A number of mills and elevators sprung up along the south side of the canal and tracks. The above image captures a number of grain trucks waiting in line. The photograph below depicts Colter Avenue in the 1950s as a well-lit, four-lane thoroughfare through Powell. (Both PCA.)

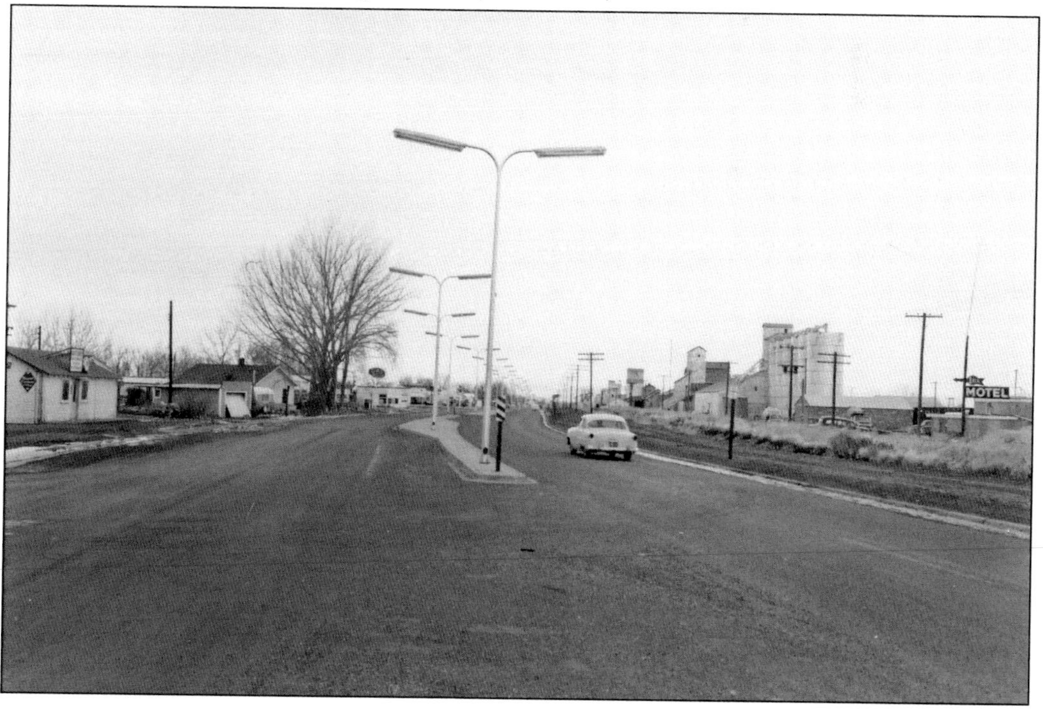

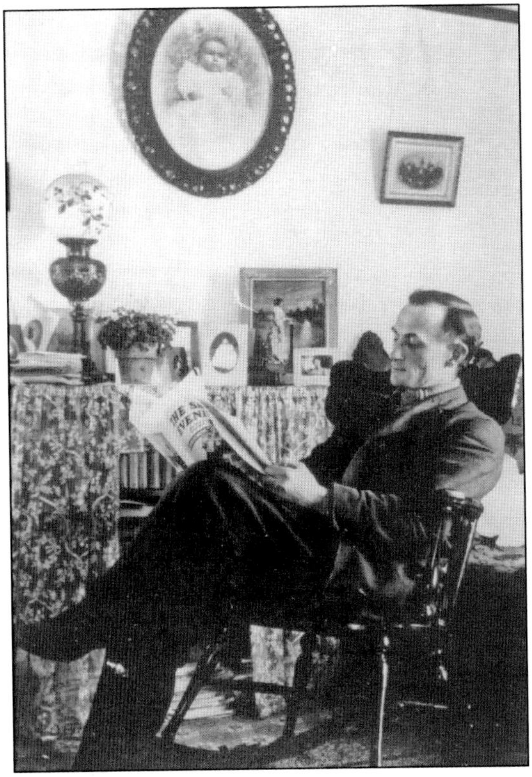

Powell's business district attracted both the prosperous and the not so prosperous. A. P. Libby, pictured at left in his study, not only was one of Powell's first successful businessmen, he also served as Powell's first mayor, from 1910 to 1911. James H. Norman, also known as Boxcar Murphy, arrived at Powell in 1966 after falling asleep in a boxcar. Boxcar bummed rides, cigarettes, and drinks. He made some money by raffling off a number of rifles and shotguns. When he walked downtown, he swung his cane all the way around and blew on a police whistle. Gregg Randall, a Northwest Community College student, managed to get Boxcar to pose for the photograph below by promising to buy him a drink. (At left, PCA; below, Gregg Randall.)

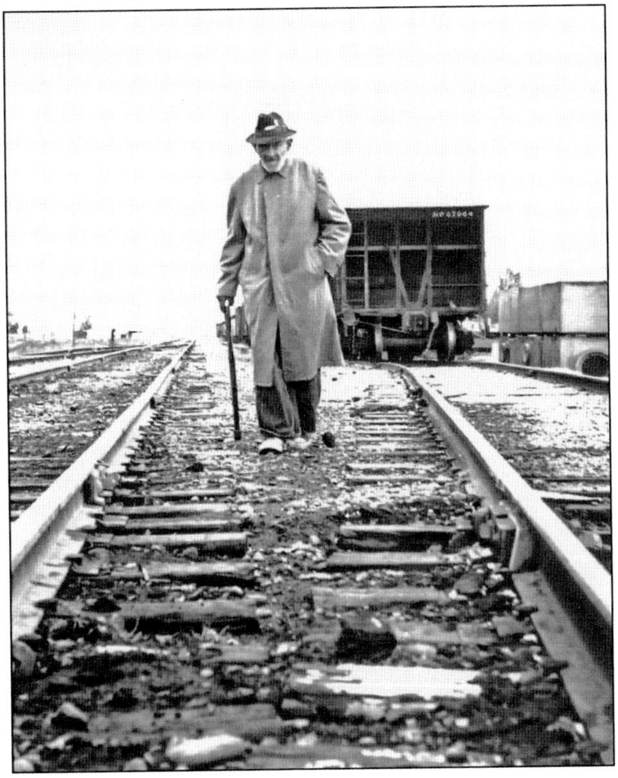

Five

EARNING A LIVING

In its first years of existence, most of Powell's residents earned a living by farming or in a position related to farming. A number of settlers also practiced a wide variety of professional trades within the community of Powell. The Bureau of Reclamation offered a number of jobs on the Shoshone Project. When the Shoshone Irrigation District was formed in 1925, it too provided jobs. Alfalfa, grain, and bean mills sprung up along the tracks to provide regular and seasonal jobs. As the community built up, more jobs were created by other economic developments. In 1915, oil was discovered in Elk Basin, some 30 miles north of Powell, and provided work to a number of oil field workers. A company town developed in Elk Basin that lasted until the mid-1950s. A small coal mine operated on Coal Mine Hill, located a few miles northeast of Powell. A few residents took advantage of the hunting in the surrounding mountains and became hunting guides.

Other sources of employment in Powell came from community institutions. School District No. 1 employed a number of teachers and staff. After World War II, Northwest Community College employed a number of instructors and staff. Powell's expanding medical services also employed a number of doctors and nurses. Some of Powell's residents found other ways to make a living. When Roy Barnes auditioned to sing for a Billings, Montana, radio station, he soon became known as the "Rocky Mountain Cowboy." His performances at dances and on Powell's new radio station, KPOW, supplemented the income he made from his gas station and as a school bus driver.

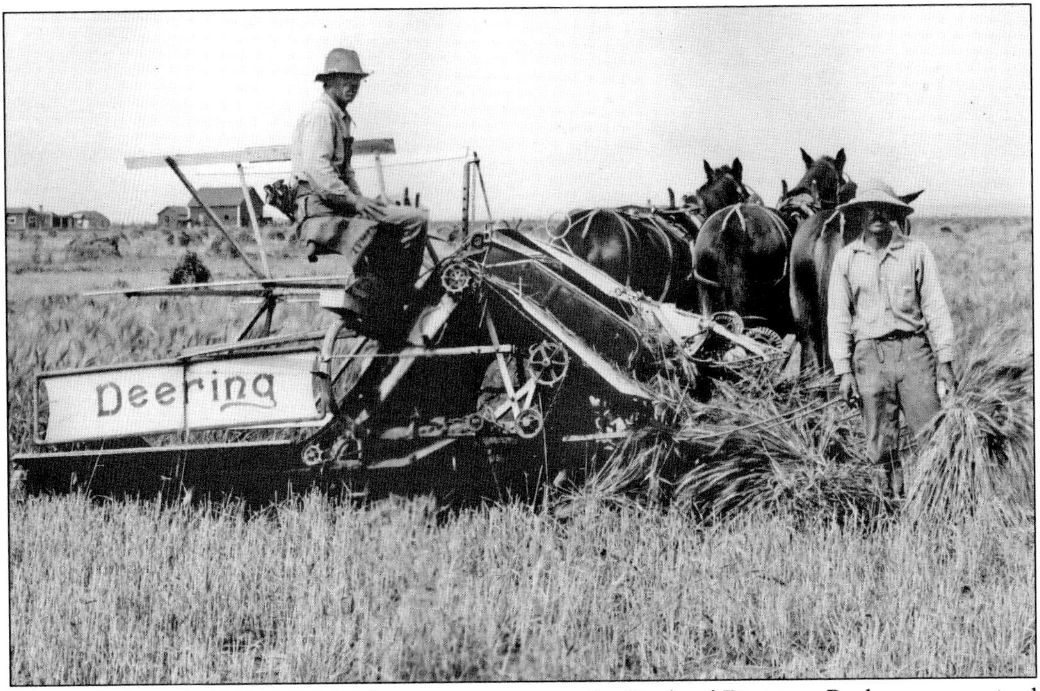

Wheat, oats, and alfalfa were the first crops grown on the Garland Division. Both crops required a tremendous amount of labor to harvest it. Once the grain was cut, it needed to be tied into shocks, as seen above. Alfalfa, grown to feed livestock, needed to be mowed, gathered, and then stacked into piles, as seen below. Both horsepower and human power were needed to harvest these crops. (Both SIDA.)

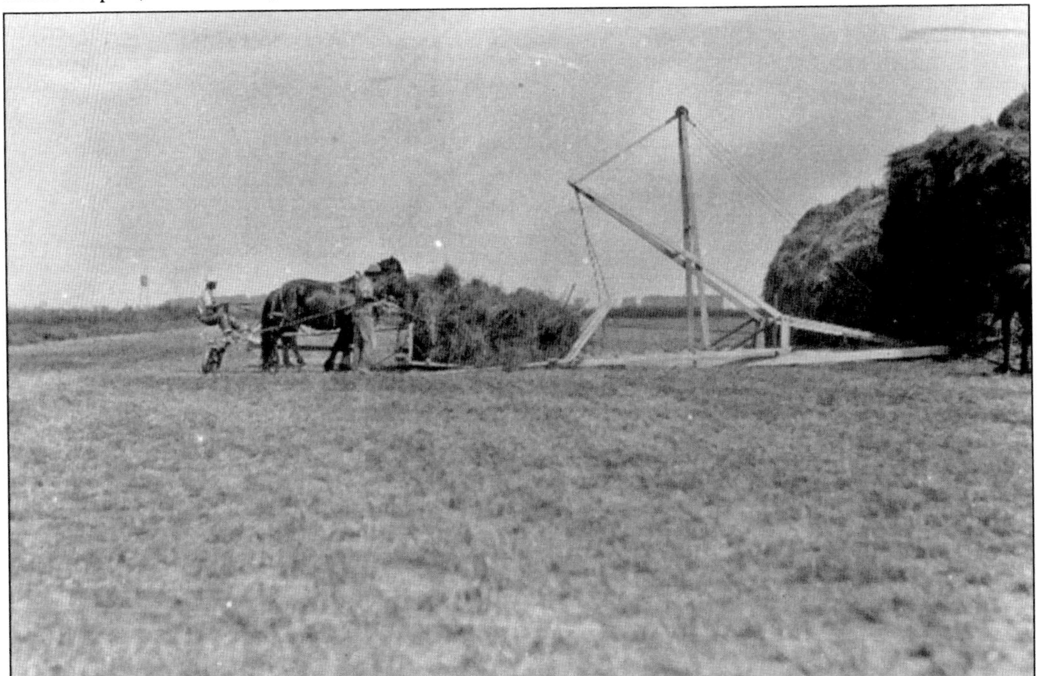

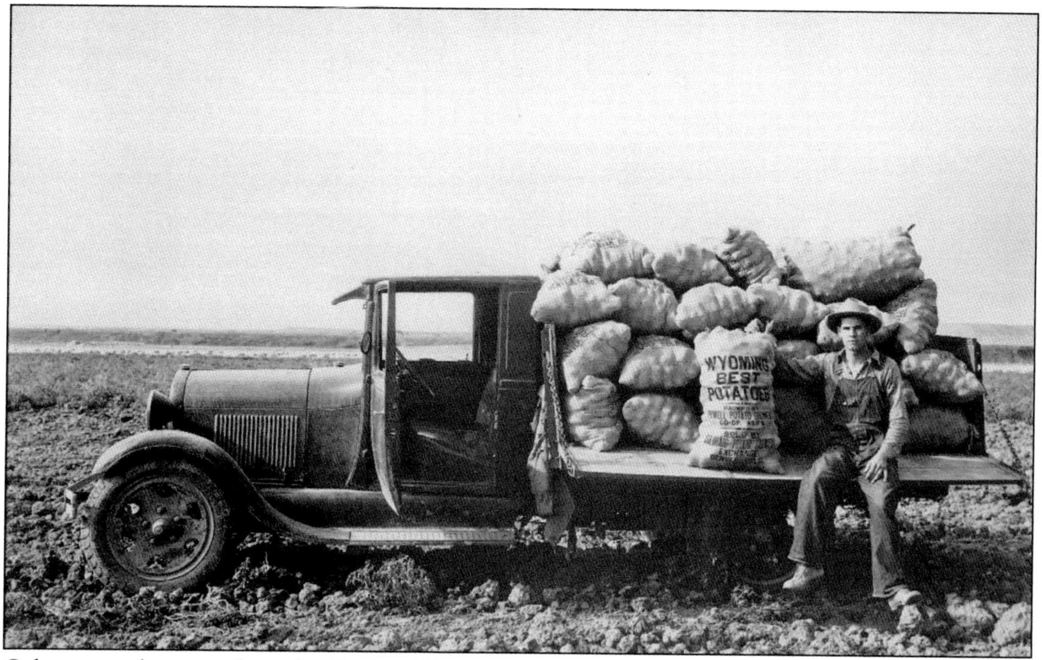

Other crops harvested on the Garland Division were beans, potatoes, and sugar beets. Potatoes were dug out by hand, often gathered by kids who wore belts with sacks attached, and then taken to the mills to be shipped out by rail to market. In the photograph above, a proud farmer is ready to haul his potatoes to market. Sugar beets were plowed out by dirt, their tops cut off by hand, and then "forked" into a vehicle and taken to market. The photograph below shows two men using beet forks to load a truck. (Both SIDA.)

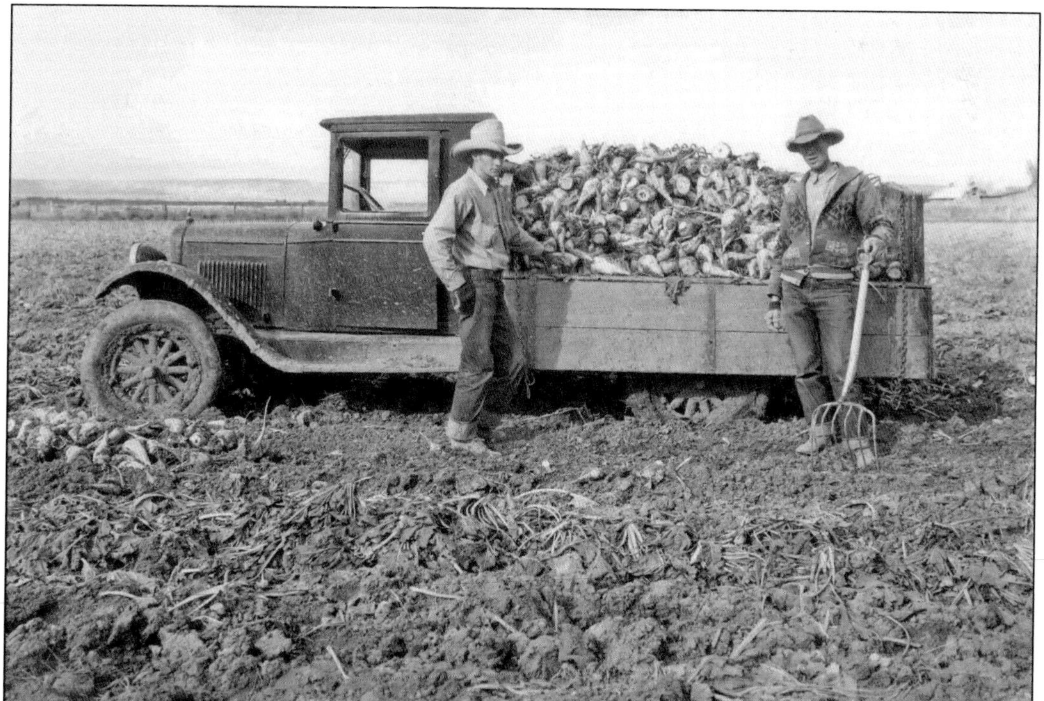

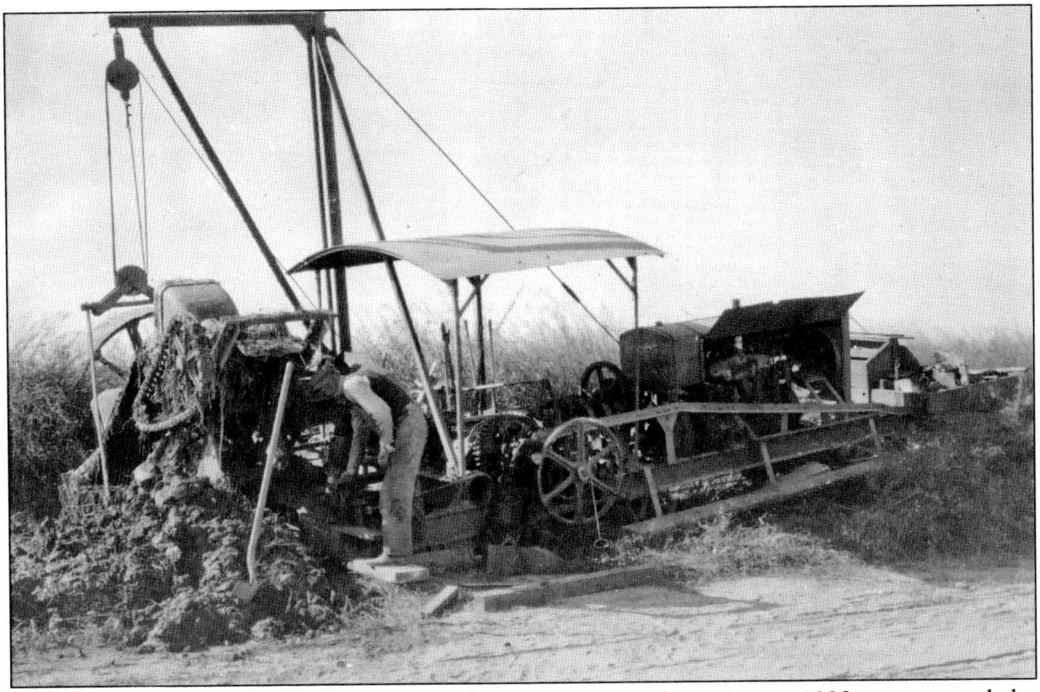

First the Reclamation Service, renamed the Bureau of Reclamation in 1923, maintained the canal and ditches associated with the Garland Division. In 1925, the homesteaders took over the project from the Bureau of Reclamation and managed it through the Shoshone Irrigation District. To keep water flowing, ditch riders were hired to manage headgates that distributed water to individual plots of land. Ditches also needed to be cleaned, as seen in the above photograph, where an employee digs out a ditch using an excavating machine. The clay drainage pipes also needed to be occasionally cleaned out. The photograph below depicts a group of men holding willow roots dug out of the Drainpipe K in 1920. (Both SIDA.)

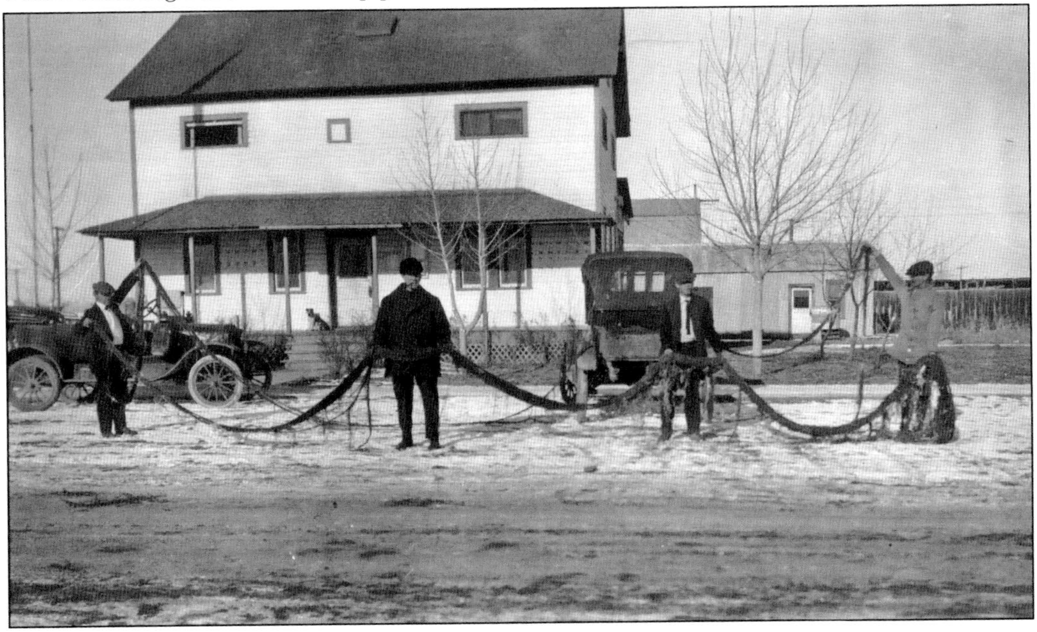

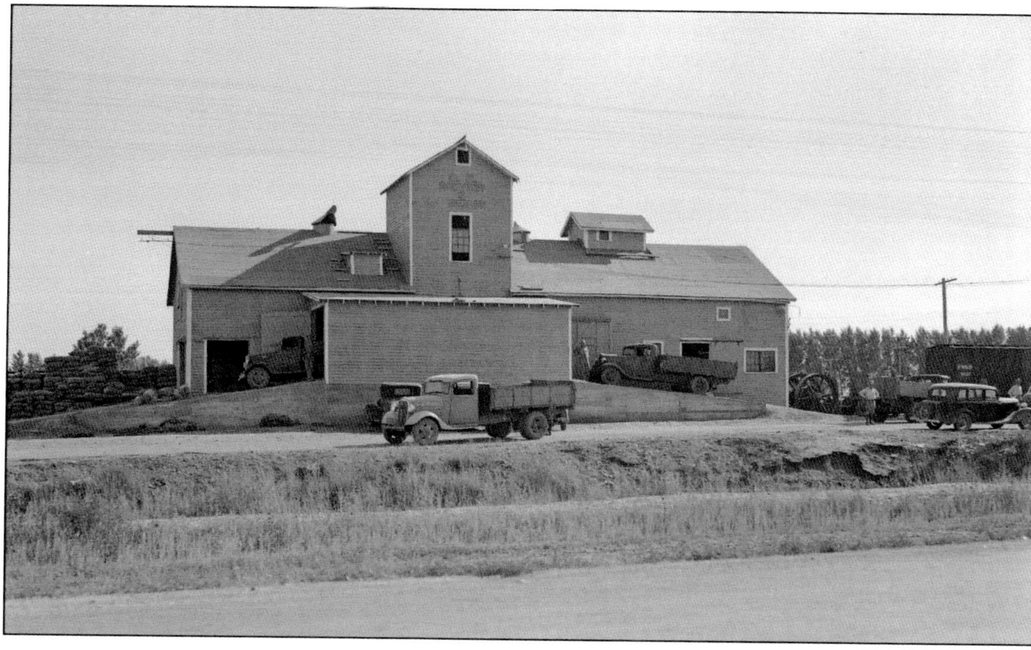

When the crops were harvested, farmers sold their bounty to the mills located along the canal. Beans were sold at O. E. Bever's and Sons mill, pictured above. The beans were sacked and stacked, as seen in the image below. Ora Bever, a former Garland Division homesteader, hired a number of Crow Indians to harvest the crops. Bever established the bean mill in the 1920s and became a prosperous businessman. At the end of the harvest, he hosted the Bever Bean Ball to celebrate. (Both FNB.)

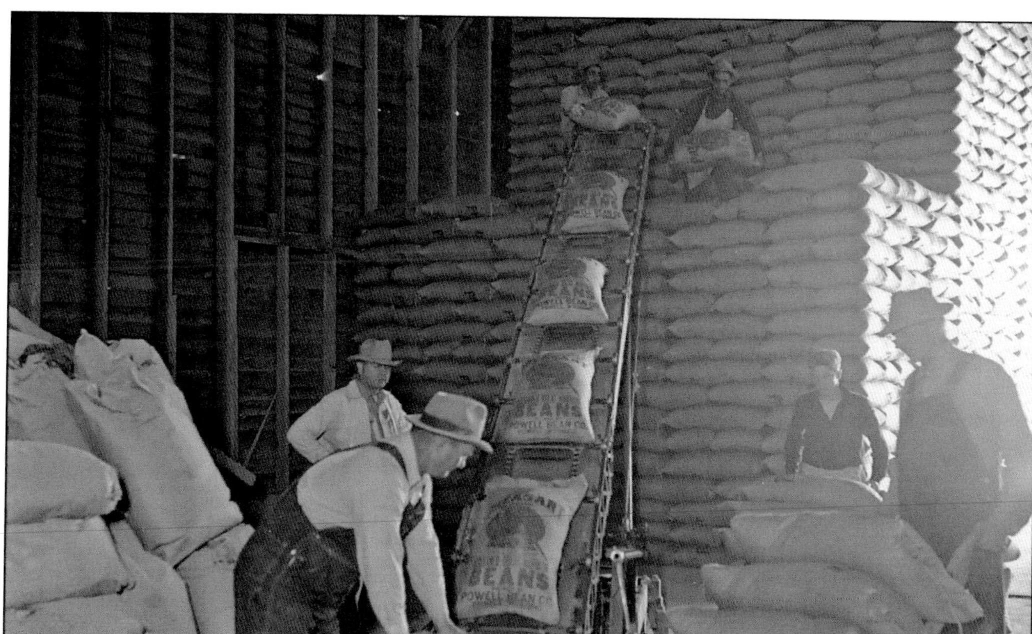

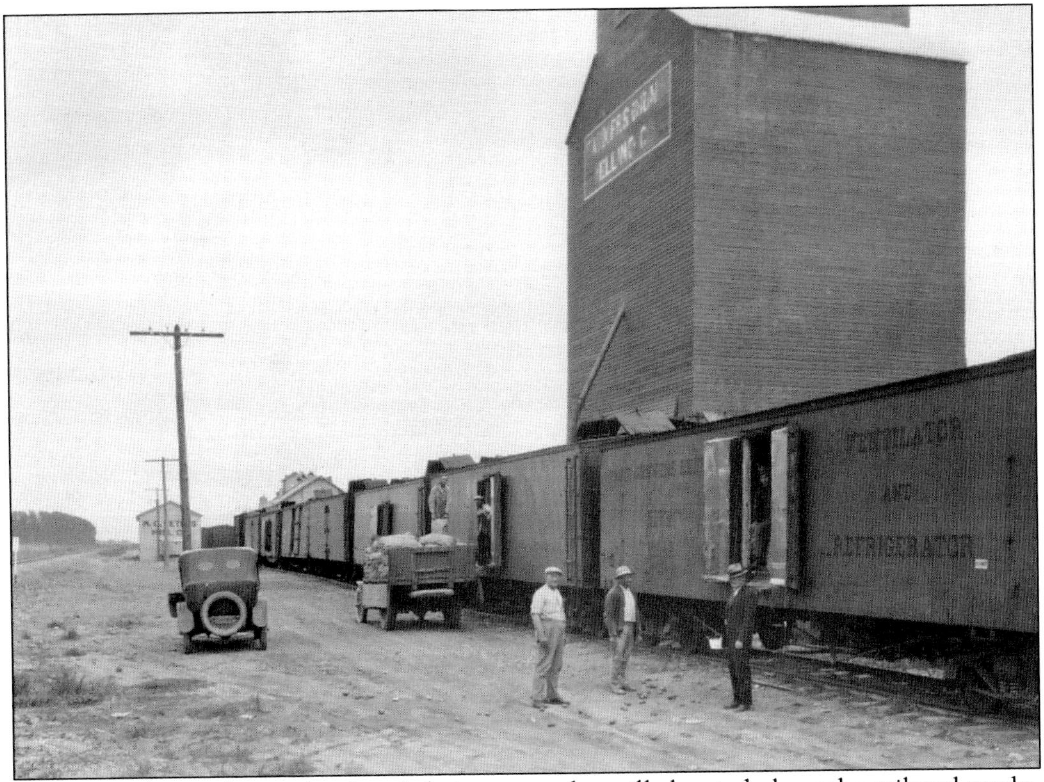

Potatoes and sugar beets also found their way to the mills located along the railroad tracks. Pictured here are men loading railroad cars with sacks of potatoes. The railroad hauled the goods to Billings, Montana, and then distant markets beyond. (PCA.)

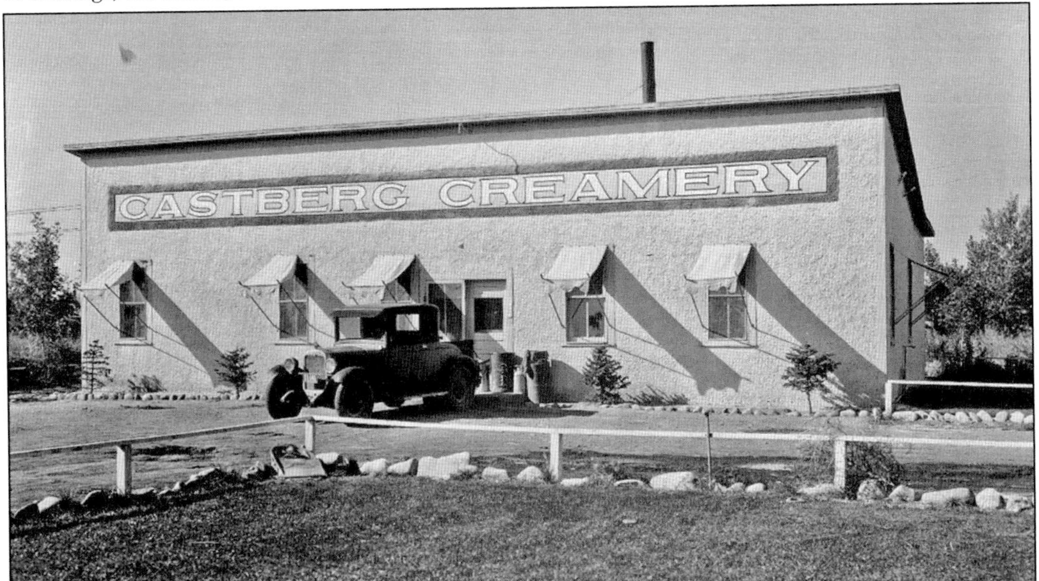

Dairy farmers sold milk to the Castberg Creamery, established in 1927. The creamery, pictured here, distributed milk, ice cream, and Eskimo pies to the community of Powell. (PCA.)

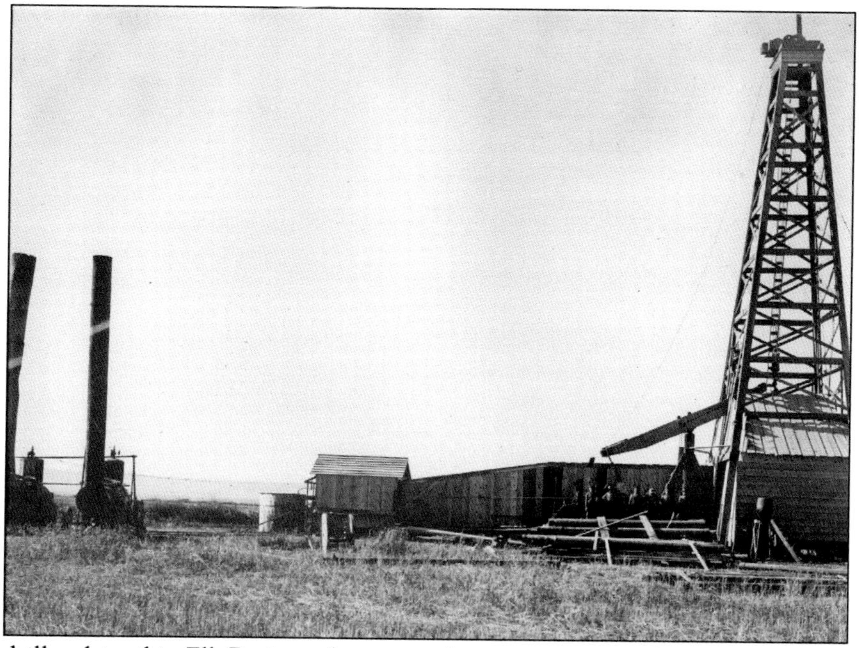

In 1915, drillers hit oil in Elk Basin and various oil companies arrived and struggled to establish control over the newly discovered oil pool. Pictured above is a well operated by the Old Colony Oil Company. Soon the Illinois Pipeline was constructed to pipe oil from Frannie, Wyoming, to an oil refinery in Greybull, Wyoming. In 1916, the town of Elk Basin was founded to house a number of oil field workers and their families, pictured below. The town later changed locations because of health concerns regarding gas fumes, which tarnished silverware and caused paint to peel. In 1955, the town of Elk Basin shut down and a number of oil field workers moved to Powell. Oil production remained a strong part of Powell's economy until Amoco limited its operations in Elk Basin during the late 1980s. (Both SIDA.)

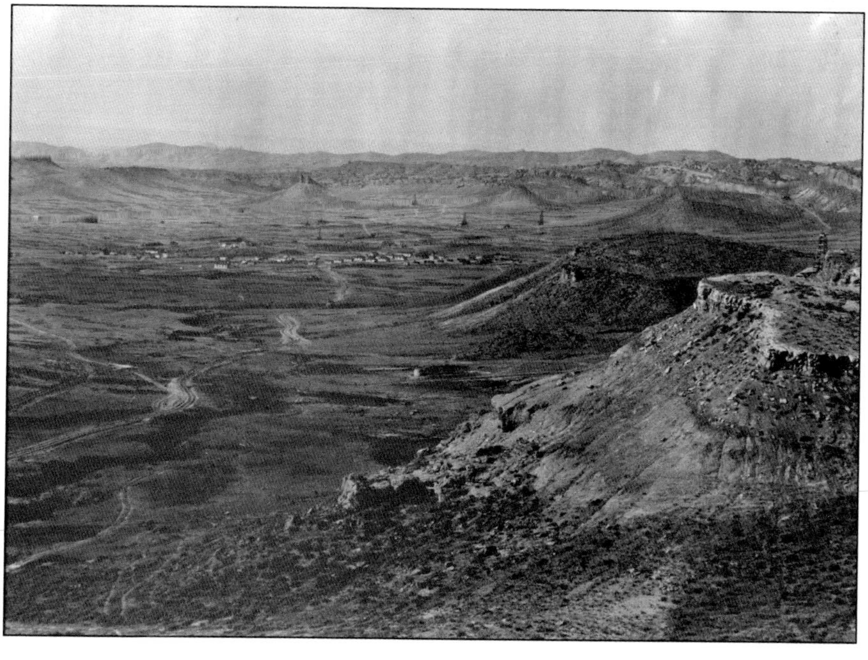

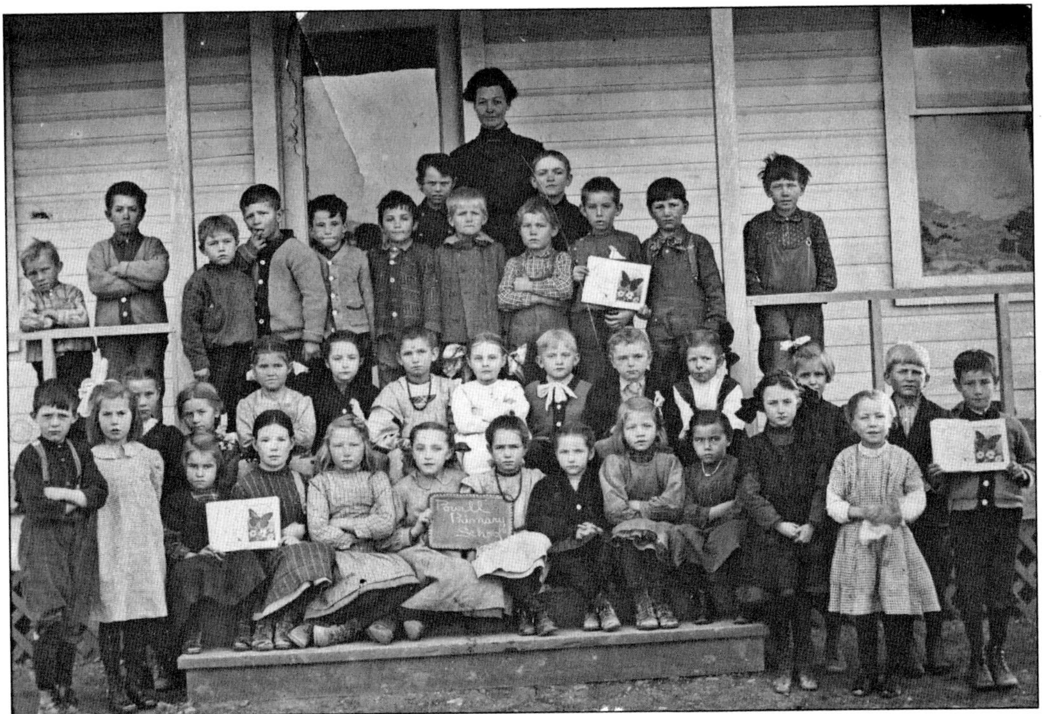

Being in the center of School District No. 1, a number of Powell's residents found employment in the public school system. This photograph depicts Powell's first teacher, Marie Haley, with her primary school class in 1908. (HM.)

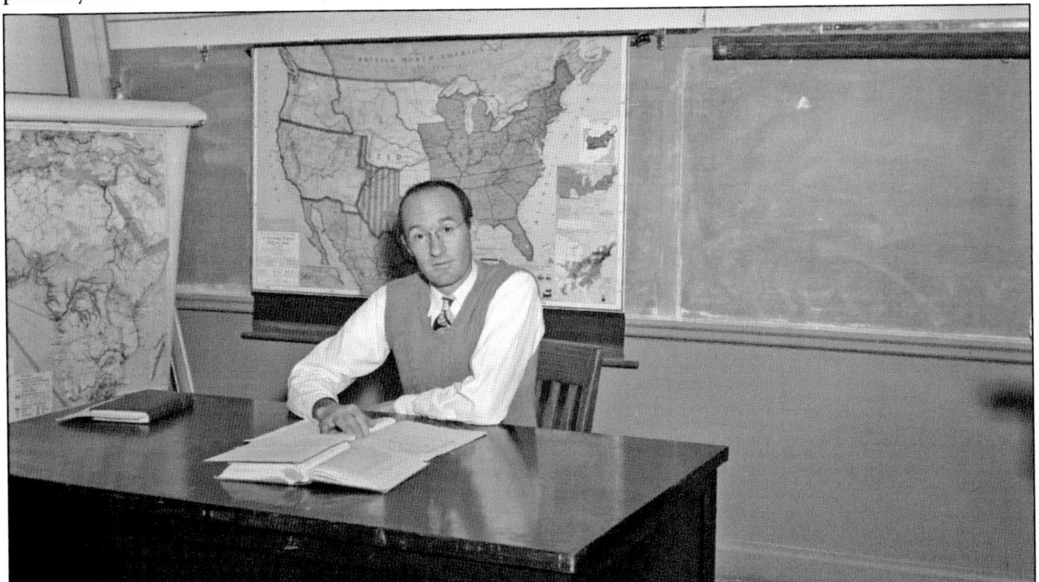

When the University of Wyoming opened up a branch campus that later became Northwest Community College, some local residents found employment teaching college courses. John Taggart Hinckley, a history instructor, poses for this photograph. Hinckley taught at Northwest Community College, now identified simply as Northwest College, from 1948 to 1980. The college library bears his name. (NWC.)

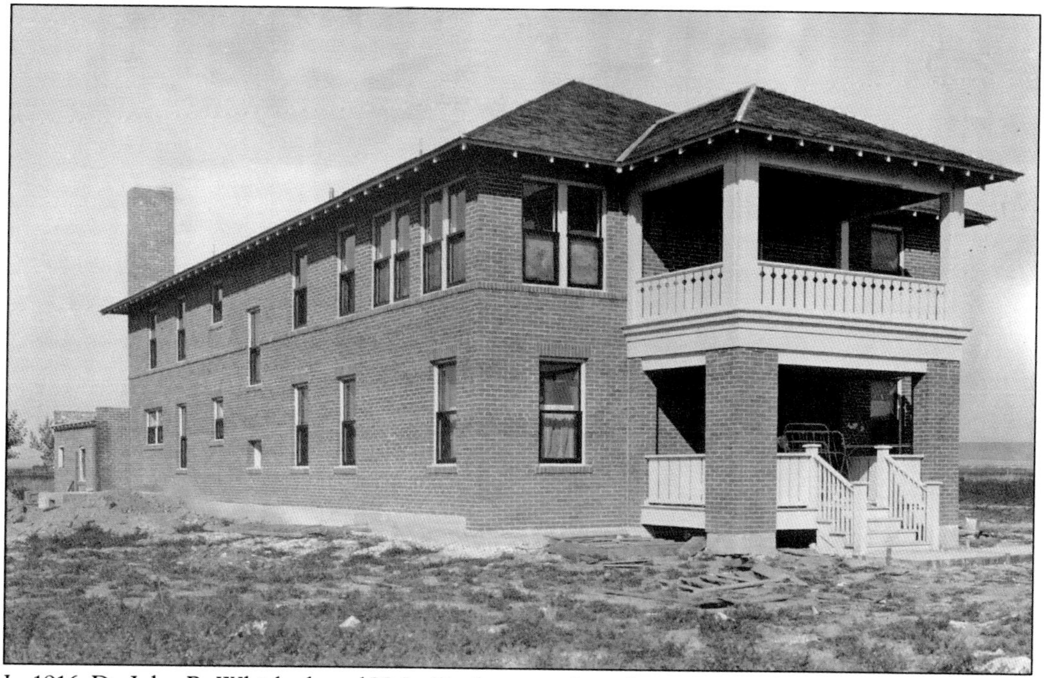

In 1916, Dr. John R. Whitlock and H. L. Gephart purchased property in the Edmond's subdivision and constructed a private 18-bed hospital, pictured above, a year later. Whitlock operated the hospital until 1936, when he sold it off to Dr. Robert Siddle. Due to Dr. Siddle's poor health, the hospital closed on a number of occasions. After Dr. Siddle passed away, three businessmen, Ernest Roney, Ora Bever, and Edgar Swallow, purchased Whitlock Hospital. Beginning in 1946, the community raised the funds to purchase land and construct a new hospital. Until it could be built, though, Whitlock Hospital was remodeled and newly outfitted with equipment acquired from the hospital at the Heart Mountain Relocation Center. Whitlock Hospital's 36 years of operation came to an end when the new War Memorial Hospital, pictured below, was dedicated in 1952. (Above, SIDA; below, PCA.)

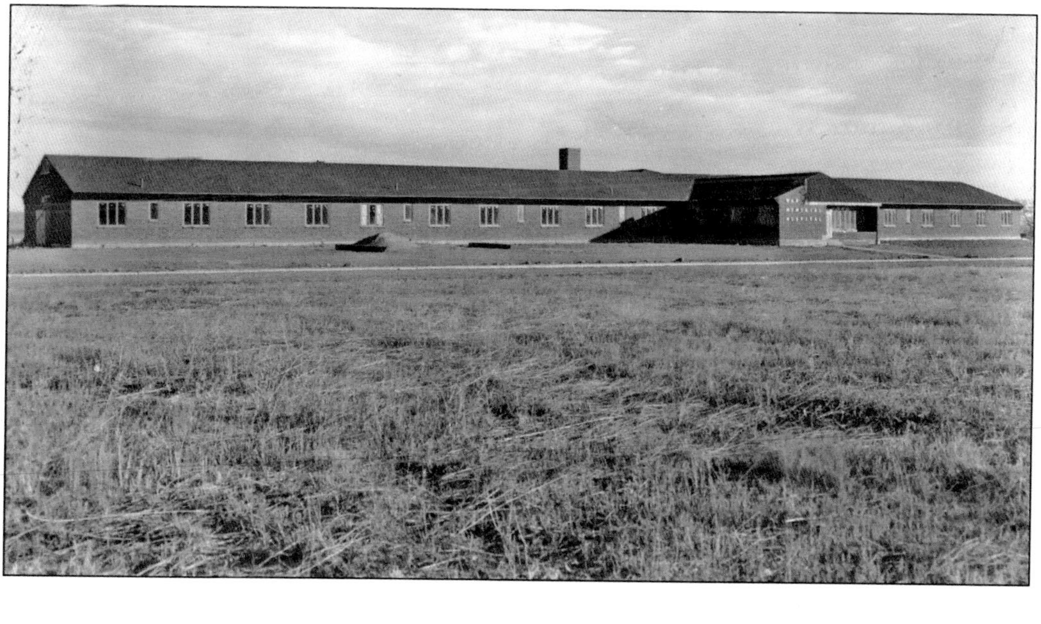

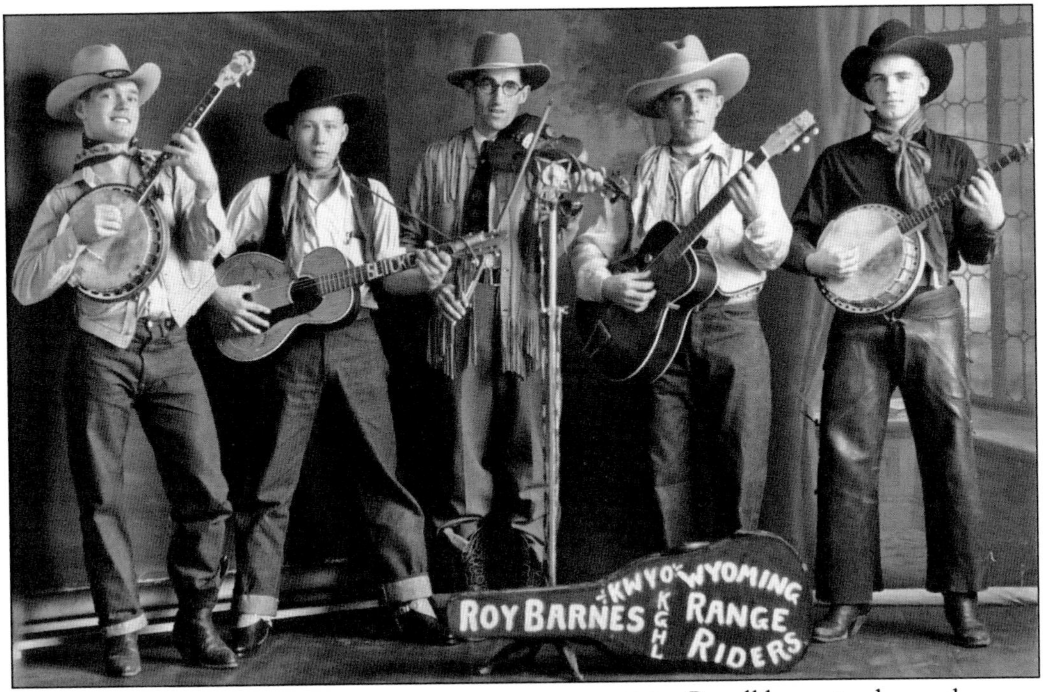

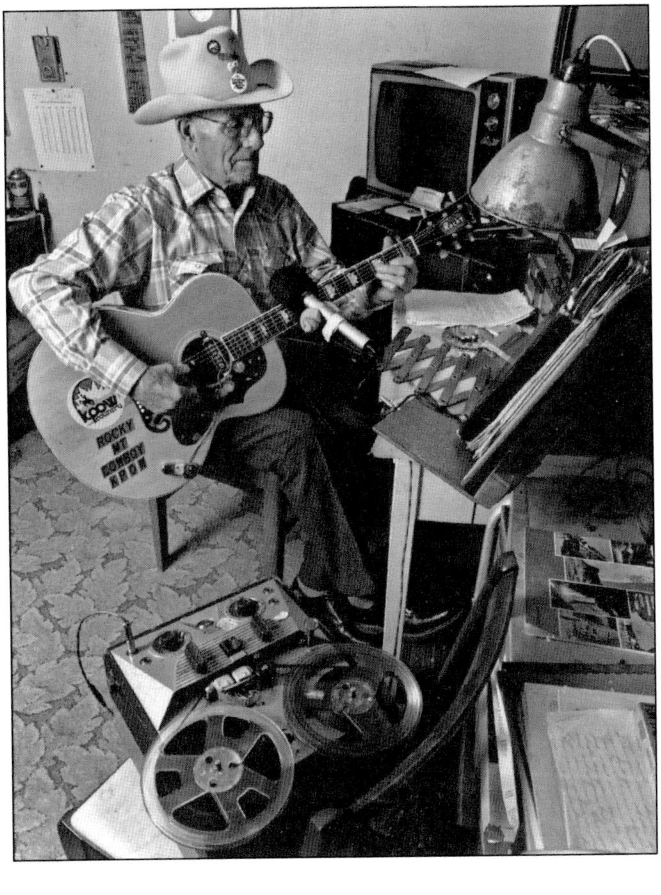

Powell homesteaders and businessmen often took on extra jobs to supplement their income. In 1934, Roy Barnes, who worked and then later owned the Husky Gas Station, traveled to Billings, Montana, for a singing audition to perform for radio station KGHL. The picture above shows Roy (second from the right) with his group. After being put on the air, Roy made a career of performing as the Rocky Mountain Cowboy and performed on the radio every morning for over 50 years. Two of Roy's World War II songs, "We Didn't Invite Them Over but We're Gonna Repay the Call" and "You Won't Know Tokyo When We Get Through," received national acclaim. His music praised the cowboy life, honored the accomplishments of homesteaders, and recalled historic events in Powell, including the saga of Earl Durand. (Both HM.)

Six

The Saga of Earl Durand

On March 24, 1939, Earl Durand walked into the front door of the First National Bank and shouted, "It's a holdup, and up with your hands." Some 40 miles west of Powell, at the base of the Beartooth Mountains, a posse led by Park County sheriff Blackburn believed Earl Durand was surrounded and would soon be captured; however, Durand managed to escape and walk down to the nearby highway. Upon reaching the highway, Durand stopped a car with three occupants and forced the driver, Harry Moore, to take him towards Powell.

The posse sought Earl Durand for a number of crimes he committed in the weeks before. Officials initially arrested Durand for poaching elk, and the judge sentenced him to serve six months in the Park County Jail. Durand escaped his jail cell by knocking the jailer, Noah Riley, over the head with a glass milk bottle and forced the dazed jailer to drive him to his parent's home outside of Powell. Hearing of Durand's escape, deputy sheriff D. M. Baker and town marshal Charles Lewis hoped to recapture Durand at his parent's home. When Baker and Lewis arrived at the Durand home, Earl Durand shot and killed both men. He eluded the law for the next few days, hiding in various locations around Powell. When the law stepped up its search for the fugitive, Durand forced two of his neighbors to drive him to the Beartooth Mountains. Here the posse finally caught up to him; unfortunately, when two men who were part of the posse, Arthur Argento and Orville Linabary, walked too close to Durand's hideout, he shot and killed them both.

After escaping the posse, Durand forced Moore to drive him to Deaver, Wyoming, where he secured more ammunition, and then to the Durand family farm so Earl could tell his parents goodbye. Durand then made Moore drive him to an isolated location where Durand left his three hostages, stole Moore's car, and drove to Powell. Durand's decision to rob the bank led to the tragic death of Johnnie Gawthorp, a bank teller, and finally brought an end to Durand's reign of crime. After being wounded in an exchange of gunfire with Powell residents, Earl Durand took his own life. Years later, songs and movies portrayed the troubled Earl Durand as a social bandit pushed too far by the establishment, forcing him to make his last stand in Powell.

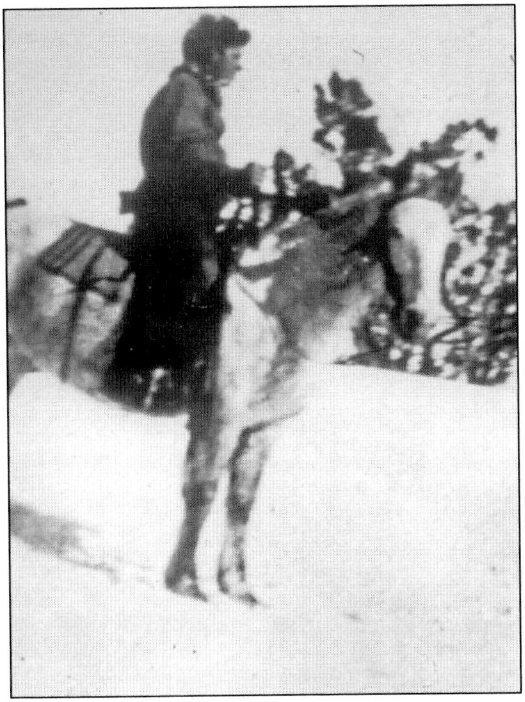

Earl Durand was known as a modern-day mountain man and an excellent shot. He dropped out of school after the eighth grade and spent a majority of his time outdoors. Durand lived in a tent outside of his parent's home, located northeast of Powell. From Powell, he would hike to the Absaroka Mountains, 40 miles west of Powell, with nothing more than a pack and rifle and not return for weeks. Durand frequently poached game for sport and to feed his family and his poor neighbors. After one hunting trip to poach elk, Durand and his companions were driving back towards home when game wardens stopped the vehicle west of Cody. Durand fled from the wardens only to be recaptured the next day. After Earl Durand pled guilty to killing two elk out of season, the judge sentenced him to pay a $100 fine and to serve six months in jail. In custody, Durand worried he would receive more jail time for killing two cattle after his initial escape from the game wardens. (Both PCA.)

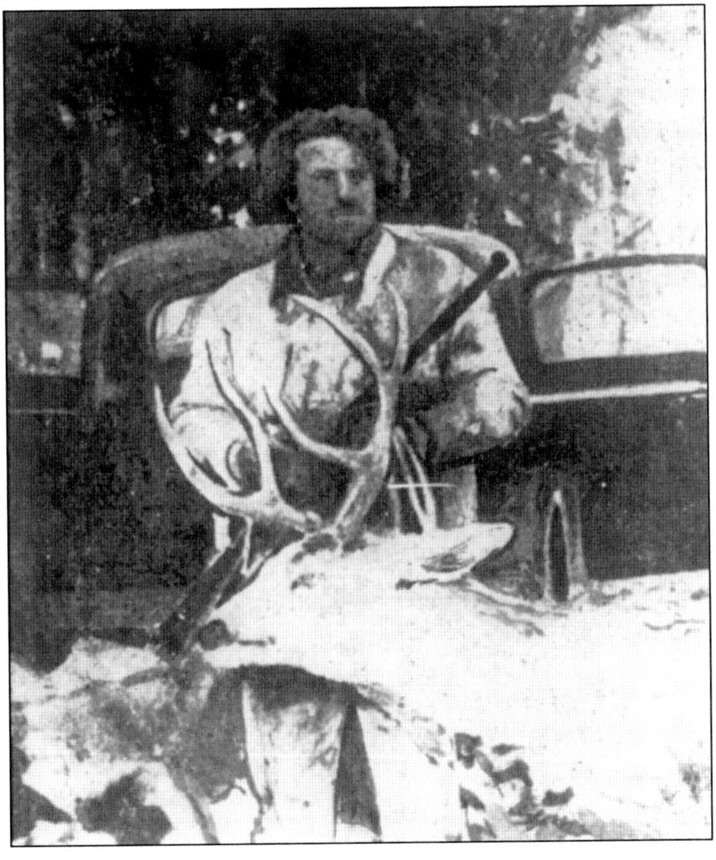

Walter Durand, Earl's father, was a well-respected homesteader in the Powell area. He arrived in Powell in 1913 from Missouri. Walter and his wife, Effie, had three daughters and one son, Earl. In 1921, Walter served as master of Absarokee Lodge No. 30, Powell's Masonic Lodge. Shortly after the death of Earl, the family wrote the lodge, "The many kind words and letters of sympathies and flowers sent us by known and unknown friends from all parts of our country has been a big help in enabling us to bear the ladden [sic] sorrows in the tragic death of our beloved son." The Durand family left Powell for Boise, Idaho, in 1945. (Absarokee Lodge No. 30.)

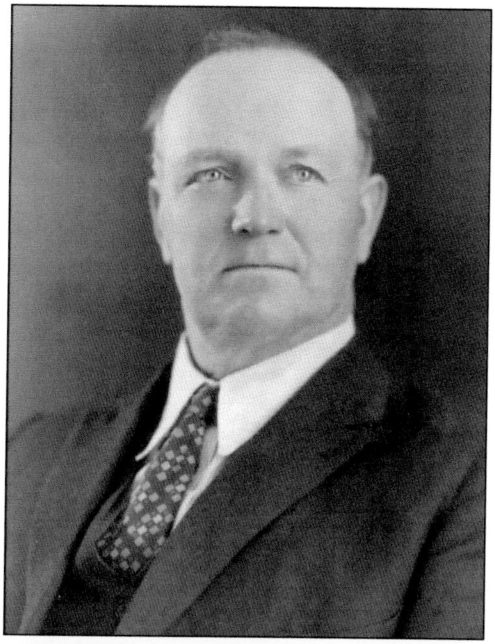

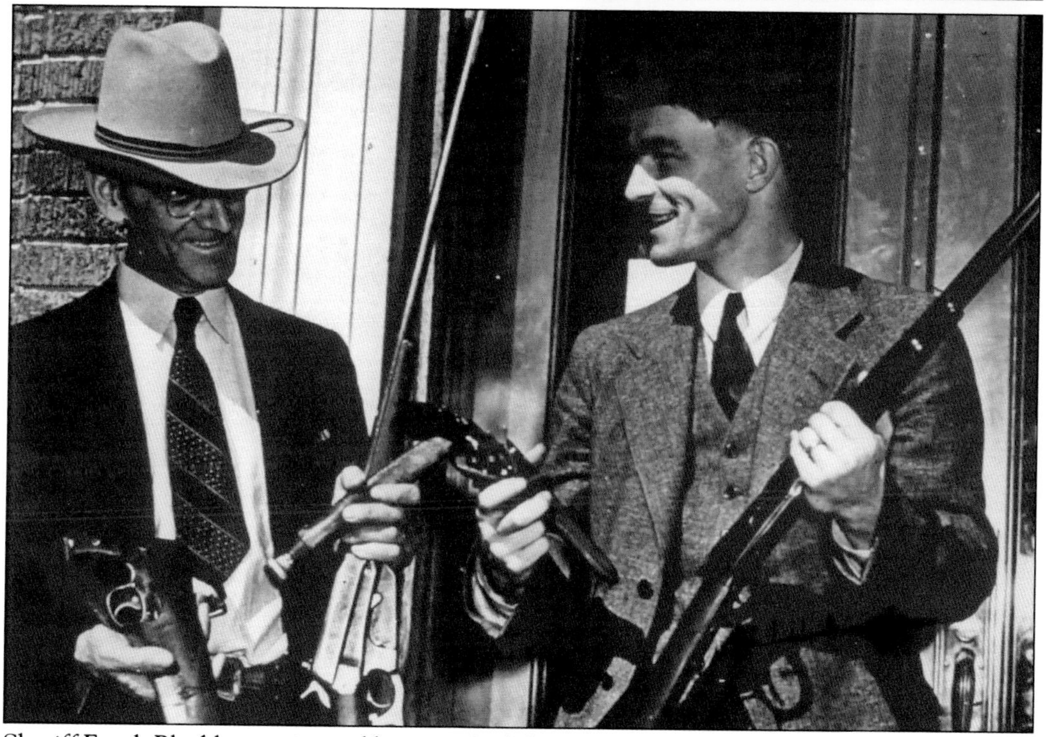

Sheriff Frank Blackburn, pictured here on the left, poses with county attorney Oliver Steadman while both men hold Earl Durand's weapons after the shoot-out in Powell. Blackburn served as Park County sheriff from 1927 to 1959. On March 16, 1939, shortly after Blackburn left for Los Angeles to pick up a prisoner, Durand escaped from his jail cell by hitting the jailer, Noah Riley, over the head with a glass milk bottle. Durand then forced the dazed Riley to drive him to his parent's house to gather supplies to sustain him while he eluded the law after his jailbreak. (PCA.)

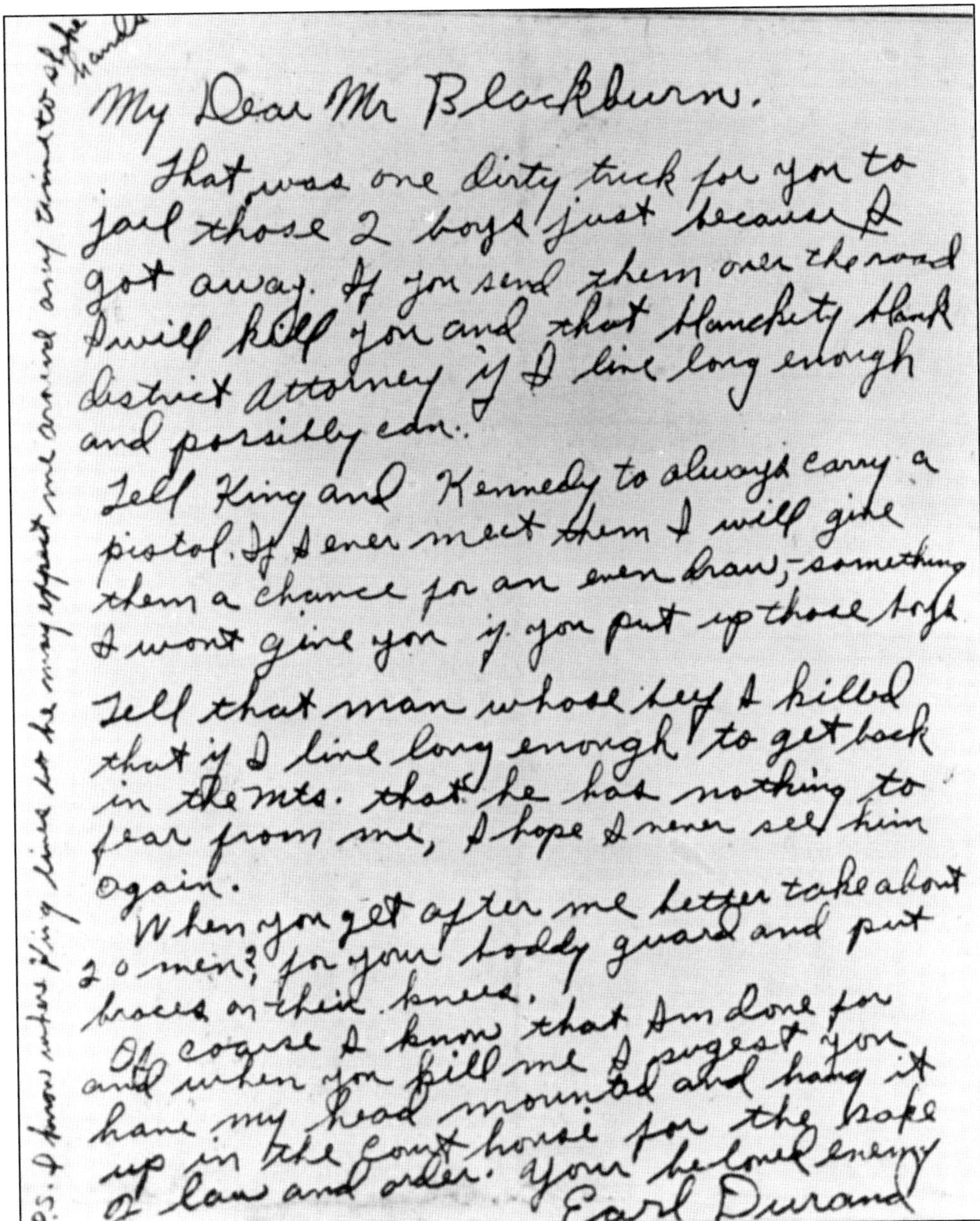
My Dear Mr Blackburn.

That was one dirty trick for you to jail those 2 boys just because I got away. If you send them over the road I will kill you and that Hanckety Hank district attorney if I live long enough and possibly can.

Tell King and Kennedy to always carry a pistol. If I ever meet them I will give them a chance for an even draw, something I wont give you if you put up those boys.

Tell that man whose key I killed that if I live long enough to get back in the mts. that he has nothing to fear from me, I hope I never see him again.

When you get after me better take about 20 men? for your boddy guard and put braces on their knees.

Of course I know that Im done for and when you kill me I sugest you have my head mounted and hang it up in the Court house for the sake of law and order. Your beloved enemy
Earl Durand

P.S. I know enters ping lines so he may expect me around any time to shake hands

Earl forced Noah Riley to drive him to his parent's farm located northeast of Powell after escaping from the Park County Jail. Deputy sheriff D. M. Baker and town marshal Charles Lewis received word of Durand's escape and return to his parent's home and they hoped to recapture the fugitive. But Earl shot and killed both men in front of the home. Upon his return to town, Sheriff Frank Blackburn took charge of the manhunt, hoping to catch Durand in the Powell area by tracking him with hounds from the Colorado State Penitentiary. Eluding the lawman, Durand went to various local residents to pick up firearms and get more ammunition. Durand then stopped at the home of Herf Graham, where he left this handwritten letter addressed to Blackburn and signed, "Your beloved enemy, Earl Durand." Durand suggests Blackburn "have my head mounted and hang it up in the courthouse for the sake of law and order." (PCA.)

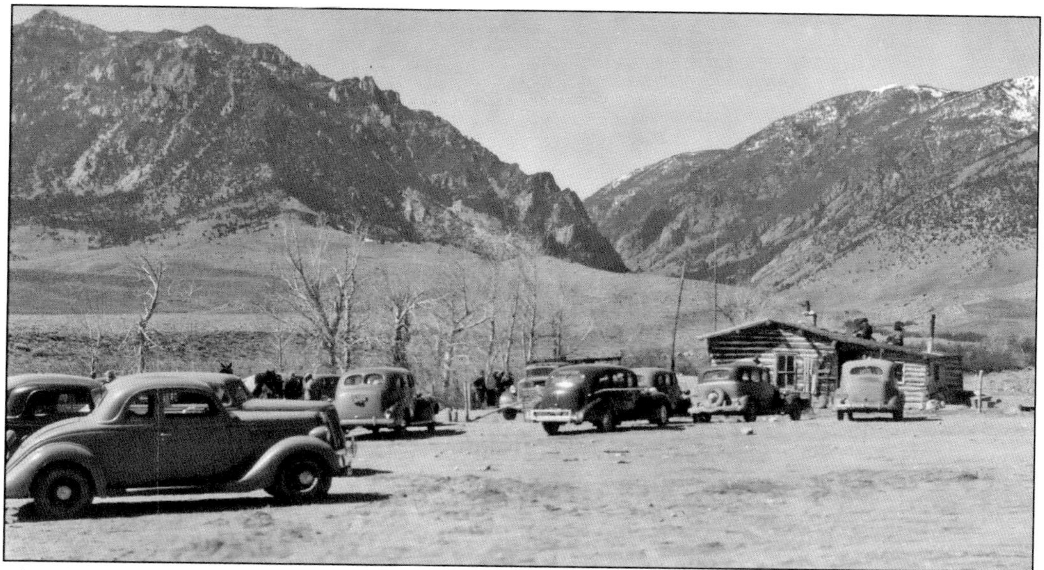

Shortly after leaving his letter to Blackburn, Earl Durand forced Art and Ester Art Thornburg to drive him to the Clark Fork Canyon region, where he sought refuge in the steep terrain on Little Rocky Creek. Upon learning that Earl Durand had fled the Powell area, Sheriff Blackburn led the posse to the Owens Ranch. The ranch house, pictured here, became the posse's headquarters while they searched the canyon of Little Rocky Creek, seen in the background. (PCA.)

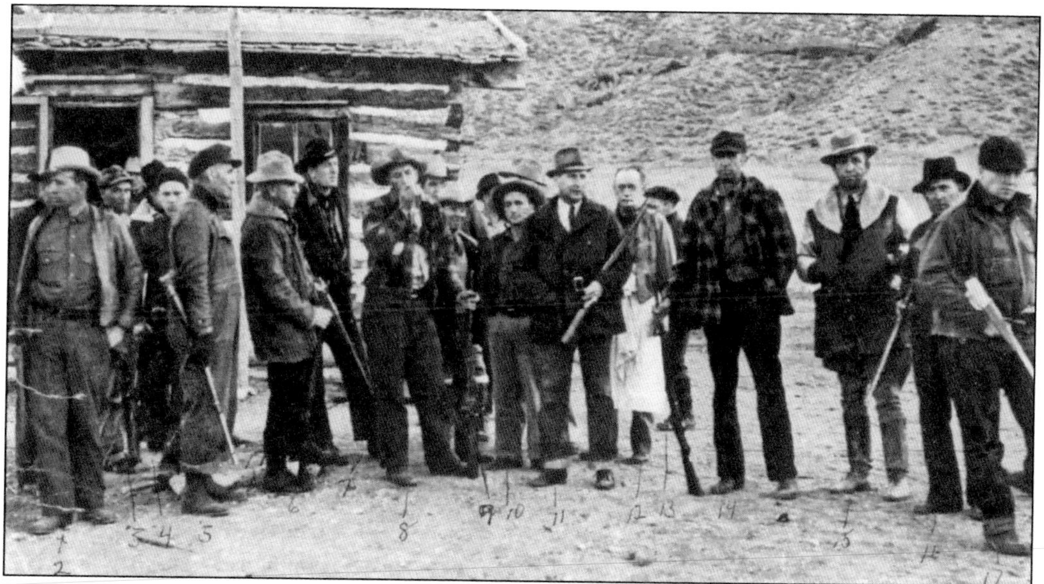

Members of the posse chasing Earl Durand pose with their weapons in front of the Owens Ranch. Tex Kennedy (identified as number 15) and Dwight King (identified as number 9) are the two men Durand referred to in his letter to Blackburn that "will give them a chance for an even draw." Both Kennedy and King were game wardens who assisted in arresting Durand for poaching. (PCA.)

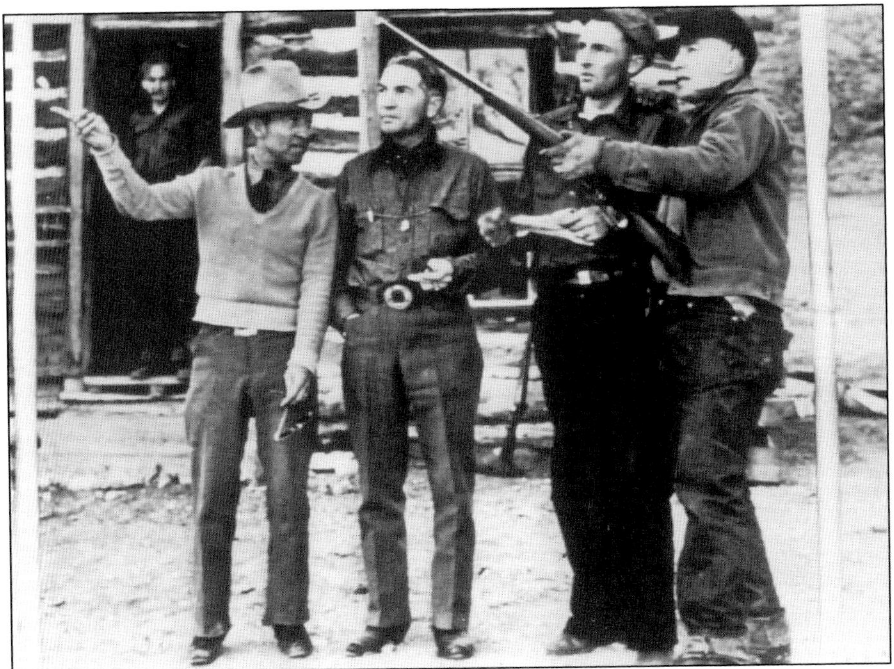

Four members of the posse confidently pose in front of the Owens Ranch with their weapons in the above photograph. The posse's confidence quickly eroded when two of its own were gunned down by Earl Durand. Hoping to surprise Durand in his lair on Little Rocky Creek, Arthur Argento, a laborer from Meeteetse, and Orville Linabary, a rodeo rider from Cody, rushed Durand's position. Durand later told Peter Simpson he shot the lawmen "because they came within 40 feet of him and were beginning to crowd him." After killing the two posse members, Durand took the dead men's rifles, Linabary's shoes, the shoelaces from Argento's boots, and Argento's deputy sheriff badge. In the photograph below, fellow posse members retrieve the bodies of Linabary and Argento. (Both PCA.)

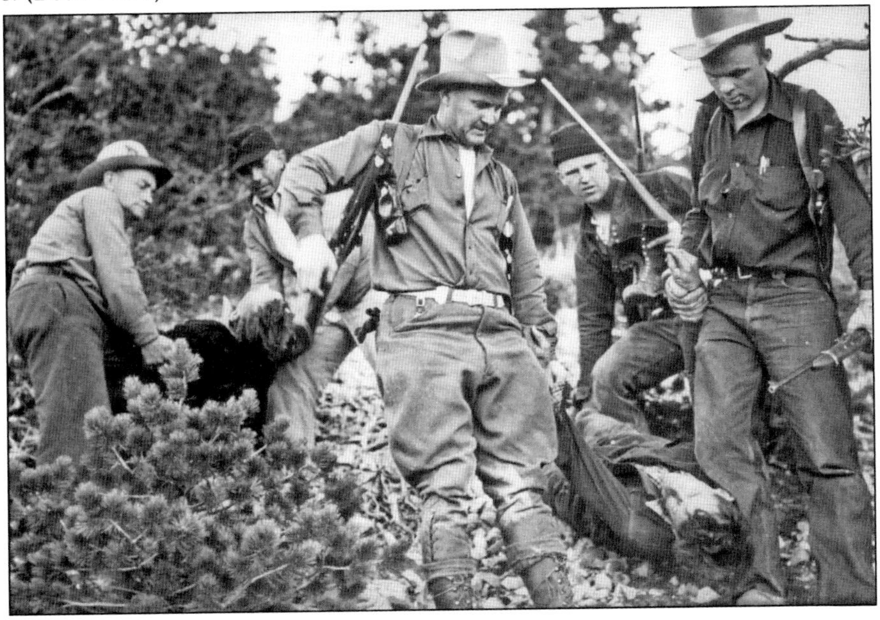

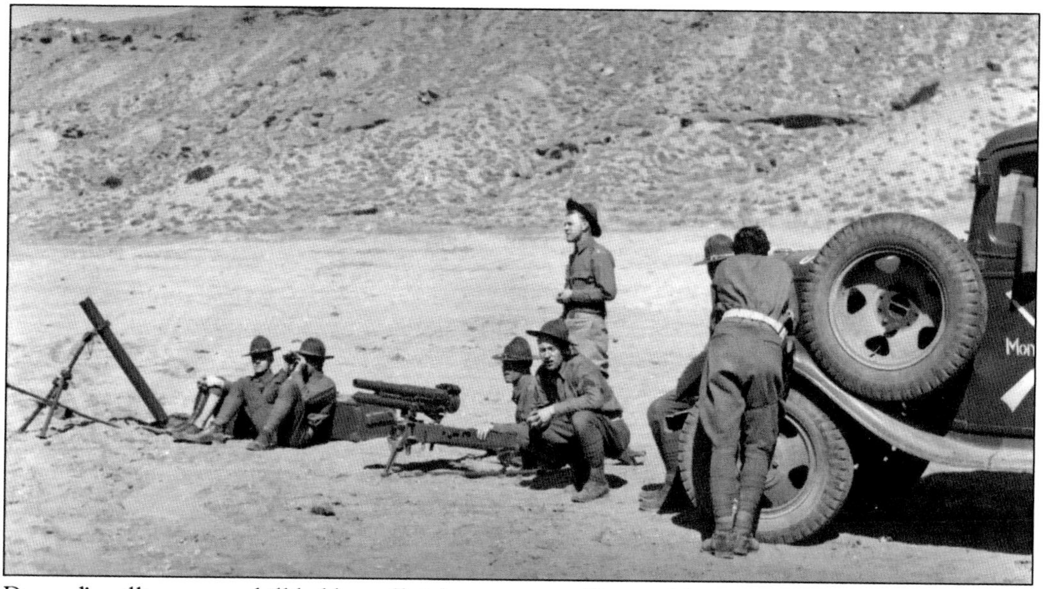

Durand's willingness to kill led law officials to recruit additional firepower. Montana governor Roy Ayers sent in a company of the 163rd Infantry of the Montana National Guard from Livingston, Montana. The Montana guardsmen are pictured above with a 37-millimeter howitzer and a 3-inch trench gun waiting to assist the posse by shelling Durand from his natural fortress. In the photograph below, local daredevil pilot Bill Monday and H. Evans inspect a teargas gun. Monday flew in the gas bombs from the Wyoming National Guard Armory in Casper hoping to drive Durand from his hiding place. After the killing of Argento and Linabary, Blackburn led 16 men hoping to catch Durand in the mountains. The *Cody Enterprise* noted Blackburn and his men "had enough ammunition and supplies to last for a number of days." Blackburn told reporters, "I think we can pick up his trail with the hounds . . . he may have come down but I think he is still up there." (Both PCA.)

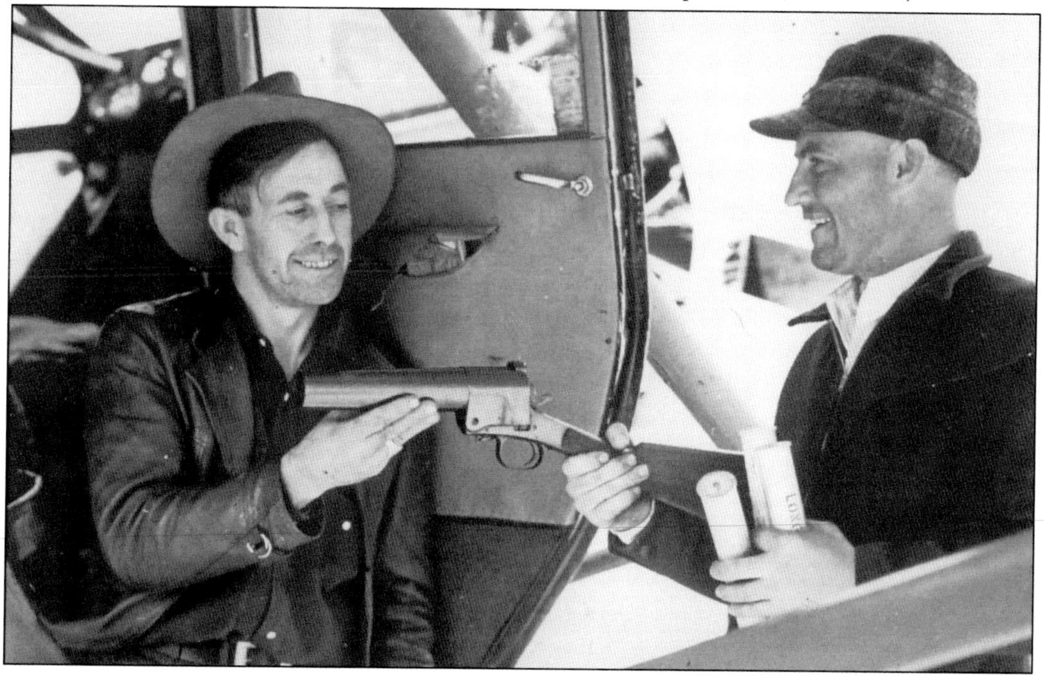

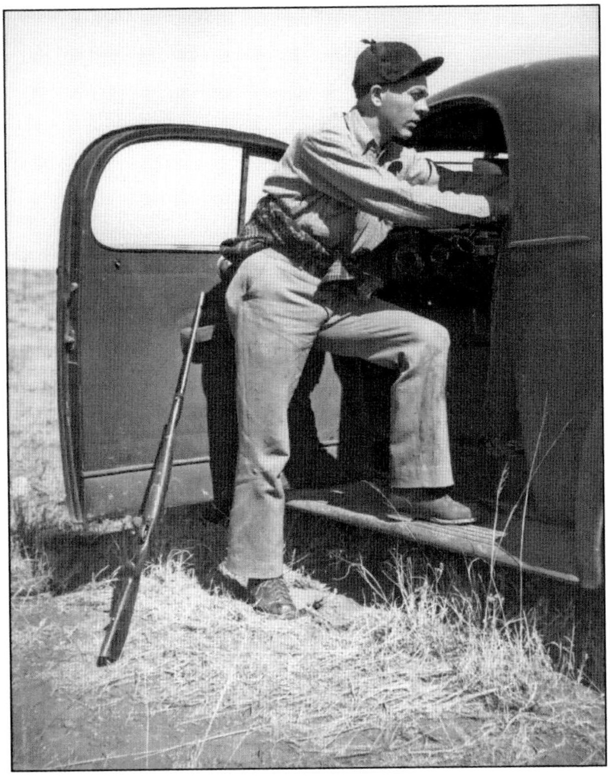

A number of local residents served in the posse hunting Earl Durand. Pictured here is Bill Garlow, Buffalo Bill's grandson. Garlow, with a rifle resting on the car door, is retrieving something from his vehicle. (PCA.)

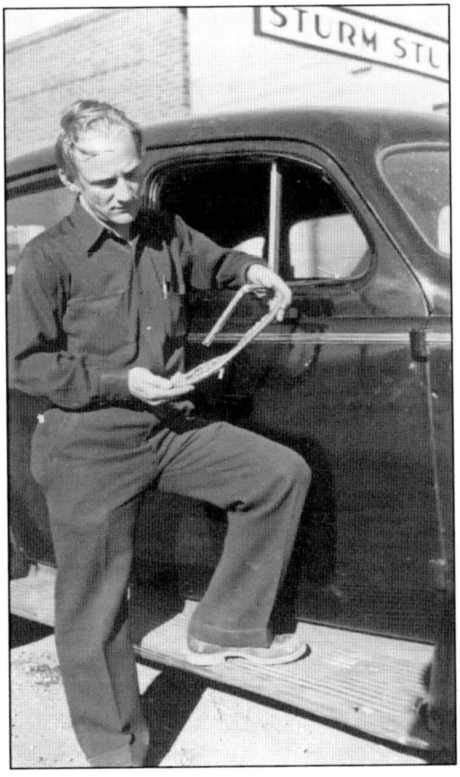

As Blackburn and his posse searched for Earl Durand in the mountains, Durand made his way back to the road, right to the spot where the Thornburgs had dropped him off a few days before. Durand waited in a clump of bushes, watching traffic and hoping for a solitary car to appear. When a lone car did appear, Durand, wearing Argento's badge, stopped the car and asked for a ride back to Powell. The car belonged to Harry Moore, a radio operator working for the posse at Owens Ranch. With Moore were two passengers, John Simpson and his elderly father, Peter Simpson. Shortly after the shoot-out in Powell, Moore poses for a photograph standing in front of his Buick. In his hand are the remains of a window broken up by Durand shortly before he drove to the bank in Powell. (PCA.)

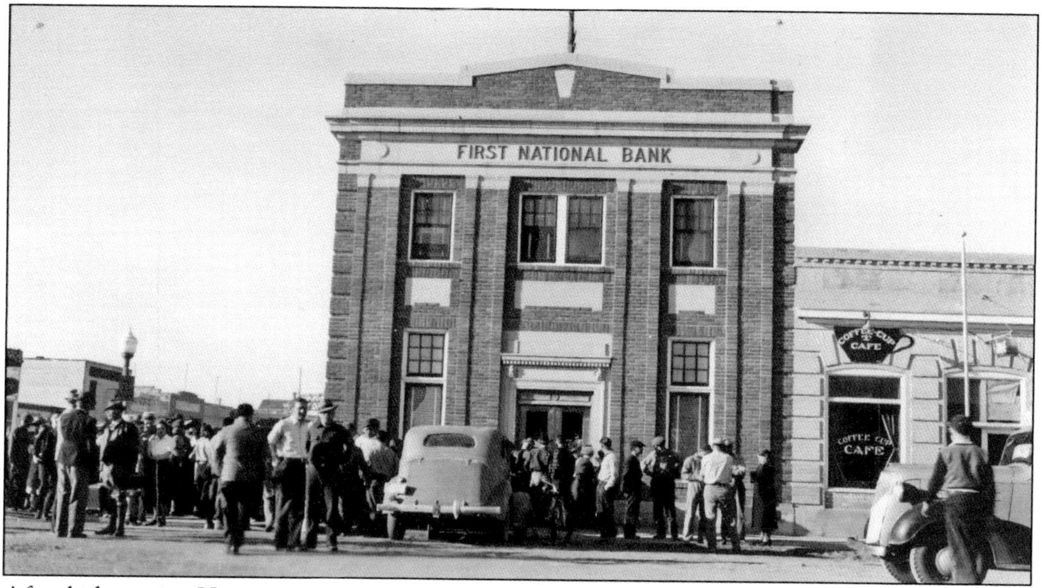

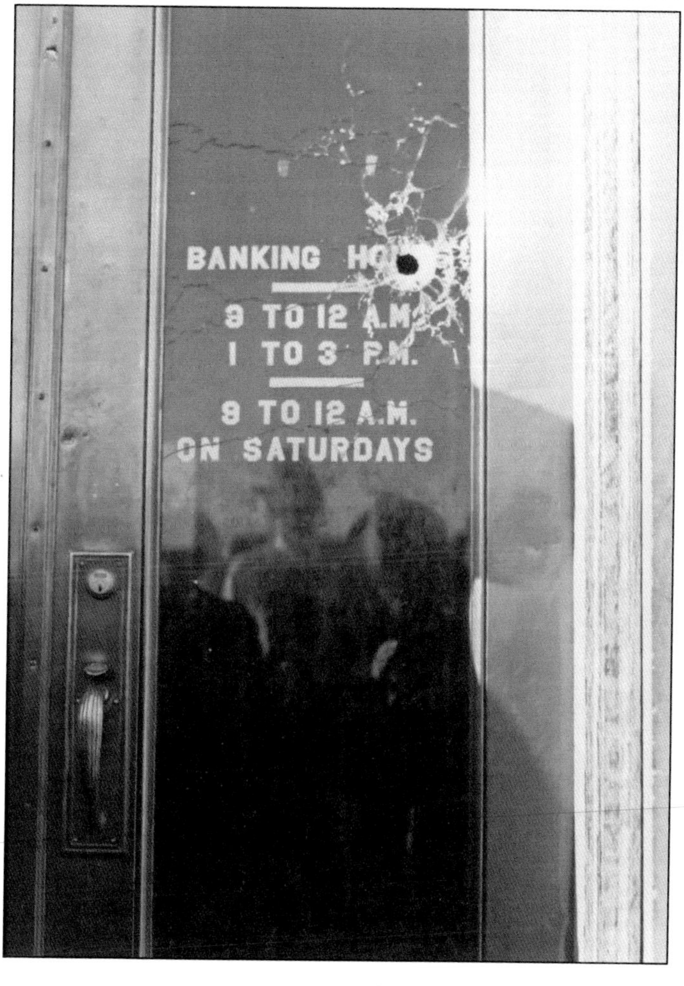

After kidnapping Harry Moore and his two passengers, Durand forced Moore to drive him to Deaver, east of Powell. In Deaver, Durand escorted Moore into the depot where Durand picked up a package containing 300 rounds of 30-30 ammunition. Durand then forced Moore to drive him to his parent's home where he acquired more items from his tent located in the backyard. After exchanging a few words with his parents, Durand took his hostages to a coal mine, located 3 miles from the nearest farm. Durand took Moore's car and called out, "Come to my funeral boys." Arriving in Powell, Durand walked into the lobby of the First National Bank, fired his rifle, and ordered everyone in the bank to stick up their hands. To emphasize his demands, Durand fired a number of shots through the bank windows. (Both PCA.)

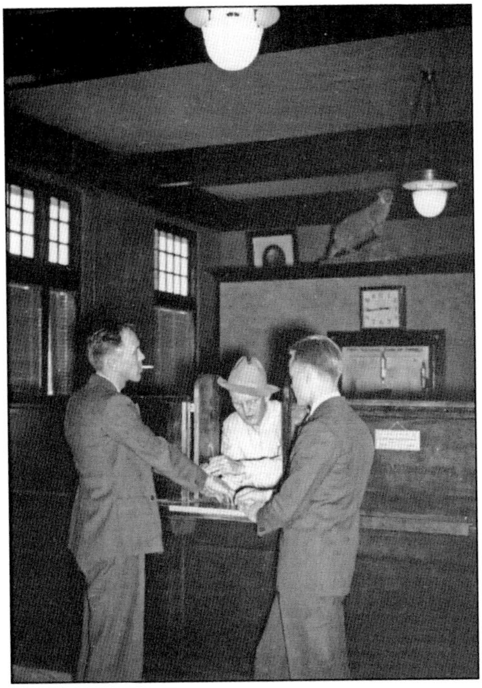

Inside of the bank, Durand demanded bank cashier Maurice Knutson and bank president Bob Nelson open the vault. Durand's demands could not be obeyed, though, due to a time lock on the vault door that only allowed the door to open at certain times. While five bank customers nervously watched Durand randomly shooting out of the bank windows, Nelson collected $3,000 and gave it to Durand. Nelson and Knutson pose for the photograph to demonstrate how Durand tied them together. (PCA.)

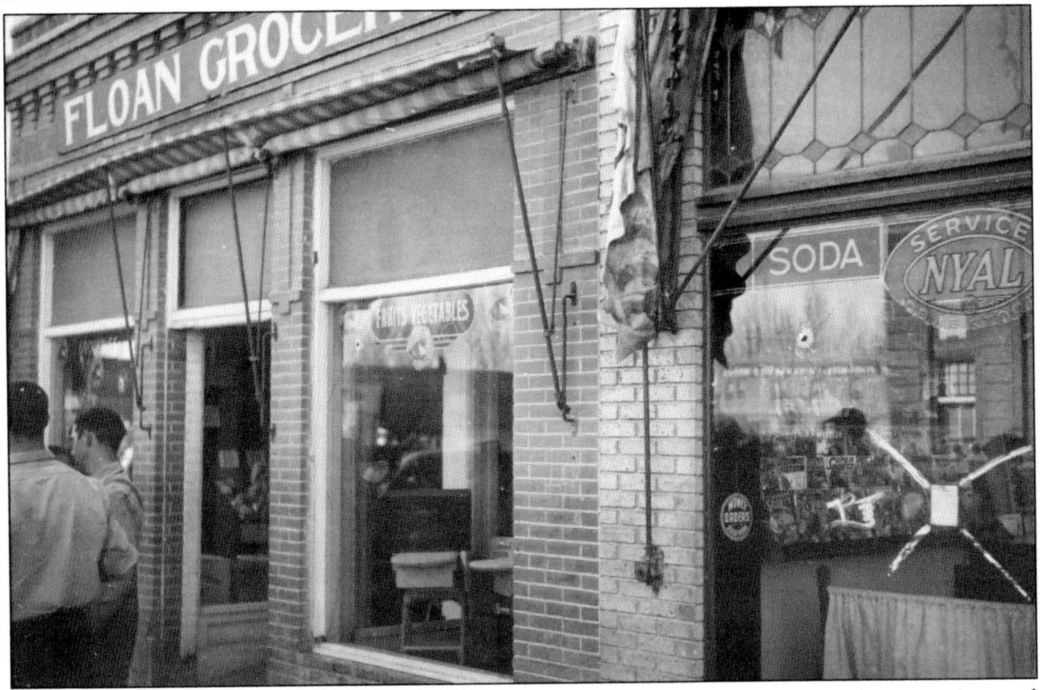

Durand's bullets hit a number of Powell businesses located across the street from the First National Bank, causing business owners and customers to take refuge. Pictured here is the window of Al Floan's grocery story. Floan crouched behind his store counter during the shootout. As he waited, one of Durand's bullets hit a large jar of French's mustard that stood on the shelf behind the counter. It shattered, covering Floan in mustard and broken glass. George Blevins, a reporter, covered the chaotic event live on the radio for Billings, Montana, station KGHL. (PCA.)

Hoping to escape from the First National Bank, Durand tied teller Johnnie Gawthorp, Maurice Knutson, and Bob Nelson together with a rope. Nelson's hands were tied together with a leather bootlace. Durand intended to use the bankers as a human shield. Johnnie Gawthorp, who was the first out of the door, received a fatal wound from an excited townsman. Gawthorp's last words were, "I'm glad it was me and not one of the married men." Durand appeared in the doorway after Gawthorp fell, firing three times. Seeing Durand, a Powell High School student, Tipton Cox, pictured here, wounded Durand with a shot from his .22 rifle from the Texaco service station (see page 62). (HM.)

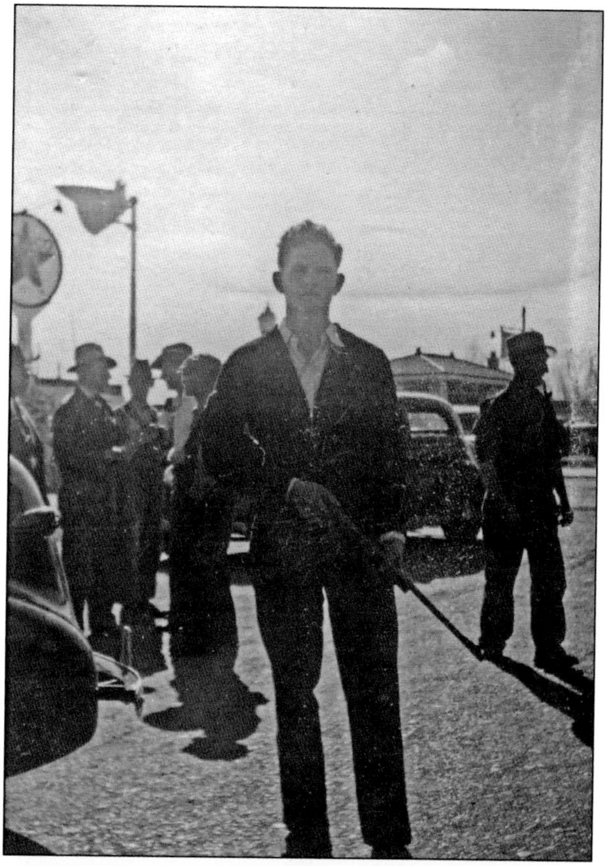

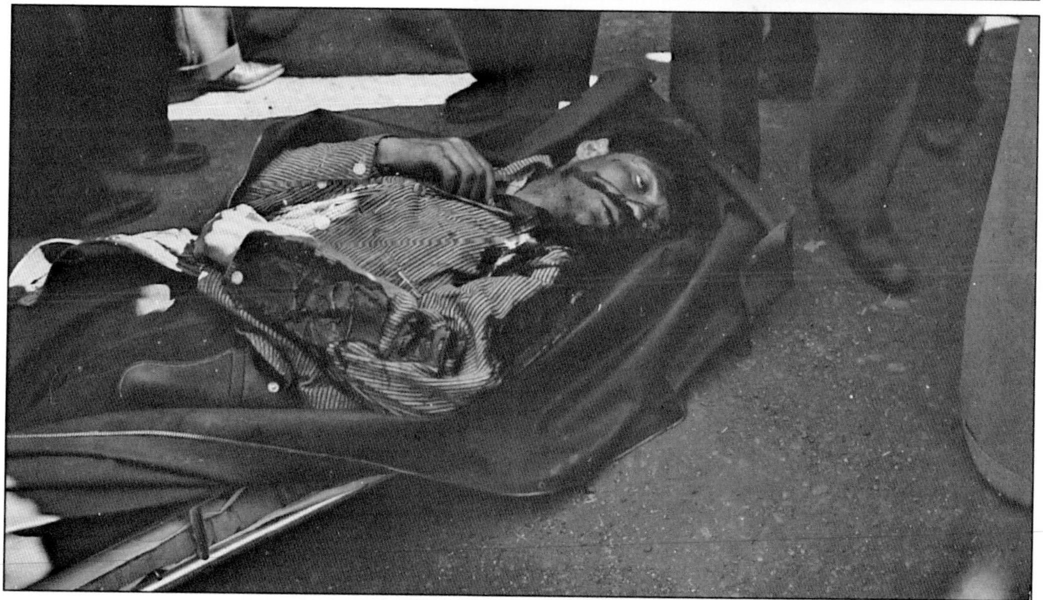

Earl Durand, wounded by Tipton Cox's shot, crawled back into the bank lobby, pulled his pistol from his holster, and shot himself in the head. Albert Lucier, a local photographer, took a picture of Durand's corpse lying on a stretcher. (JTHL.)

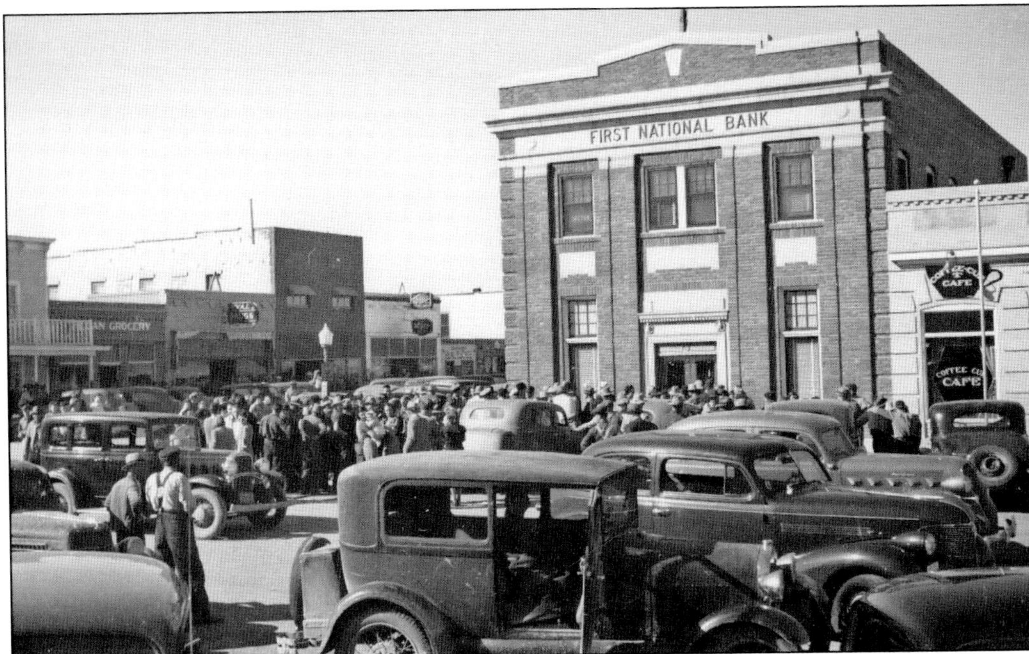

During the shootout between Earl Durand and his fellow Powell citizens, crowds gathered around the scene to witness the event. Laness Northrup later told the author that his dad, Dan Northrup, and Jim Bever decided to drive down to the bank. The two men brought Laness, a young boy at the time, along for the ride but with strict orders that he keep himself crouched on the floor of the car near the back seat. These two photographs show the number of people and vehicles gathered around the bank shortly after Earl Durand shot himself. (Both PCA.)

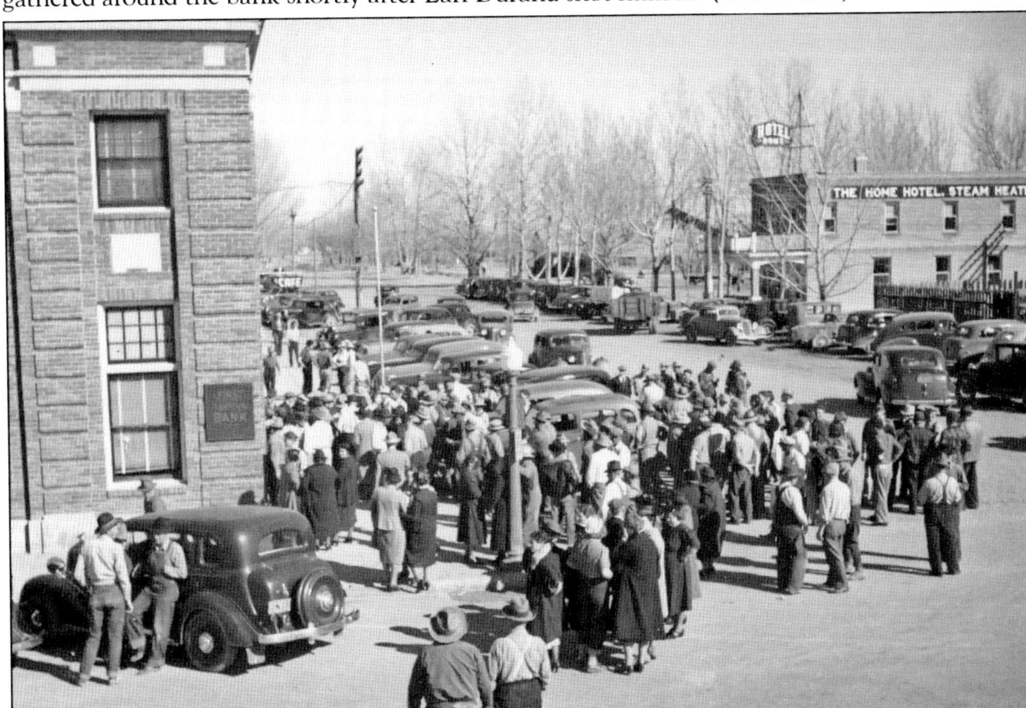

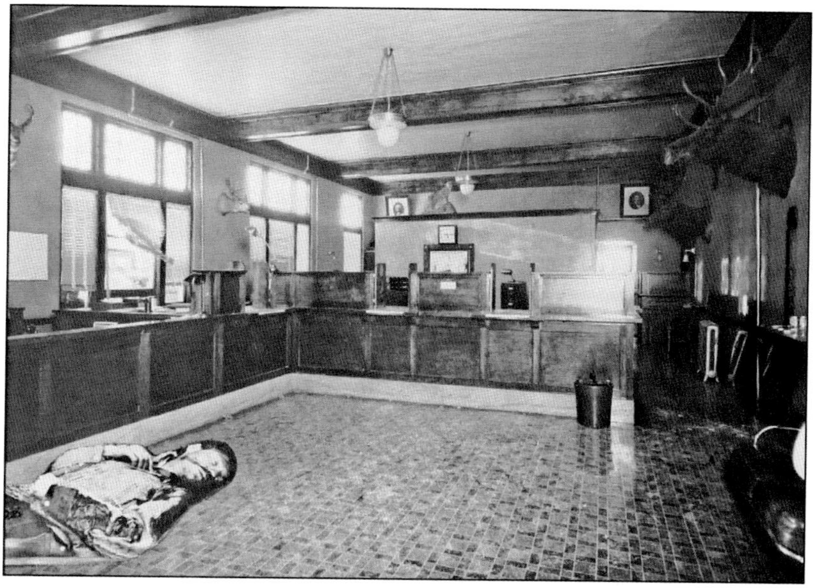

Sometime after Earl Durand took his own life, Albert Lucier imposed this image of Durand's body on a photograph of the First National Bank lobby. Note the damaged windows and blinds on left. (JTHL.)

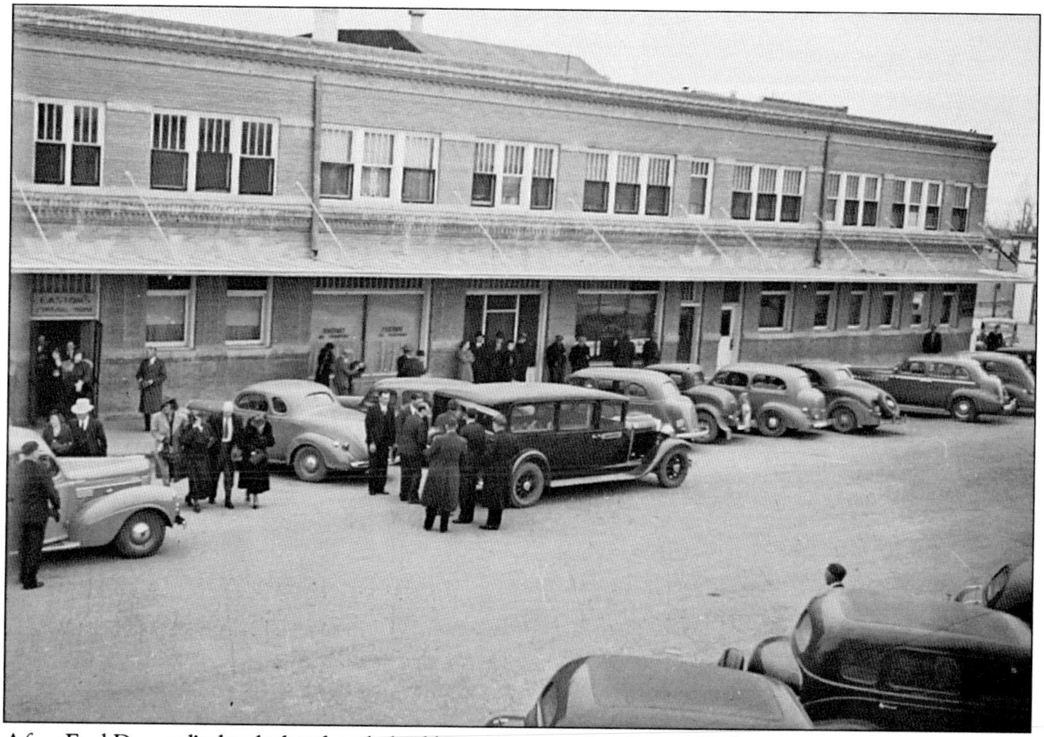

After Earl Durand's death, his family laid him to rest in the Crown Hill Cemetery. This photograph captures pallbearers placing the casket into the hearse as Durand's family leaves the mortuary. Durand's friend, Allen Richardson, later recalled loaning Durand a book about Billy the Kid, "I can still remember how Earl was intrigued by the Kid's ability to break out of jail. And I had lost three friends, Durand, Baker and Lewis." (JTHL.)

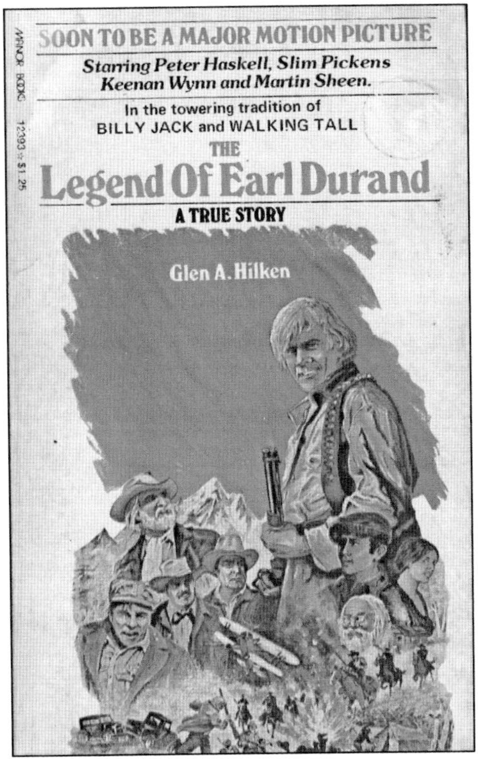

Earl Durand's saga attracted a lot of publicity, and newspapers nicknamed him "Tarzan of the Tetons." Durand's story soon found its way into film. Shortly after his death, a character similar to Durand, in the film *Wyoming Outlaw* named Will Parker, appeared. John Wayne, the hero of the film, attempted to help young Parker but was too late to save his life. In 1974, the Teton Theater in Powell hosted the world premiere of *The Legend of Earl Durand.* One of the stars, Slim Pickens, attended the premiere. Ticket holders enjoyed free champagne and Coke before the film while listening to Roy Barnes sing a song retelling the saga of Earl Durand. This photograph shows the front cover of a book by Glen A. Hilken based on the movie. Hilken's book also included snippets from various local newspapers that covered the events surrounding Earl Durand. (Author's collection.)

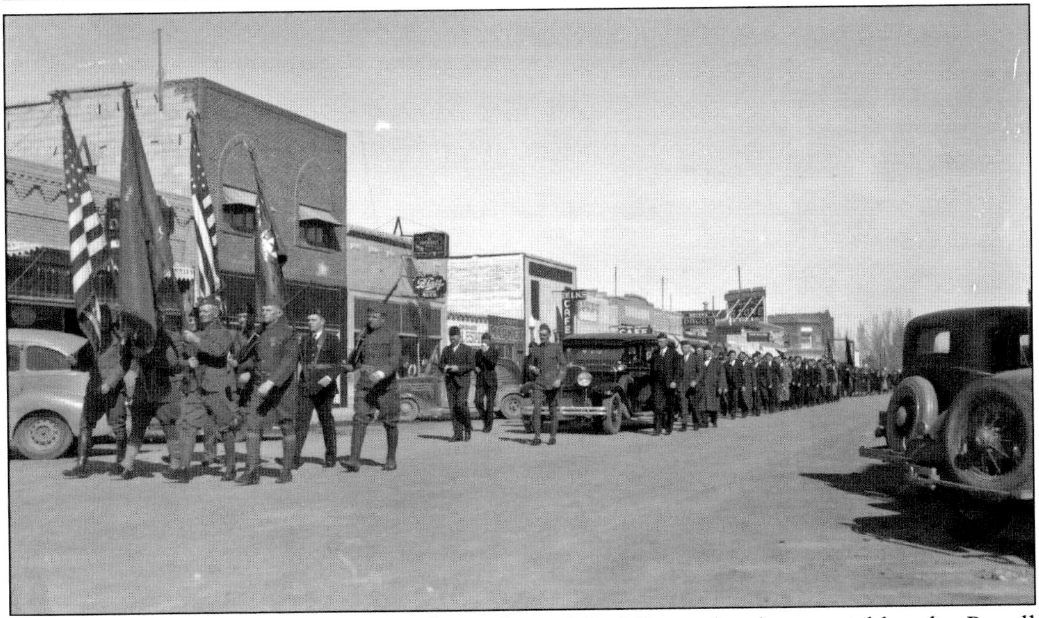

While distant newspapers and newsreels proclaimed Earl Durand to be a social bandit, Powell grieved those citizens who lost their lives because of Durand's actions. Pictured here is the funeral procession for town marshal Charles E. Lewis. Lewis was a well-respected member of the community, and his early death at the hands of Durand shocked Powell residents. On March 16, 2009, seventy years after Lewis's death, the community of Powell named the Powell Law Enforcement Center in his honor. (PCA.)

Seven

School District No. 1 and the College

A good portion of the Garland Division homesteaders belonged to the professional working class, and they greatly desired a strong educational system in the Powell region to ensure the proper education of their children. The first school in Powell opened in 1908 with Marie Haley teaching in a small boxcar top building provided by the Reclamation Service. This first class contained 36 students from ages 6 to 21. The next year, 61 students enrolled in Marie Haley's class. In 1911, School District No. 1 was formed, and over the years this district expanded through the consolidation of surrounding school districts. Lacking classroom space, the Powell School Board worked towards constructing a large brick school building, which was completed in 1912.

The school board also provided busing to ensure students from distant farms could attend classes; soon Powell had the largest busing system in the state. Through the years, Powell's School District No. 1 continued to build various educational facilities and provided busing for numerous students.

After World War II, the demand for college education greatly increased with the passage of the GI Bill. Powell responded to this demand by acquiring the Northwest Center of the University of Wyoming in 1946. In 1953, efforts began to form a college district when voters approved a 2.5 mill levy to fund construction of Northwest Community College. On May 20, 1956, Northwest Community College, now Northwest College, dedicated a new building providing a library and classroom space. By 1959, it had enrolled 65 students and employed 21 faculty and staff. Through the remainder of the 20th century, Northwest Community College expanded its facilities to include two gymnasiums, five residence halls, an expanded library, a student union building, and various classroom facilities.

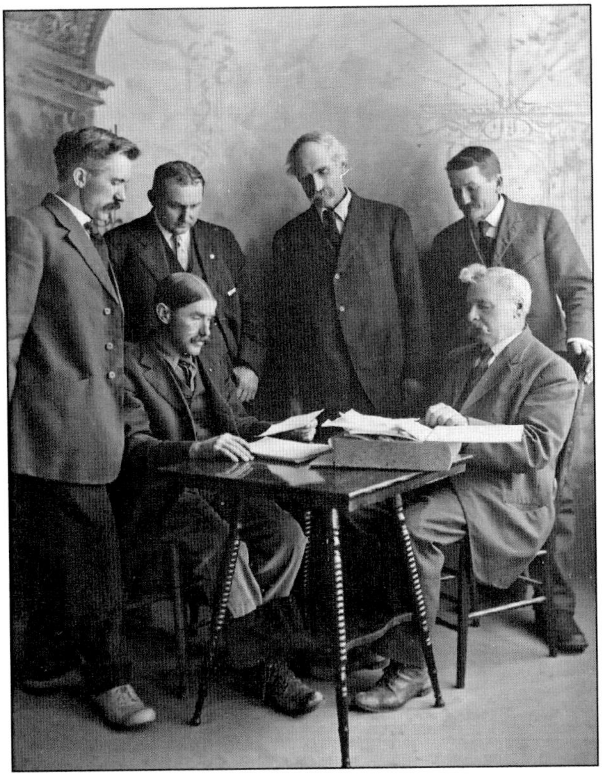

Powell's first school board poses for a photograph. The men, in no particular order, are George Pyatt, Mr. Wilcox, Dr. William A. Graham, Mr. Charles Hill, Dan Bagley, and Dr. Barney, veterinarian. (HM.)

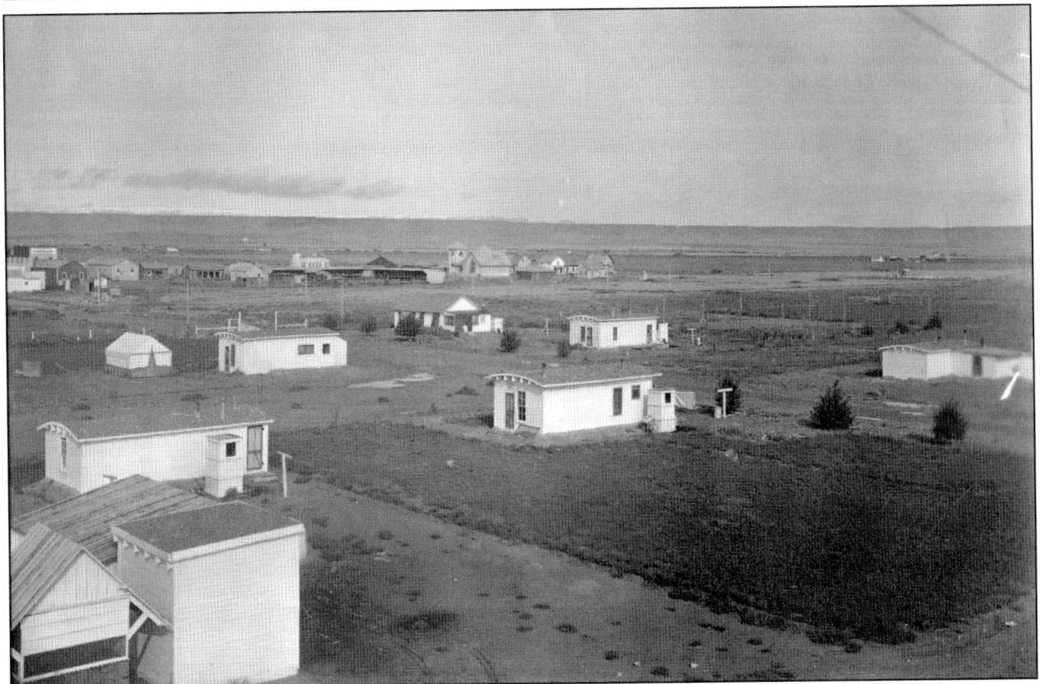

Powell's first school met in one of the boxcar top houses provided by the Reclamation Service, which were very numerous in Powell. Marie Haley taught a crowded class of 36 students in this small schoolhouse, which measured 14 feet by 28 feet (see page 76). (SIDA.)

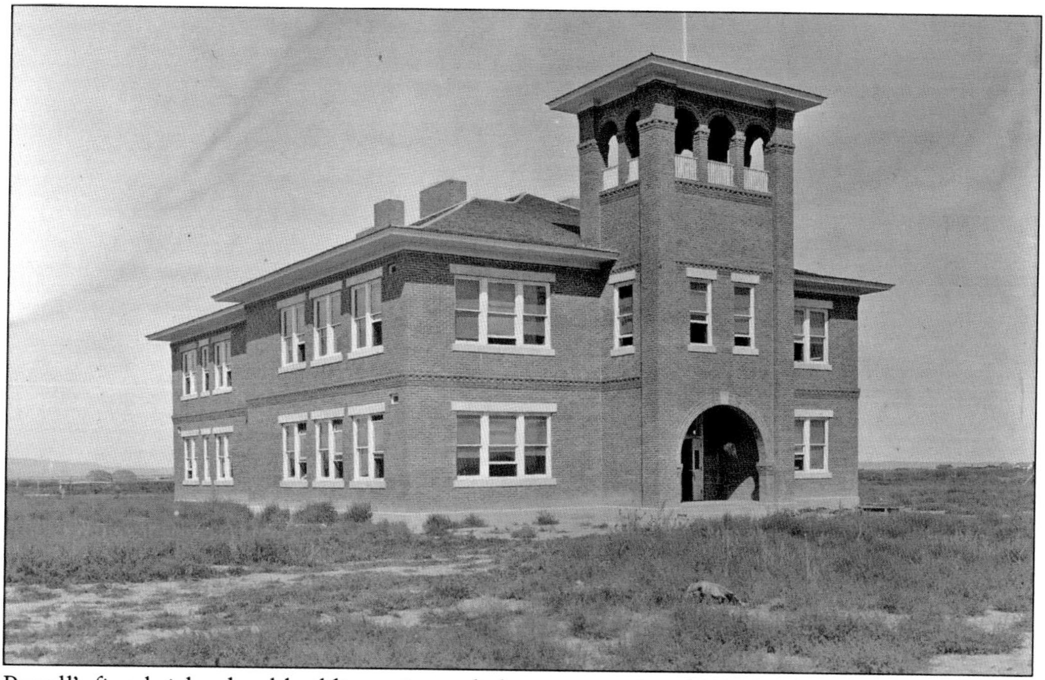

Powell's first brick school building, pictured above, opened in 1912. By that time, 175 students attended Powell's school, which had been meeting in various locations around town, including town churches. In 1915, enrollment increased to 498 students, leading Powell to pass a $5,900 bond to complete an addition to the brick school, as seen in the photograph below, and to expand the bus routes. This was also the year of Powell's first graduating class of eight students. The 1915 class motto was "We have started." (Above, PCA; below, SIDA.)

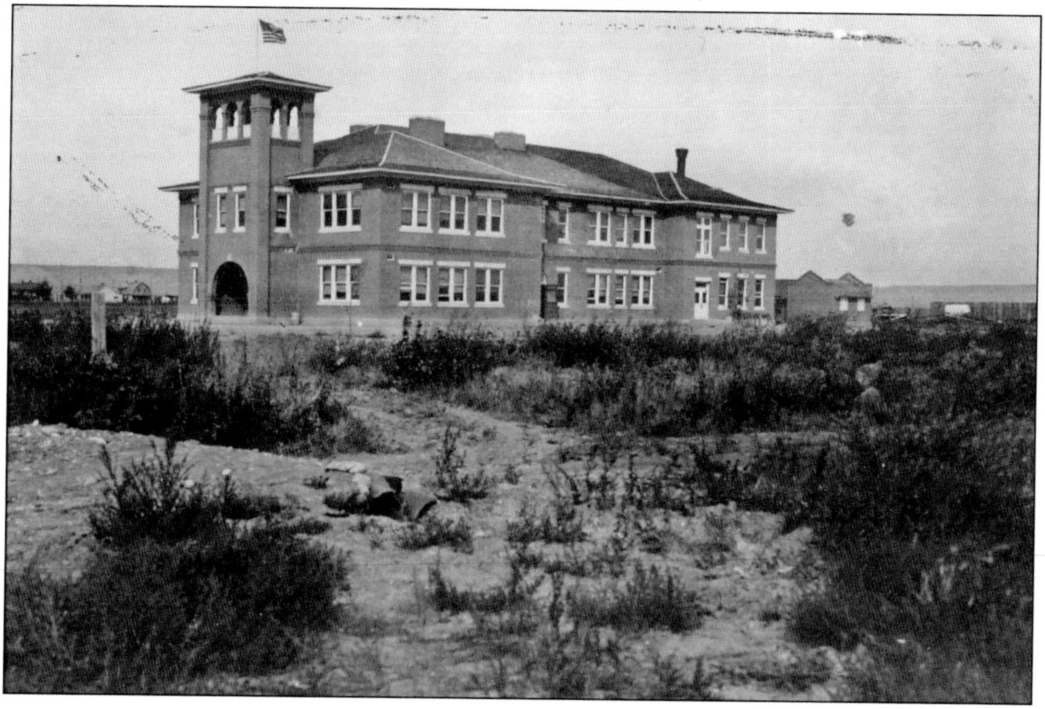

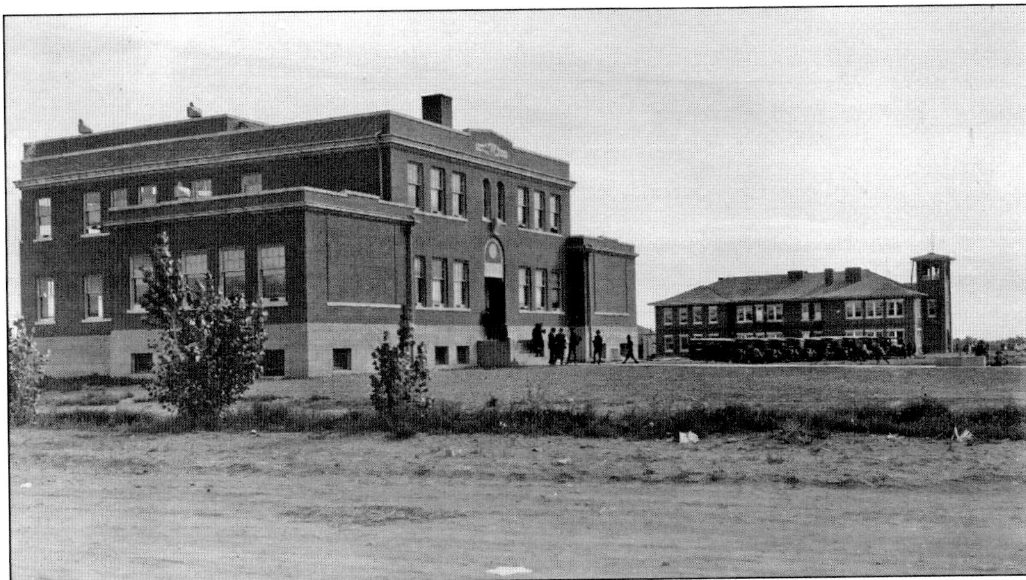

By 1920, nearly 200 students enrolled at Powell High School, creating the need for a high school building. After one trust company's bonds failed, the school district issued another bond to complete a new $75,000 high school building, pictured above. The new school contained an auditorium and a gymnasium. The gymnasium not only housed a growing athletic program, it could also be used to show off the produce from the Powell area in the 1921 Northwestern Wyoming Fair, as evident in the photograph below. (Both SIDA.)

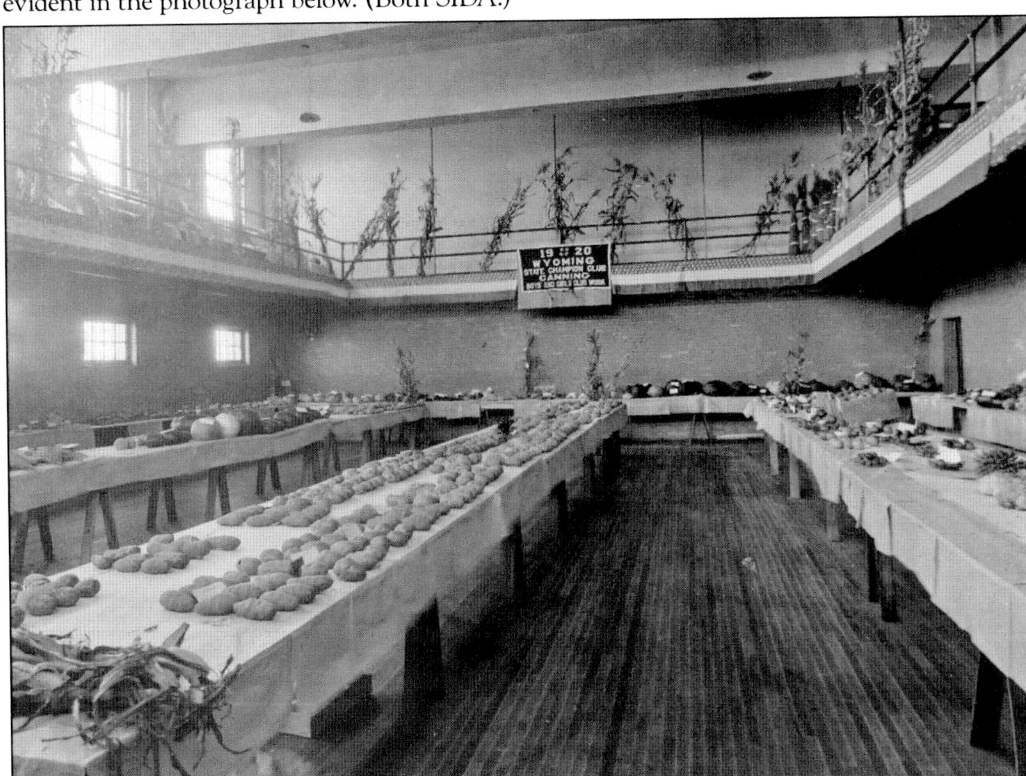

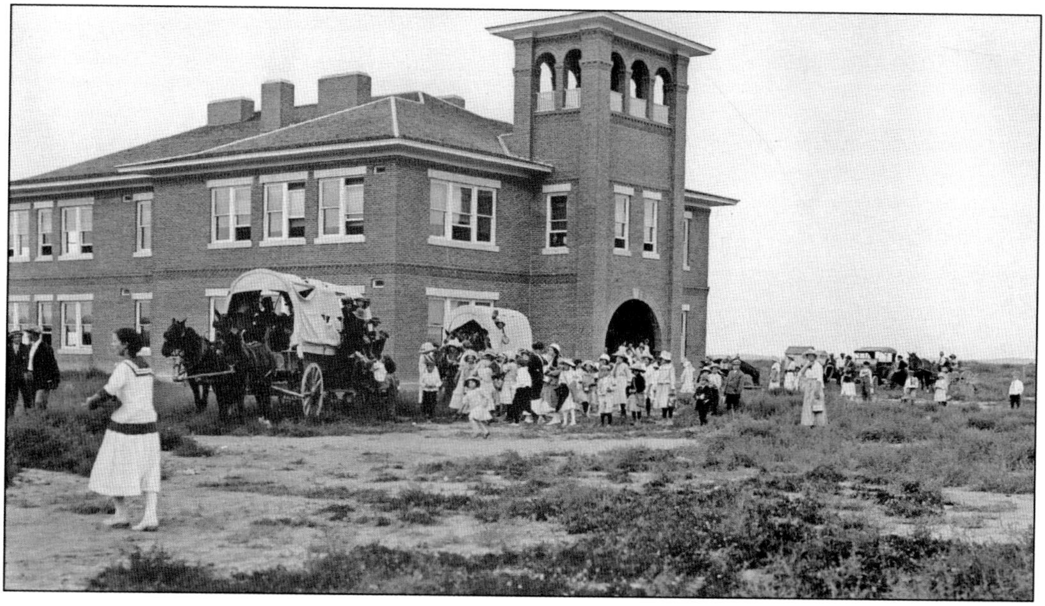

In 1911, the Powell schools offered bus service for children on two separate routes, approximately 10 to 12 miles long. The school provided wagons, warmed with kerosene heaters, but the drivers provided their own horses as seen above. Soon the wagons gave way to autobuses, as seen below. This group of students is being bused from the Willwood Division in 1930. Due to the expansion of the Shoshone Project and the consolidation of other school districts into Powell School District No. 1, the Powell schools operated and maintained the largest school busing system in the state of Wyoming. (Both SIDA.)

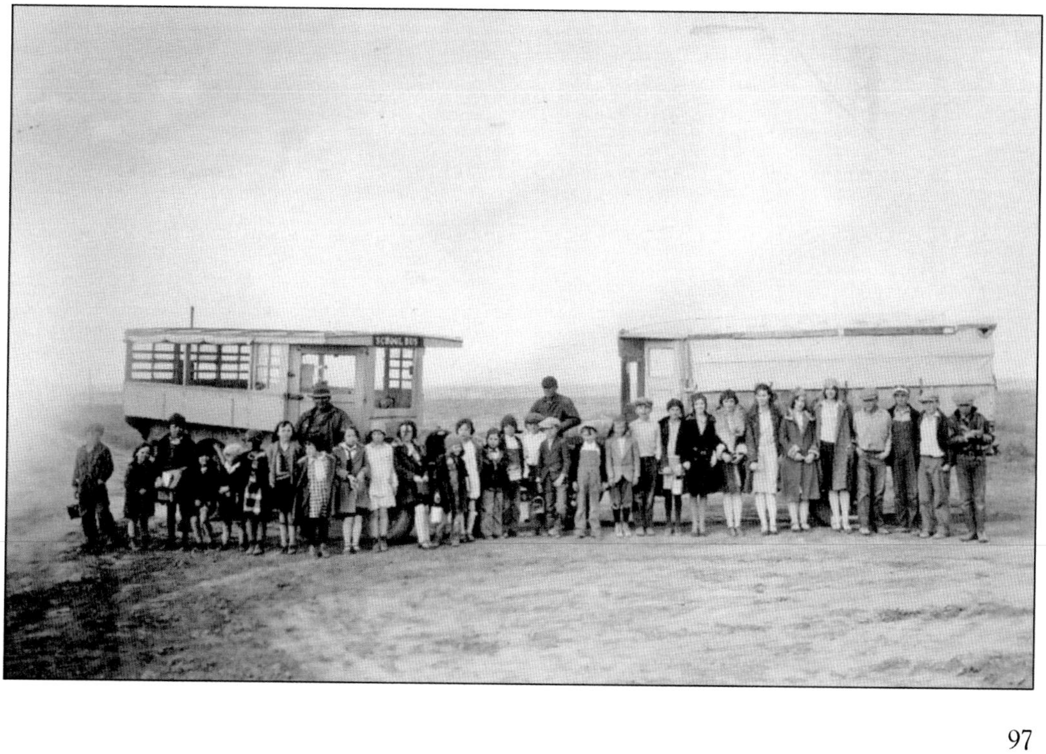

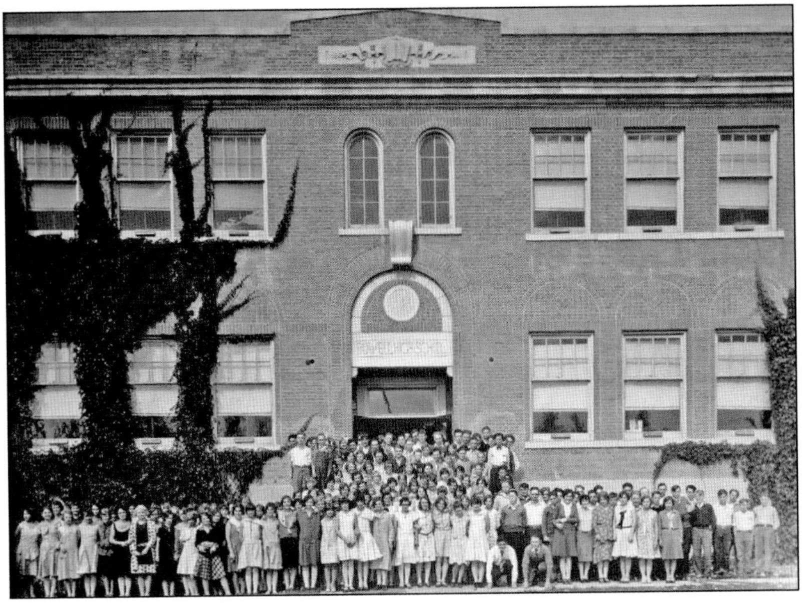

In this photograph, students enrolled at Powell High School stand in front of the high school building in 1930. Clearly within 15 years, Powell's school system greatly expanded and improved. Its facilities now catered to a number of students. (SIDA.)

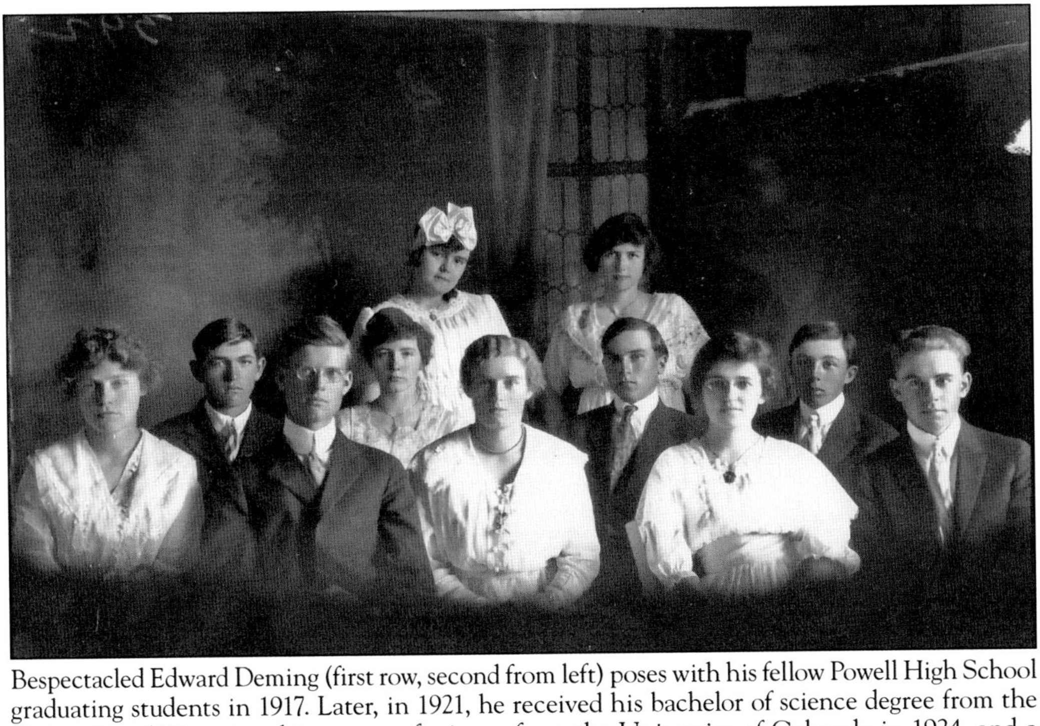

Bespectacled Edward Deming (first row, second from left) poses with his fellow Powell High School graduating students in 1917. Later, in 1921, he received his bachelor of science degree from the University of Wyoming, his master of science from the University of Colorado in 1924, and a doctorate from Yale University in 1928. After World War II, Deming served in Tokyo under the Supreme Command of the Allied Powers led by Gen. Douglas MacArthur. Deming's theories of business management restored Japan's economy from the ashes of World War II. In 1952, the Japanese Union of Scientists and Engineers established the Deming Prize for the outstanding practice of statistical quality control. Deming authored a number of books on business management techniques and also wrote a number of orchestral songs. (FNB.)

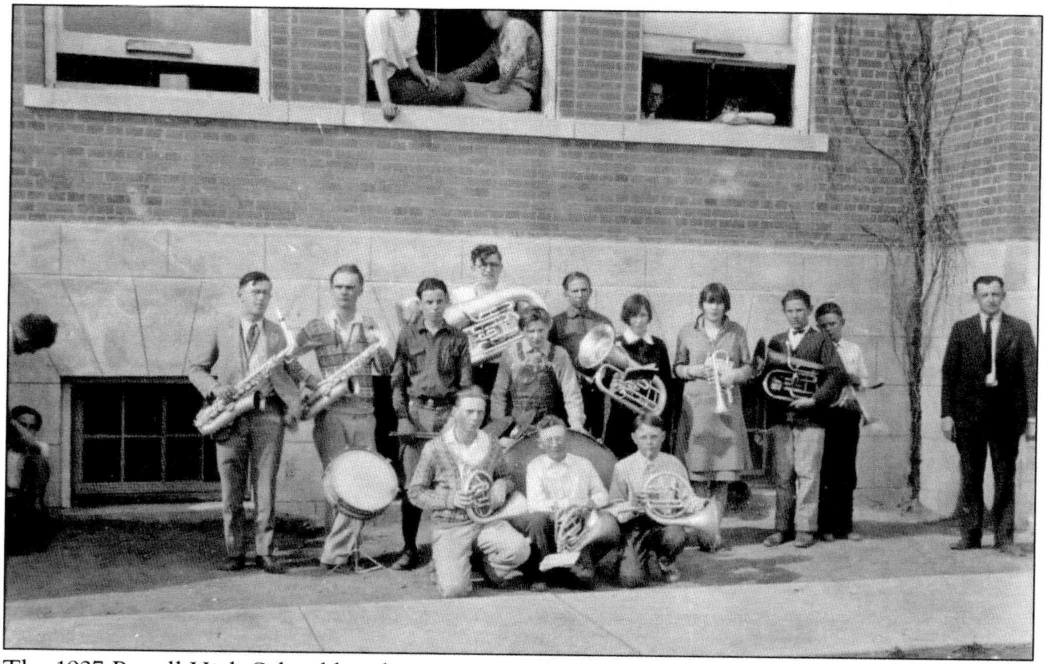

The 1927 Powell High School band stops to pose during a performance to celebrate Arbor Day. The students are standing next to the 1920 high school building. Note that the band did not have any uniforms and students wore a variety of outfits. (SIDA.)

Powell schools also provided students with the opportunity to play sports. Pictured here is the Powell High School girls basketball team in the 1920s. In 1922–1923, the boys basketball team won their first state championship. (FNB.)

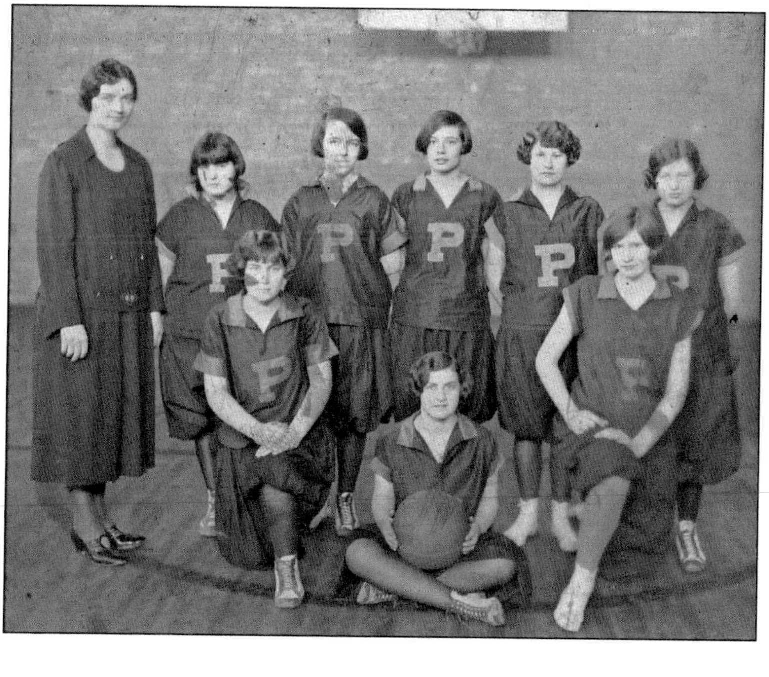

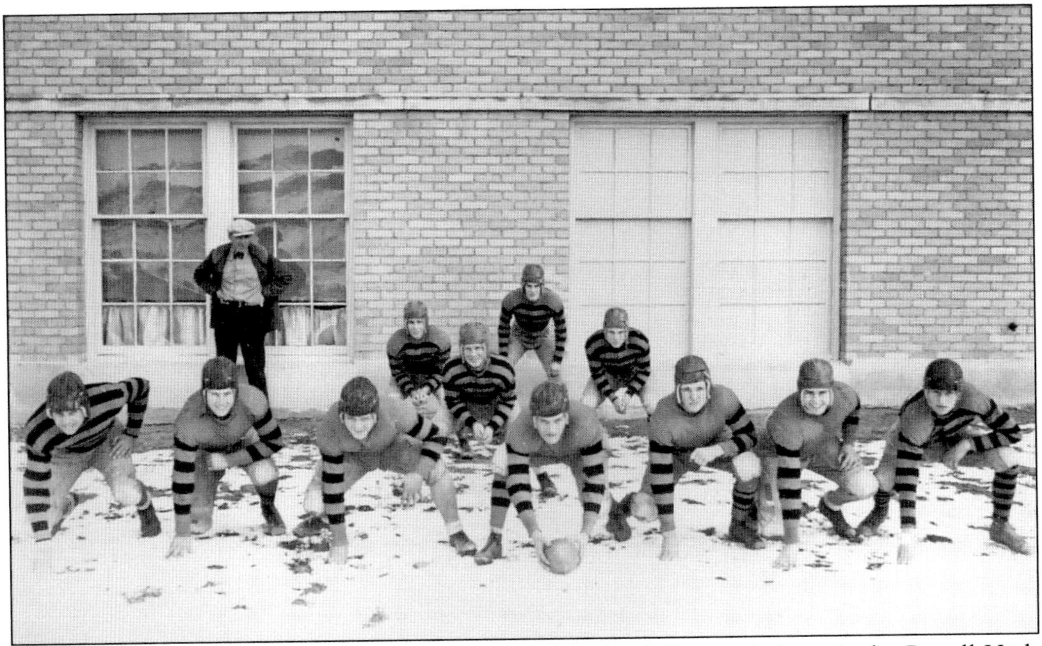

Boys also played football and track for Powell High School. Pictured above is the Powell High School football team sometime during the 1920s. The coach looks tougher than the rest of the squad. Pictured below is the Powell High School track team in the same time period. The football team claimed its first championship during the 1923–1924 school year. The track team won the Big Horn Basin Championship in 1937–1938. (Both FNB.)

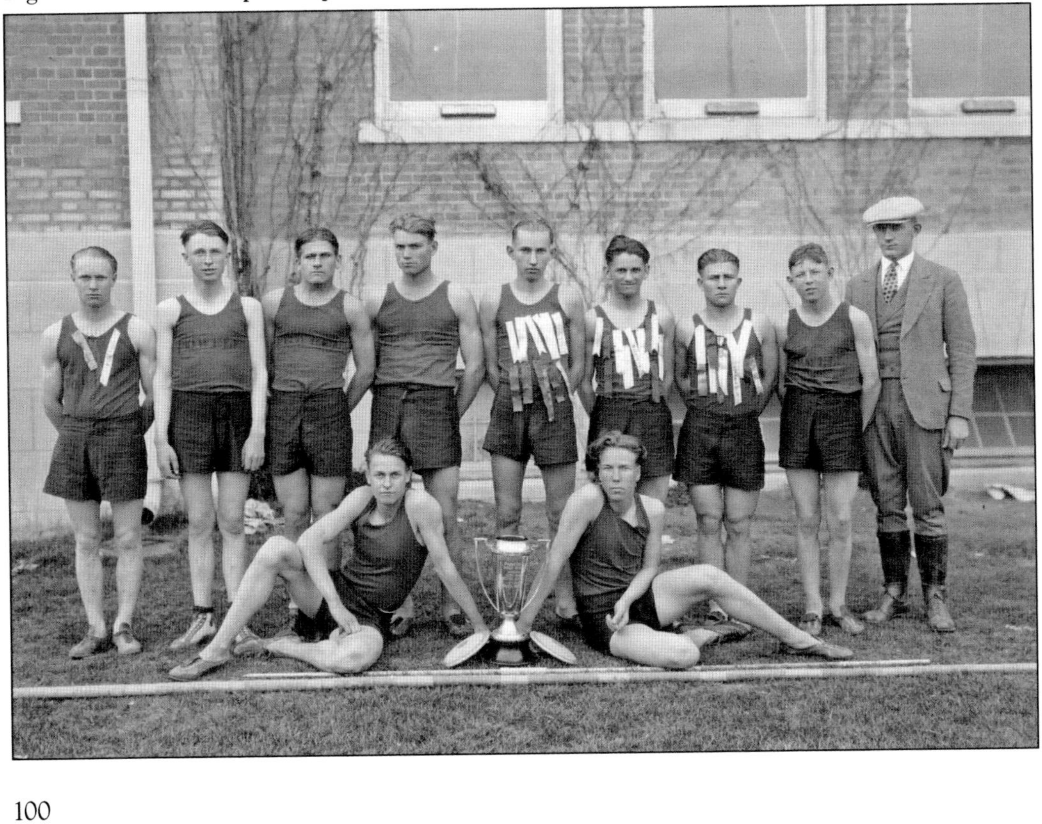

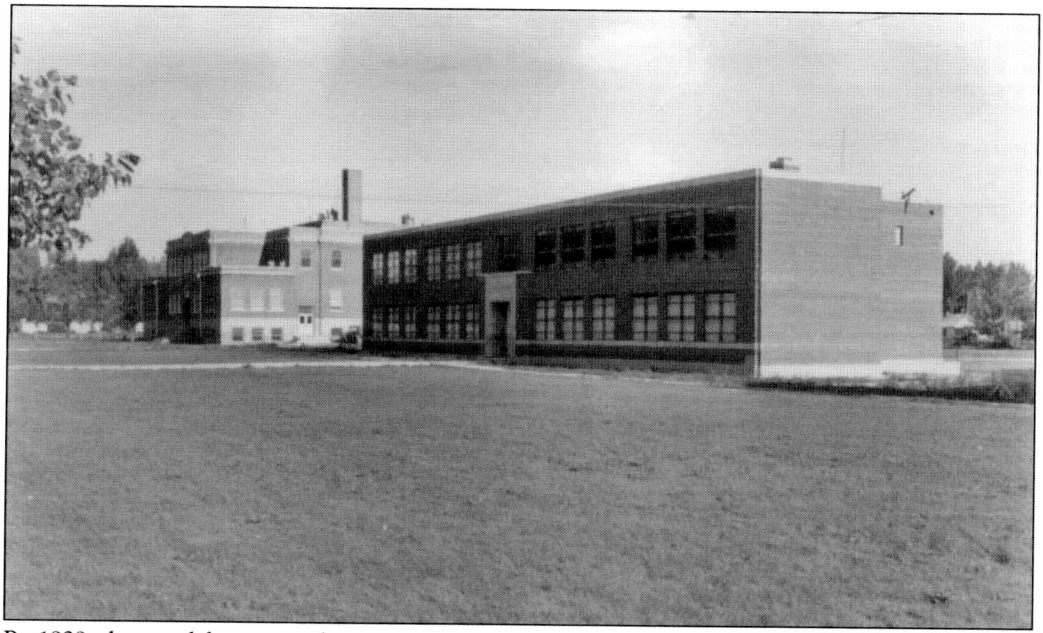

By 1939, the need for more educational facilities led to the construction of this building, which housed a grade school and the junior high school at various times. That same year, more than 1,000 students were enrolled in schools located in Powell School District No. 1. (HM.)

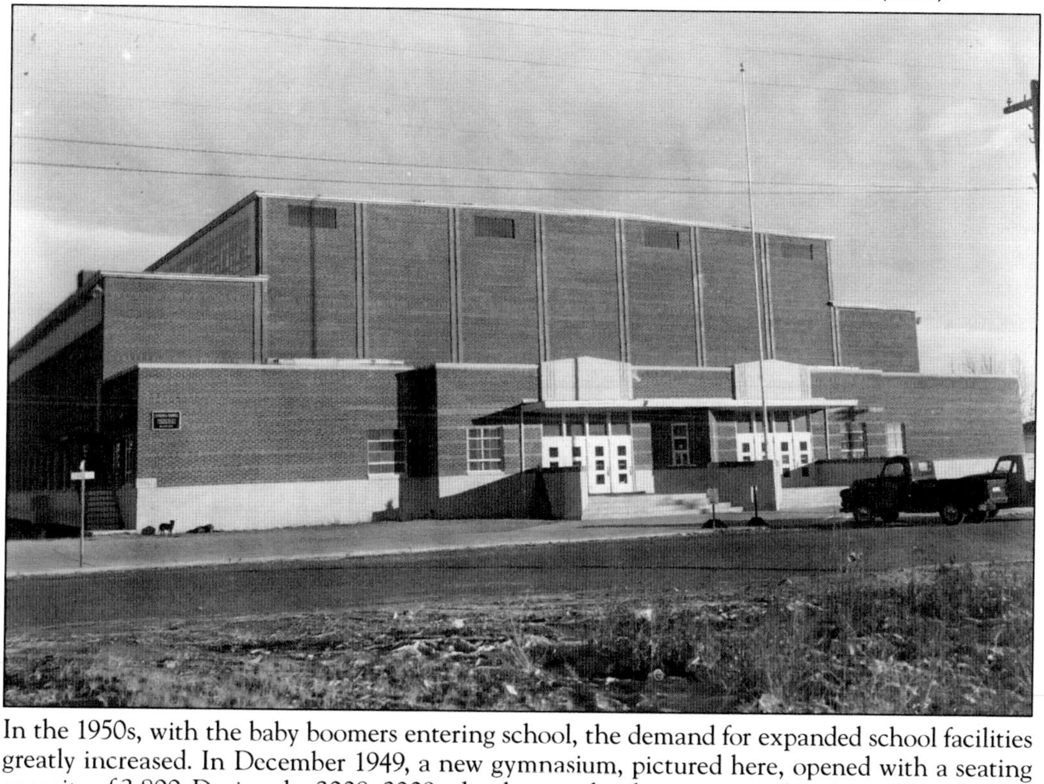

In the 1950s, with the baby boomers entering school, the demand for expanded school facilities greatly increased. In December 1949, a new gymnasium, pictured here, opened with a seating capacity of 2,800. During the 2008–2009 school year, school events moved to the new high school gymnasium located east of town. (HM.)

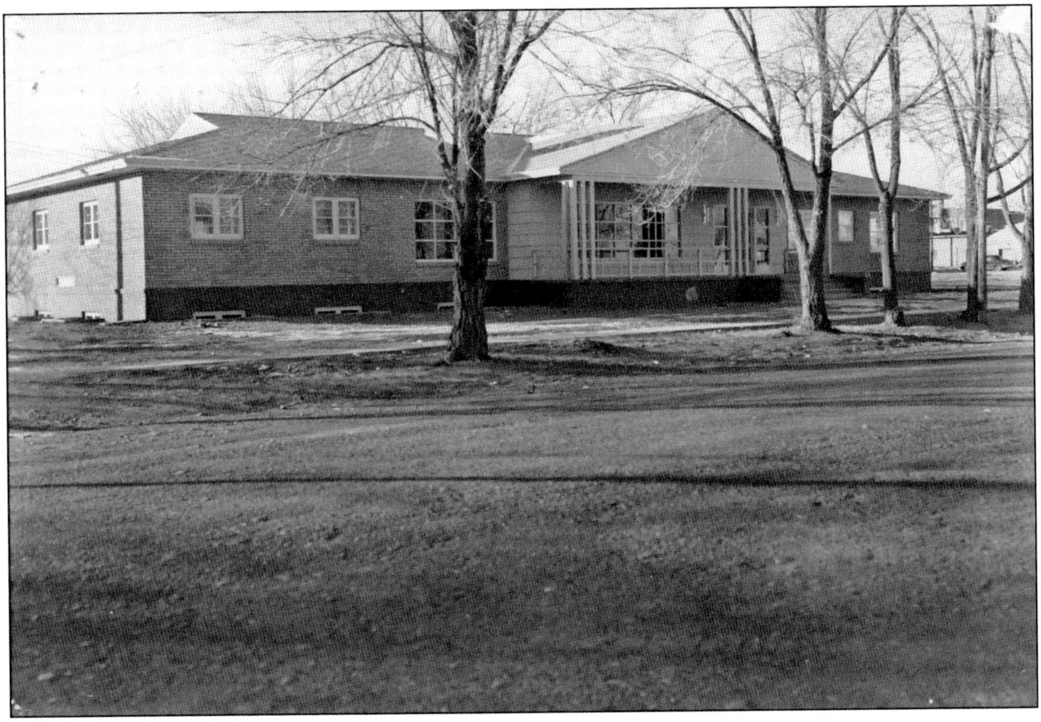

More school facilities were built in the early 1950s. In 1952, the home economics cottage, pictured above, opened. By 1956, the new swimming pool and auditorium opened. Powell residents wondered about the tremendous cost; in the summer of 1955 alone more than $821,000 was spent on construction projects. From the 1950s into the 21st century, these facilities served a great number of Powell students. (Above, PCA; below, HM.)

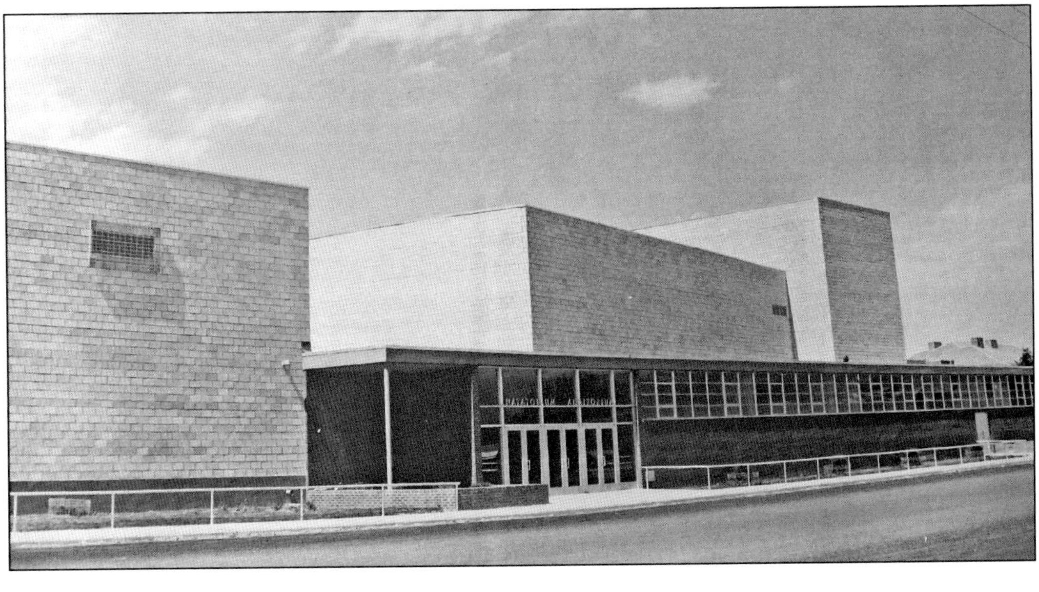

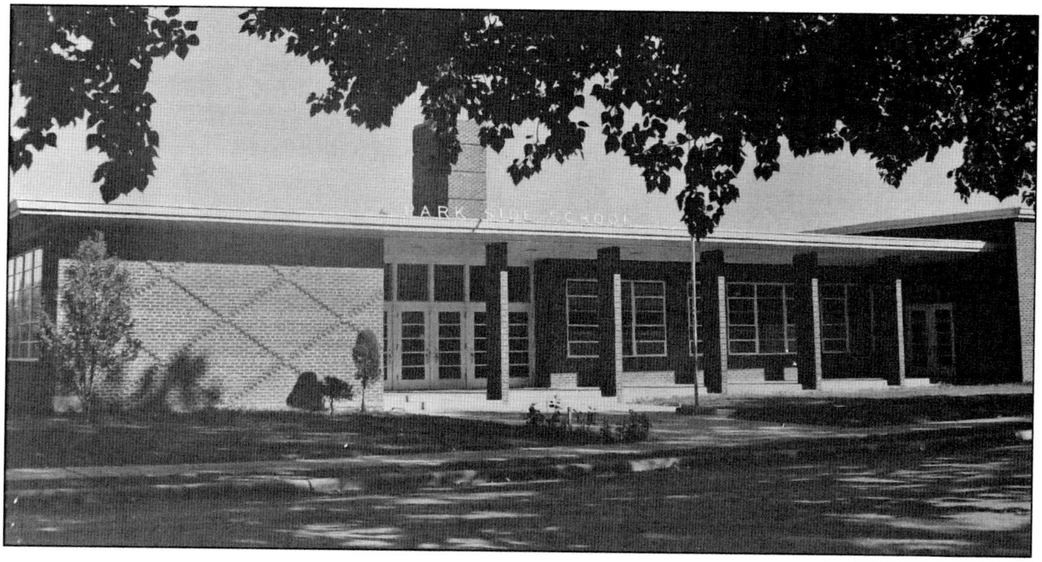

The need for grade school classrooms led Powell School District No. 1 to build schools located in various parts of the community, away from the traditional school grounds in the central part of town. Along with the bond passed to fund the construction of the new gymnasium, funding was also secured to remodel the old grade school building, to be known as Eastside School, and to construct Parkside School, pictured above, which was complete in 1949. Southside School, pictured below, opened in 1956 to serve students living in the expanding residential area south of Coulter Avenue. (Both HM.)

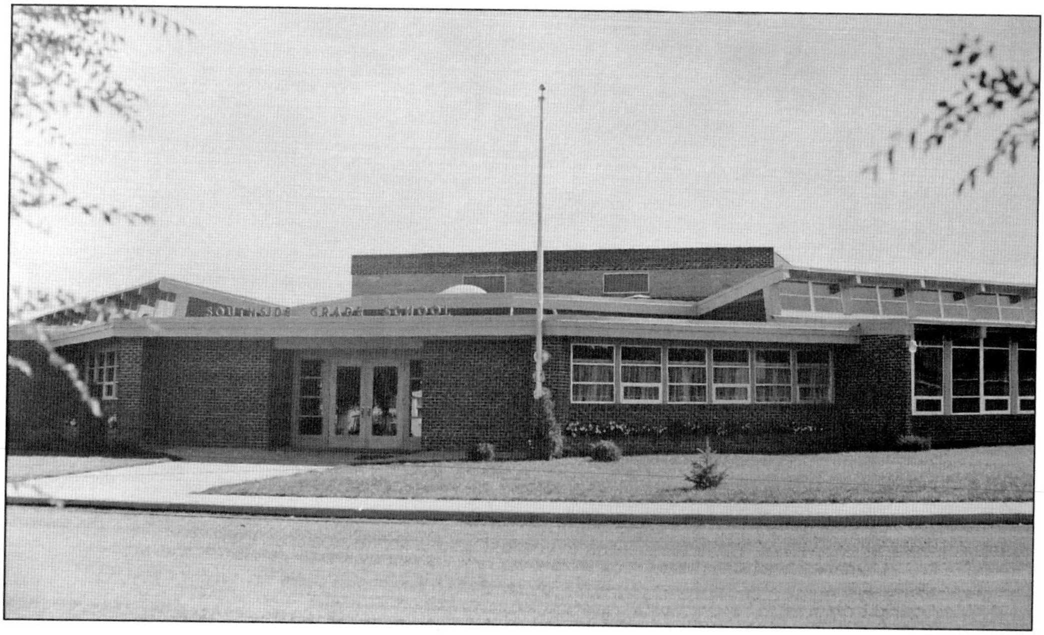

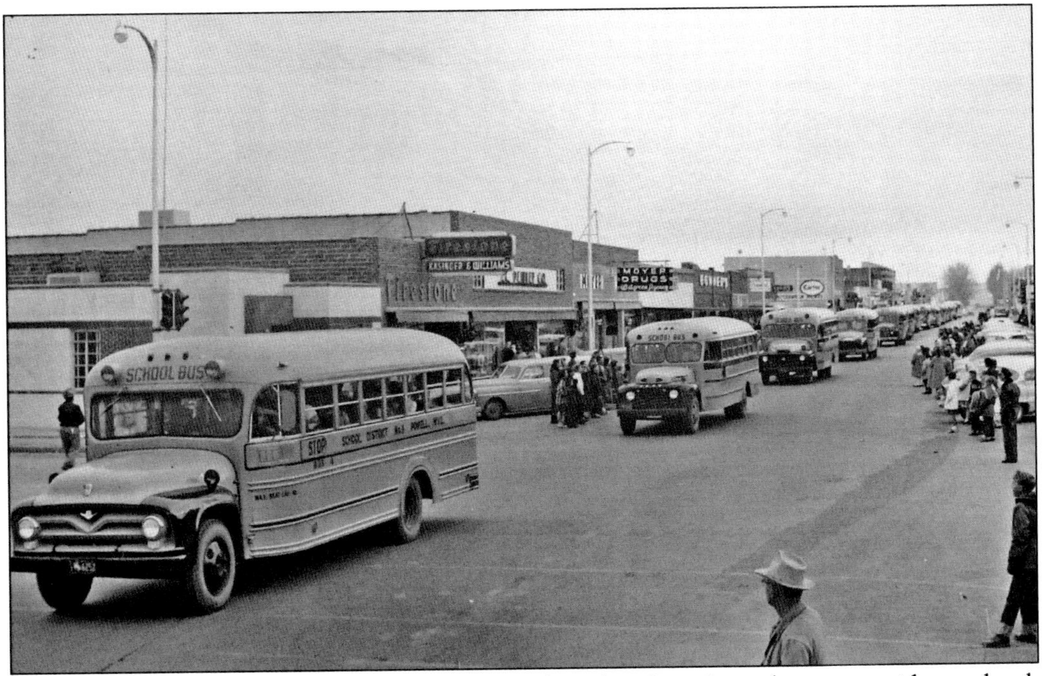

By the 1950s, Powell's busing system carried a number of students from the countryside to school. In 1955, Powell School District No. 1 showed off its great number of buses by parading them through town. In 1959, the Powell School District had an enrollment of 1,978 students, 869 of whom rode buses to school. This photograph was taken from the corner of Bent and Third Streets, looking south. (HM.)

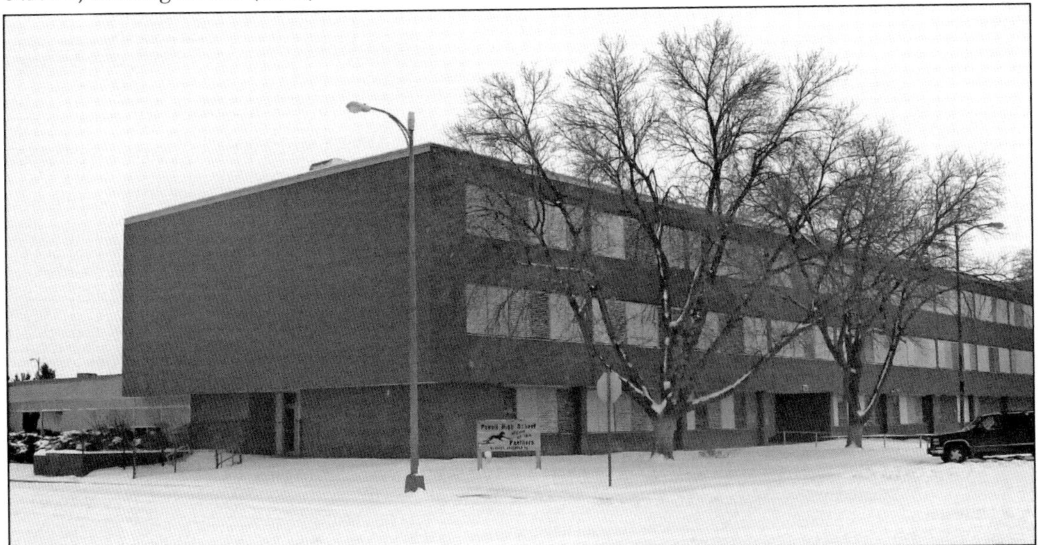

By 1959, the need for a new high school building led the community of Powell to support a $1.7 million bond. The new high school opened in 1960 to serve 700 students. This structure remained in use until the 2008–2009 school year, when Powell's high school students moved into a new building constructed east of town. The use of most of the old high school facilities, such as the gymnasium, auditorium, and swimming pool, will most likely be discontinued in the next few years. (Author's collection.)

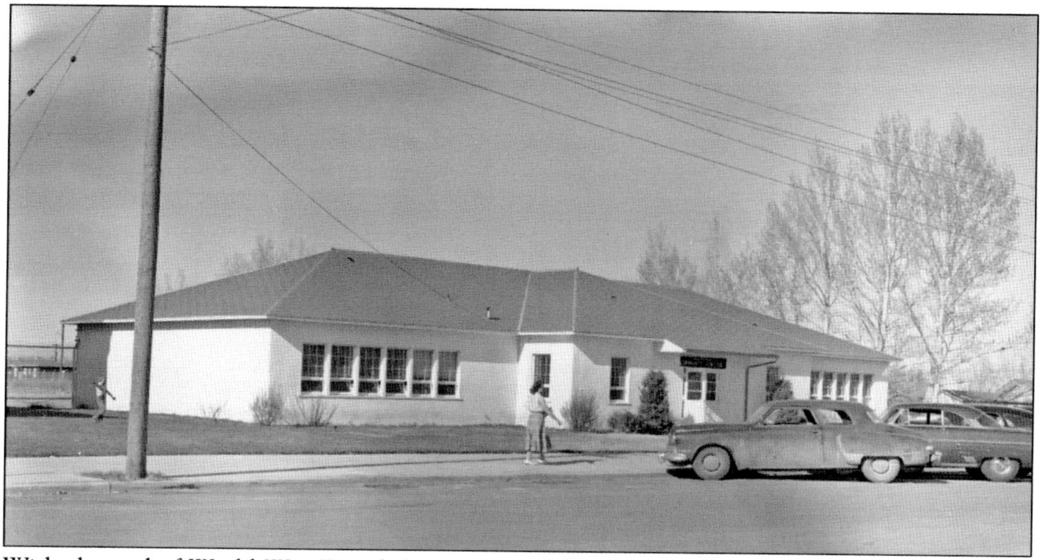

With the end of World War II and the passage of the GI Bill, a number of returning veterans sought a higher education, and Powell residents examined the possibility of opening a college in their community. In 1946, the Northwest Center of the University of Wyoming opened in Powell. The first courses taught through the Northwest Center were held on the second floor of Powell High School using three faculty members. The college and high school students shared use of the library, gym, and laboratories. In 1949, the Northwest Center moved into a small cottage, nicknamed the "Little White House," pictured above, just east of the gymnasium. The center still shared facilities with the high school, and some classes met in the basement of the Presbyterian church. Also in 1949, J. E. Christensen, pictured below, replaced Clarence Moore as director. Christensen would later become the first college president of NWCC. (Both NWC.)

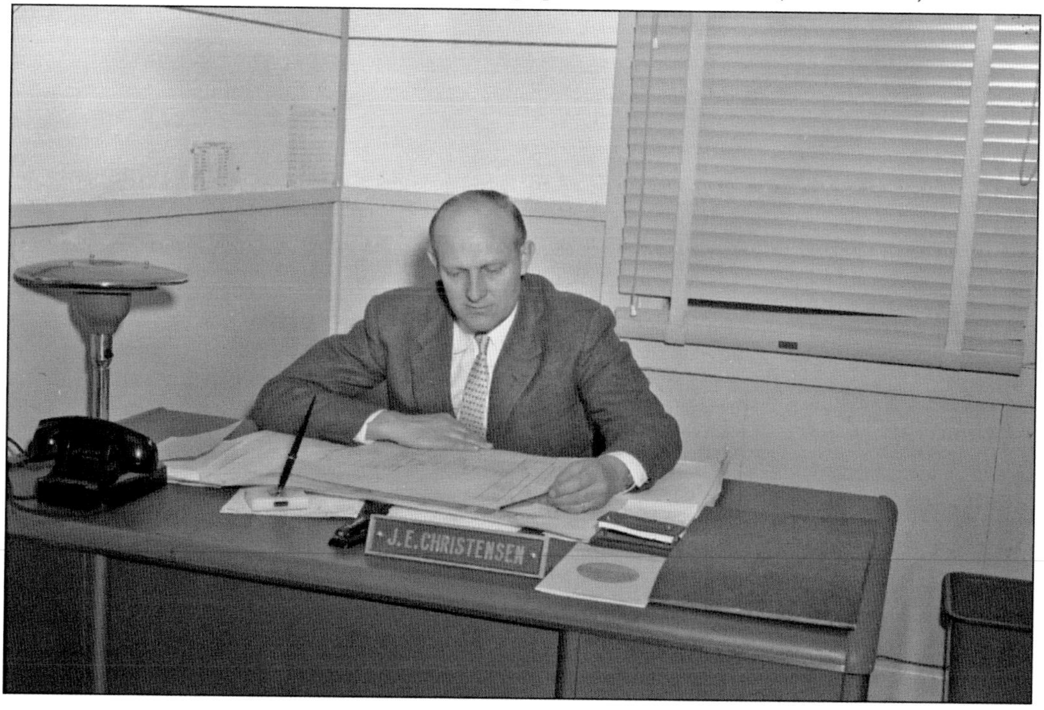

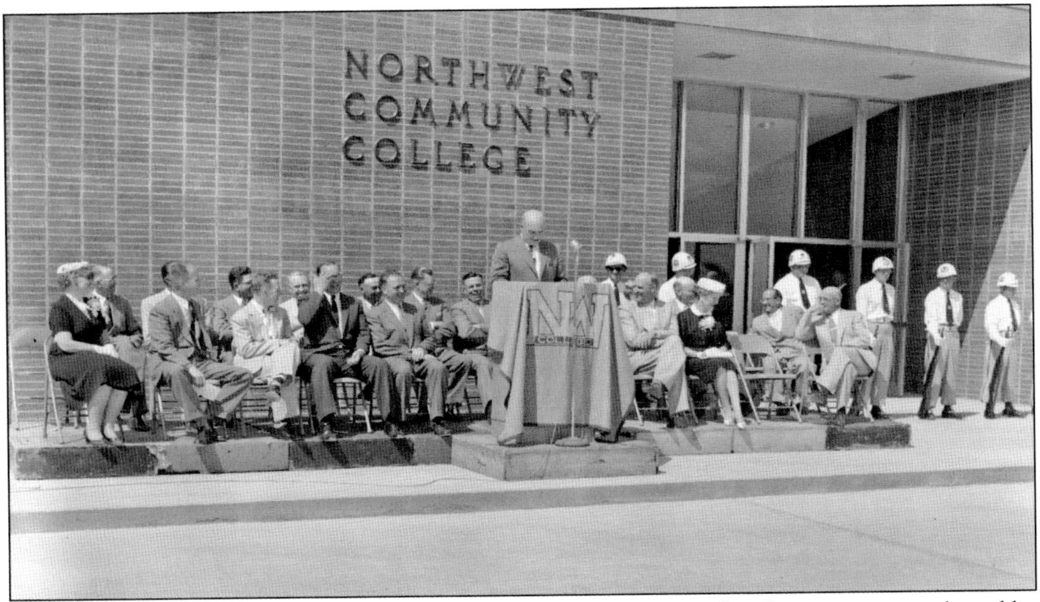

In 1953, Powell's citizens recommended a college district be created and a seven-person board be elected to oversee Northwest Community College (NWCC). After acquiring land from Eleanora Hancock between Fifth and Sixth Streets and Bernard and Division Streets, Northwest Community College constructed a new building, passing two separate bond issues that totaled nearly $450,000. The dedication of the new building occurred on May 20, 1956, as seen in the above photograph. A reception followed, as seen below. Nearly 1,600 people attended this dedication. (Both NWC.)

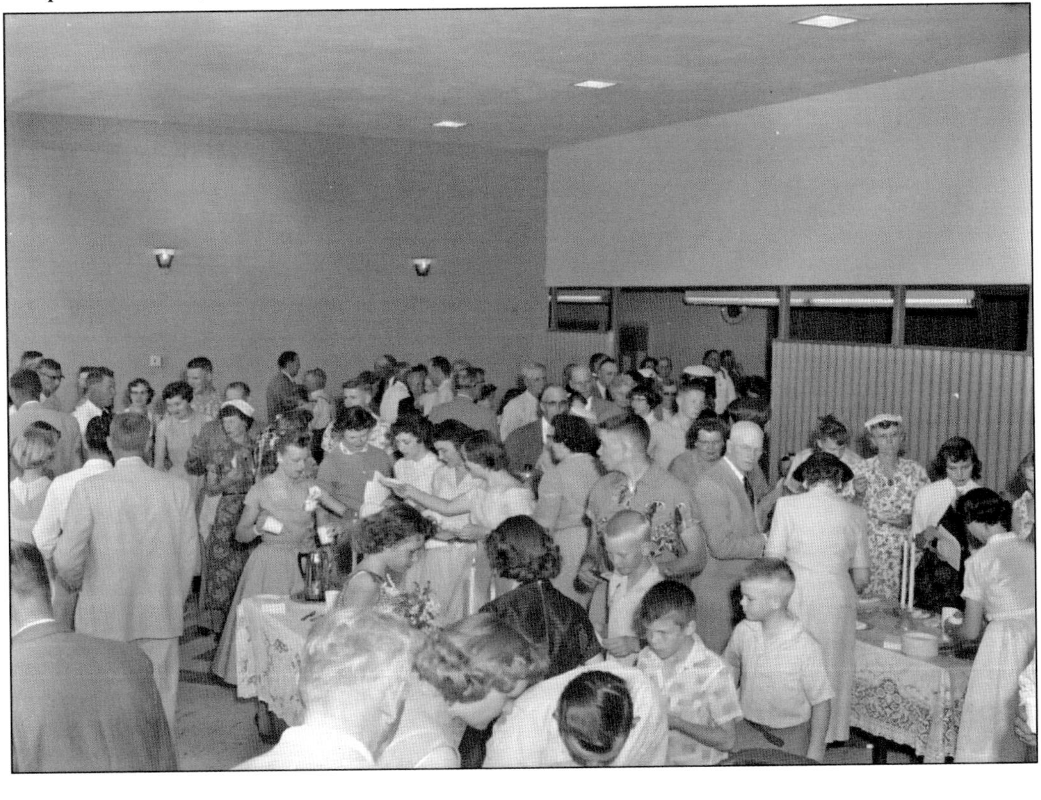

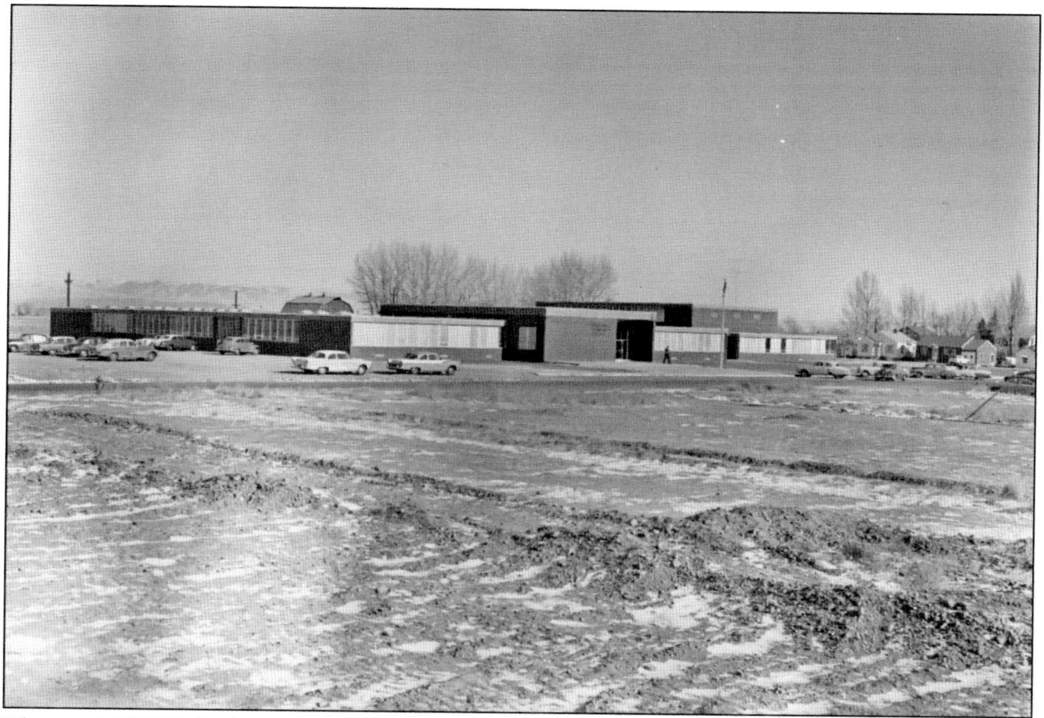

The new NWCC facilities included offices, classroom space, a gym, and a library with over 6,000 volumes. The above photograph shows the new college campus surrounded by undeveloped land. In 1956, one hundred seventy-five students enrolled for classes at the new community college. Below, students arrive to class on a cold winter day. (Both NWC.)

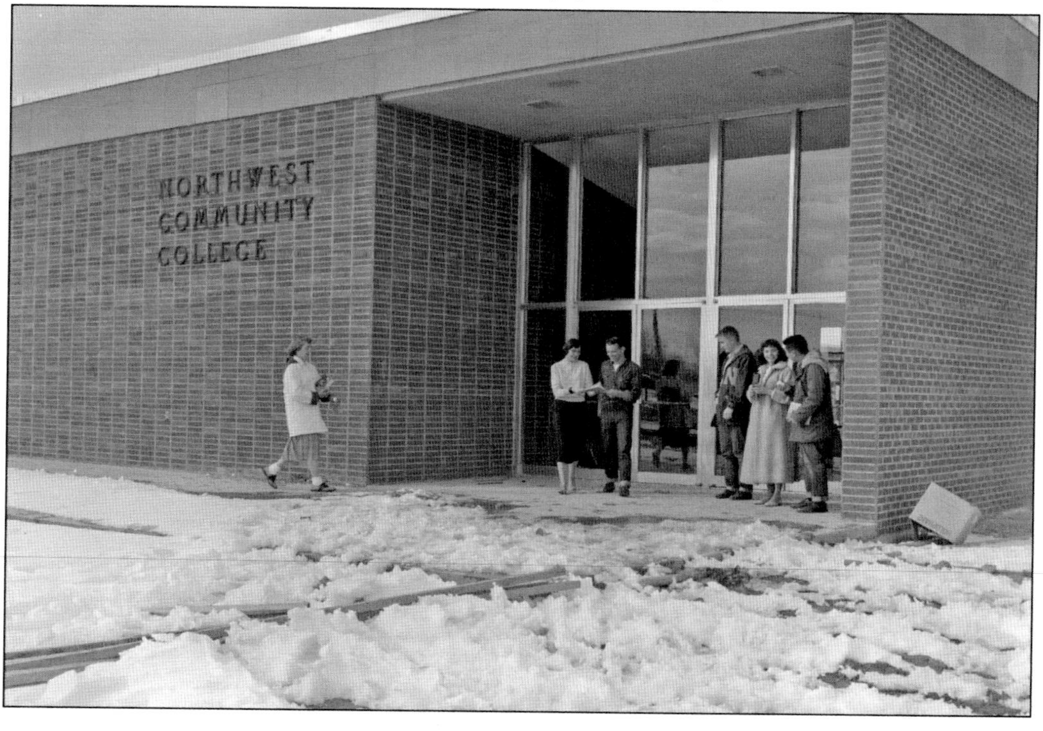

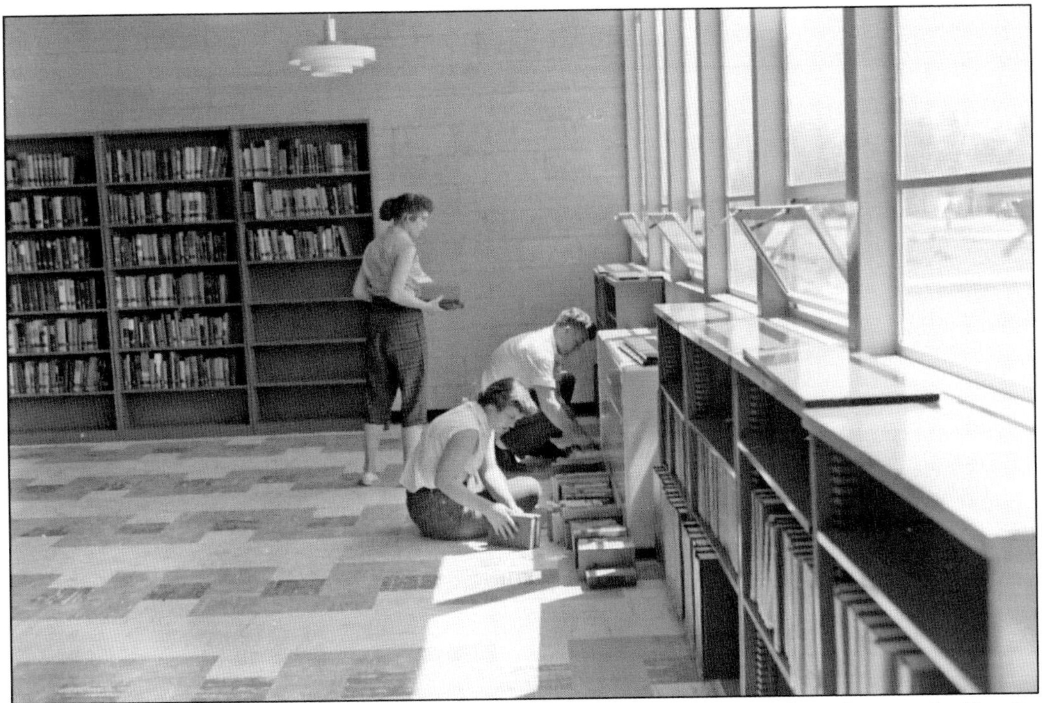

Students volunteered to move equipment from the "Little White House" to the new facility. In the photograph above, students sort through and organize various books to be placed in the new library facility. Below, various office and classroom equipment waits in the courtyard, now the site of Northwest College's natural history dioramas. (Both NWC.)

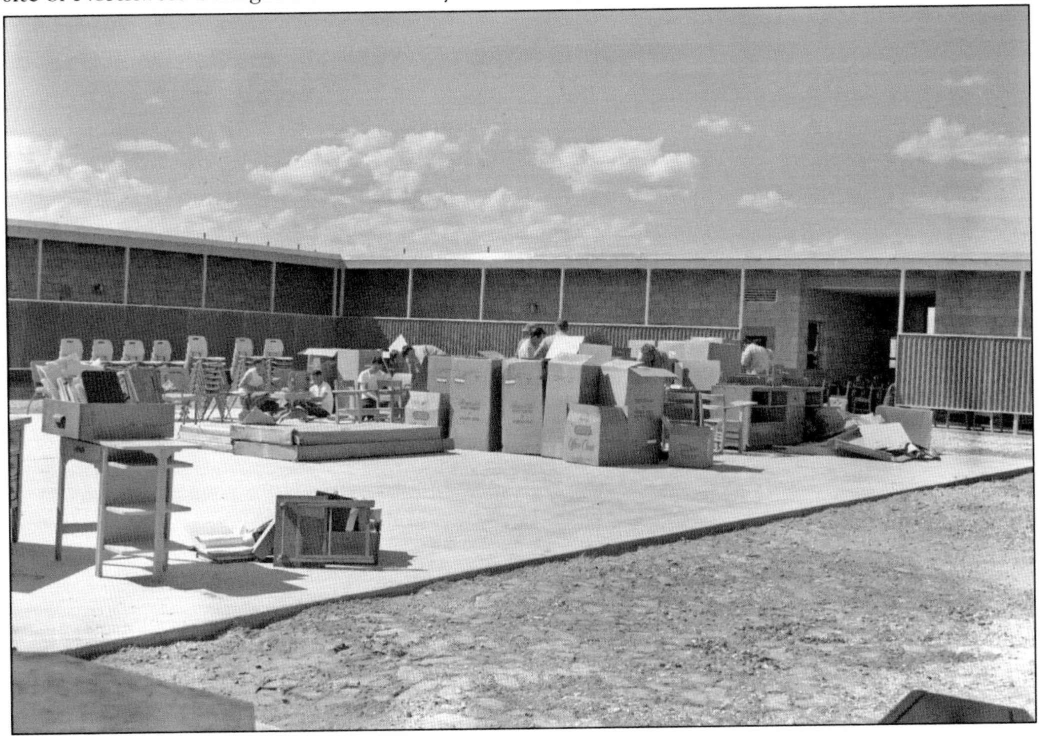

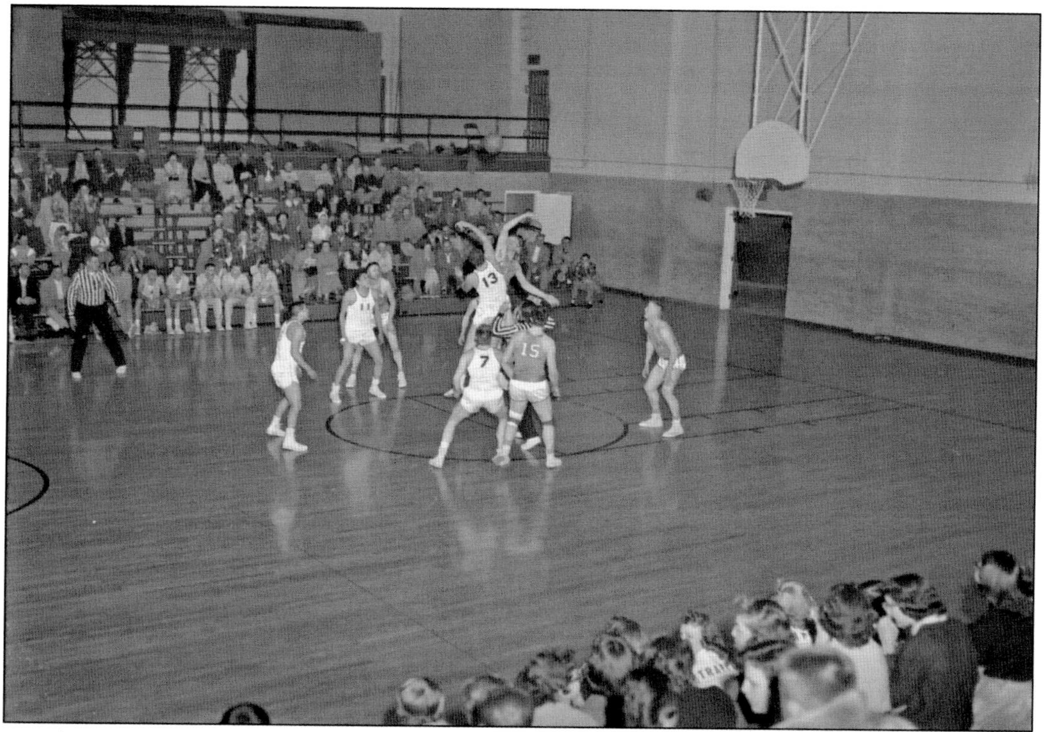

Northwest Community College provided its students with an athletic program. In 1946, the Northwest Center offered basketball, and in 1954 football was added. The basketball team, known as the Northwest Lions, later renamed the Trappers, plays a game in the Powell High School Gymnasium around 1956. Below, a group of Northwest Community College cheerleaders show off their moves in front of the new campus building. Pictured from left to right are Leatha Nelson, Loretta Wales, Norma Griffen, and Nancy Brubaker. (Both NWC.)

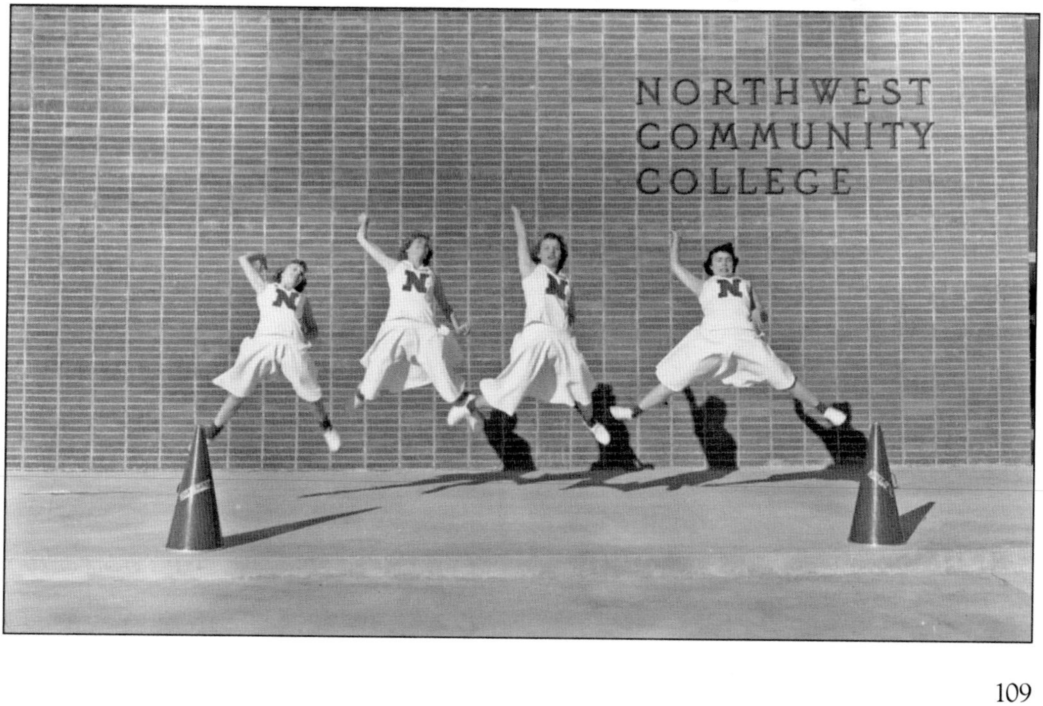

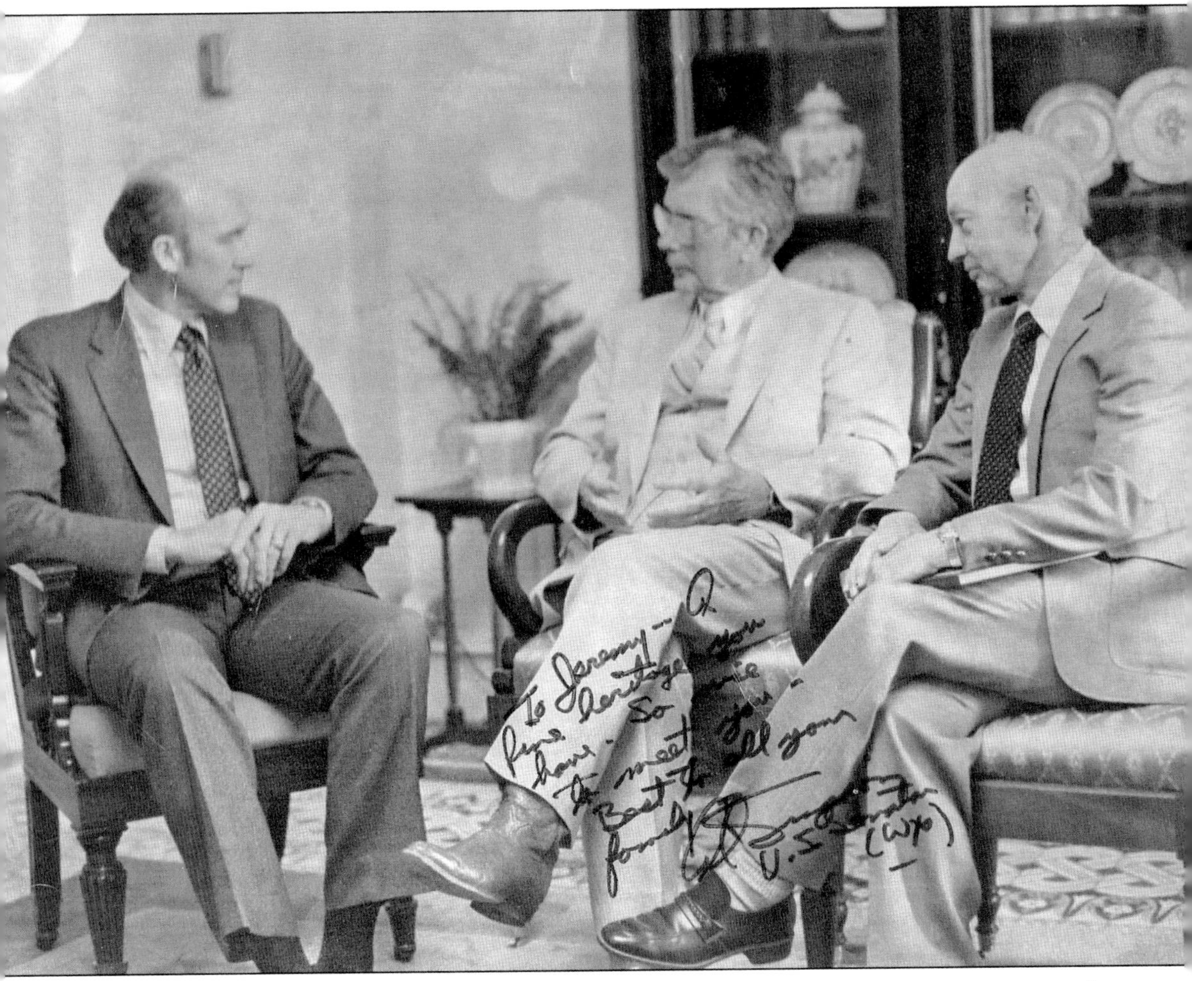

In 1966, Northwest Community College entered a period of chaos. Due to a controversy regarding faculty tenure and various financial concerns, J. E. Christensen stepped down as college president after 18 years. The board hired Sinclair Orendorff as the new president. Orendorff, working with a strong board that included Rev. Ray Nott, Warren Smith, and Bob Fagerberg, expanded the college district from just Powell School District No. 1 to all of Park County. The extra revenue generated from the expansion saved the college and allowed it to grow its facilities. Pictured are, from left to right, Wyoming senator Al Simpson, a strong advocate of the redistricting; Sinclair Orendorff; and Dan Oliver, who developed the first vocational programs for the college. (Author's collection.)

Eight

LIFE IN POWELL

A number of people have made Powell their home over the last 100 years. Some families resided within the town while others lived in houses built on the original family homestead. Because of Powell's distance from any major metropolitan area, residents did their best to entertain themselves and their children. A number of social organizations such as the Masons, Eagles, American Legion, and the Veterans of Foreign Wars (VFW) provided men with fraternal organizations that created strong bonds of friendship. Various women's clubs and auxiliaries also sprung up in the countryside and within town to provide women the opportunity to bond with fellow women. A number of churches also developed in town not only to meet the community's various spiritual needs, but to also provide another opportunity to gather with neighbors.

The movie theater, library, and community events provided an immediate source to meet Powell residents' entertainment needs. The more adventurous families would travel to the distant mountain ranges for hunting and fishing. Powell established Washington Park, and additional parks through the years, to allow its citizens the opportunity to hear a band concert, enjoy a family or community picnic, and for children to run and play. After a rivalry with its neighbor Cody, Wyoming, Powell abandoned a Fourth of July Parade and ceremonies in exchange for hosting the Park County Fair. Every year, citizens of Powell host a number of visitors at the Park County Fairgrounds and sponsor a Park County Fair parade. The bonds of community also helped Powell and its residents suffer through the international conflicts of the 20th and 21st centuries. The loss of a Powell soldier's life often solicited community assistance to ease the family's grief. Powell also remembered these soldiers' sacrifices in monuments and participation in national holidays of remembrance.

This community bond has not always been welcoming to outsiders. During World War II, more than 11,000 Japanese Americans found themselves interned at the Heart Mountain Relocation Center, 10 miles west of Powell. Powell's citizens fought the Relocation Authority, and fought amongst themselves, over how these new residents should or should not be welcomed to the region. Despite these painful tests of community bonds, Powell residents continue to feel a strong sense of community spirit. As Powell celebrates its centennial year with a variety of celebrations, it continues to honor its past and looks forward to the next 100 years of community progress.

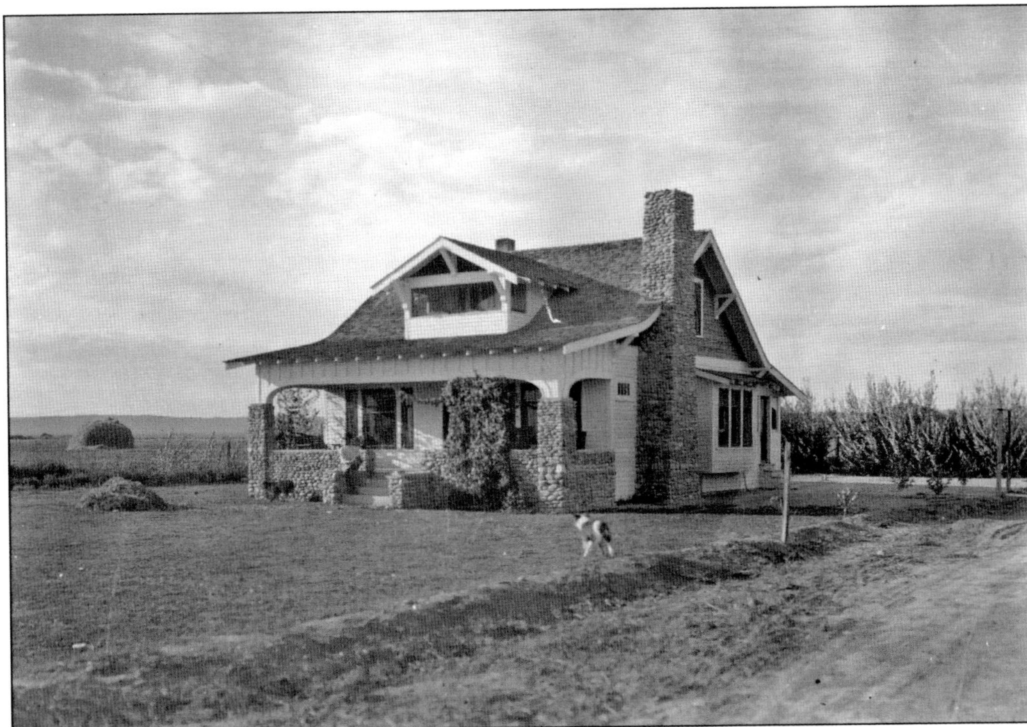

The ultimate proof of success for Powell's homesteaders and settlers was moving the family out of the homestead shack and into a two-story house. This photograph depicts Otto Smith's home in 1921. The Smith family still owns this residence. (SIDA.)

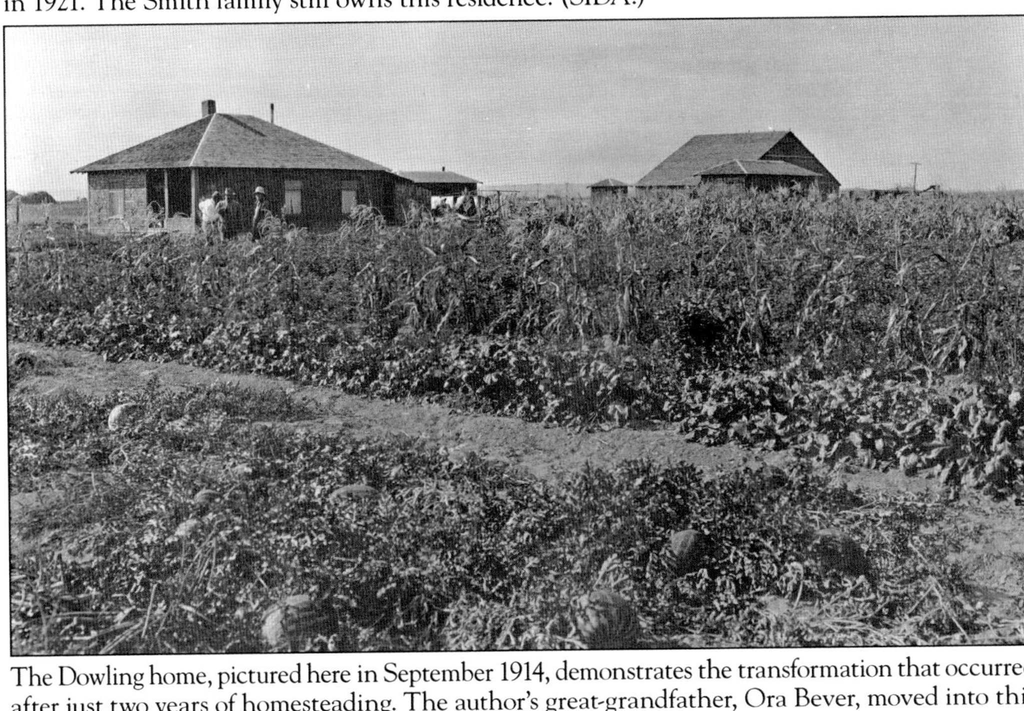

The Dowling home, pictured here in September 1914, demonstrates the transformation that occurred after just two years of homesteading. The author's great-grandfather, Ora Bever, moved into this house in 1918. The author's grandfather, James Bever, was born here that same year. (SIDA.)

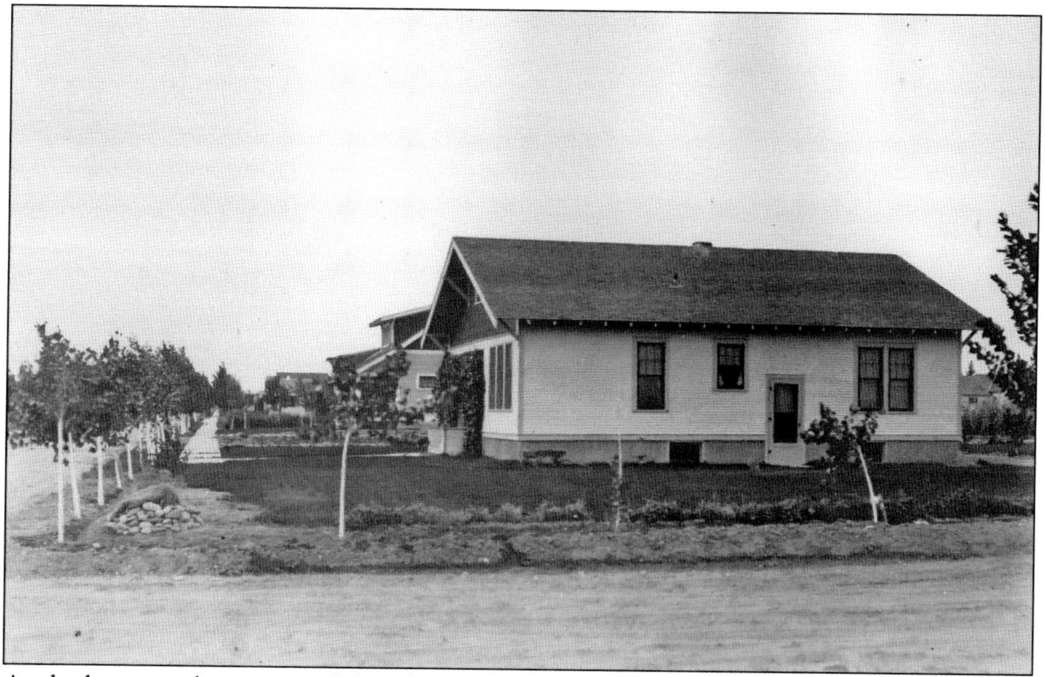

As the homesteaders improved their living conditions in the countryside, residents within the city limits also built new homes and the town quickly expanded its residential area. Henry D. Edmonds and W. A. Deming developed their 40-acre plots, located west of town, as the town's first subdivision. Officials from the Reclamation Service protested the development, not wanting promoters to profit from real estate development on the Shoshone Project lands. Edmunds Street bears H. D. Edmonds name and marks the western boundary of the Edmonds subdivision. The photograph above depicts a house, built in 1920, at 370 North Bernard Street. The photograph below shows the Dunlavy home built at 411 West Third Street in the 1920s. (Both SIDA.)

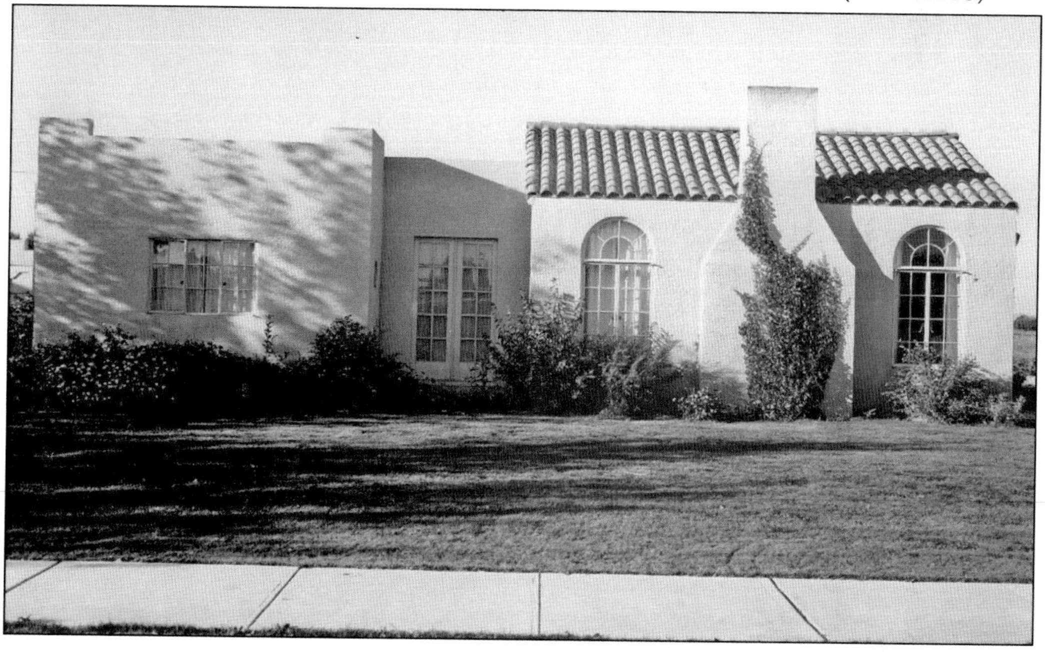

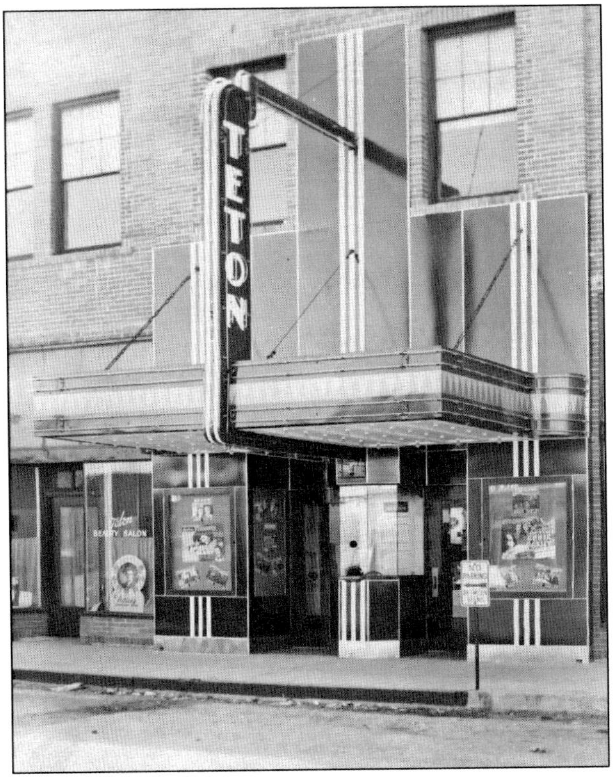

The theater on Bent Street provided community members entertainment with stage shows and movies. The image below depicts the inside of the movie theater with its screen surrounded by various local advertisements. At left is the theater's marquee. The theater has had various names throughout the years: the Lyric Theater, the Teton Theater, and the Vali Cinema. (At left, HM; below, PCA.)

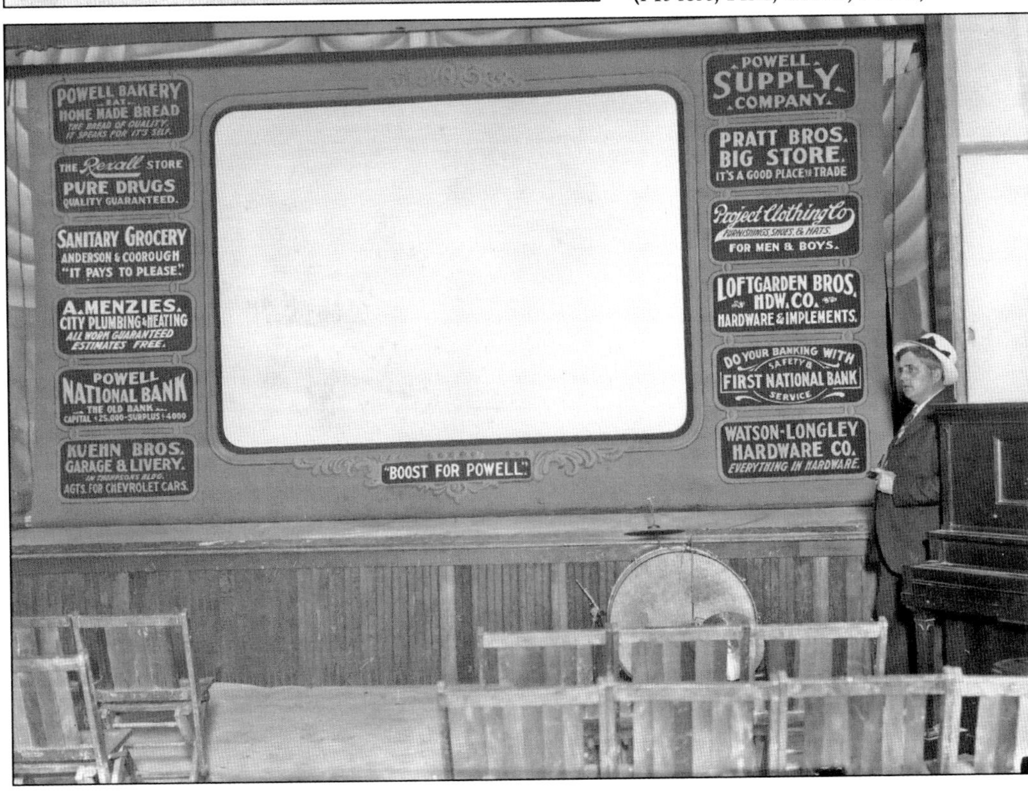

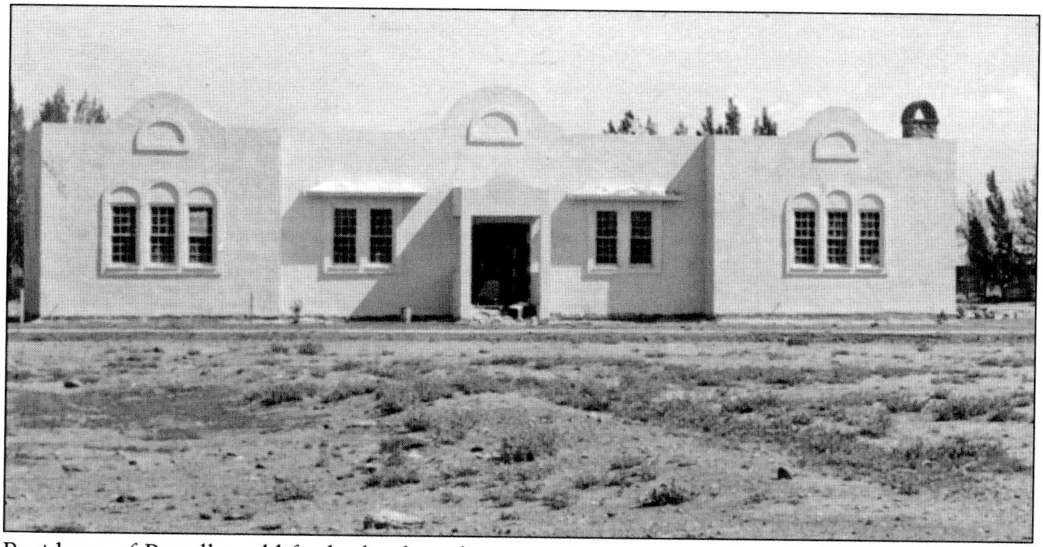

Residents of Powell could find a book and some quiet space to read at the community library. The Ladies' Union began the Powell Library Club in 1910 to establish the first town library. The library consisted of four shelves made by A. P. Libby and was housed in his home. Later the book collection moved several times, to Dr. Lewellen's Drug Store, to the Wyoming Hotel, and then to the basement of the Baptist church. In 1921, the old Fairview School Building was purchased for use as a library and moved to the corner of Clark and Third Streets. The library building, pictured here, was completed in 1934. (SIDA.)

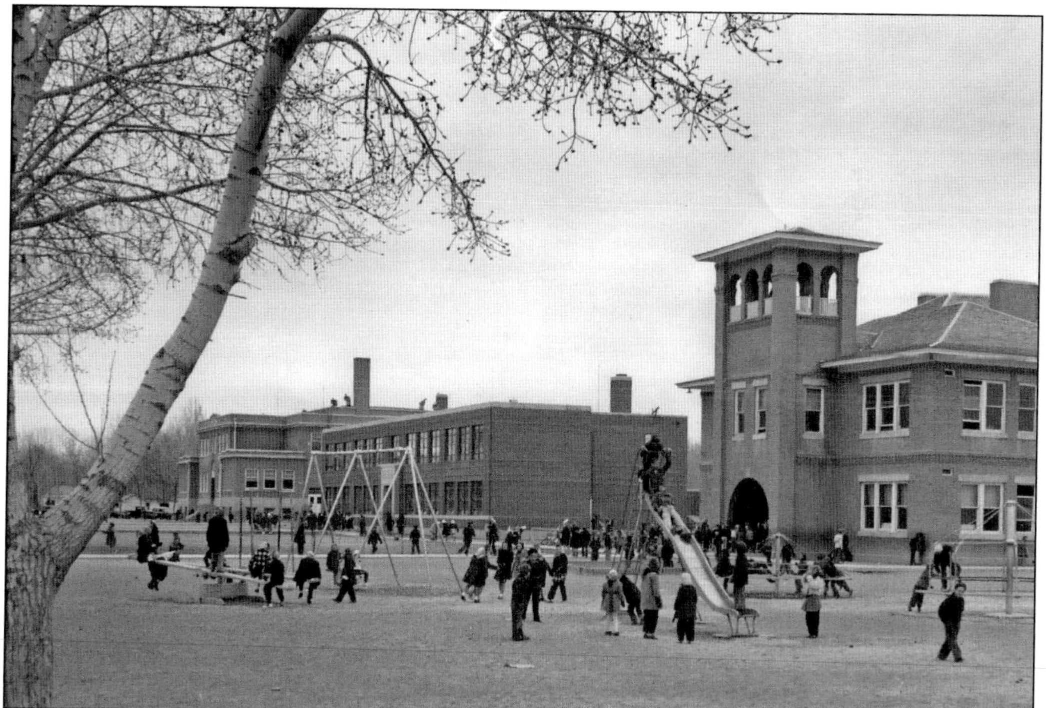

Schools not only offered an educational opportunity, they also provided an area for children to play at recess, after school, and through the summer months. This image depicts a number of children playing on the playground equipment in front of Eastside School. (PCA.)

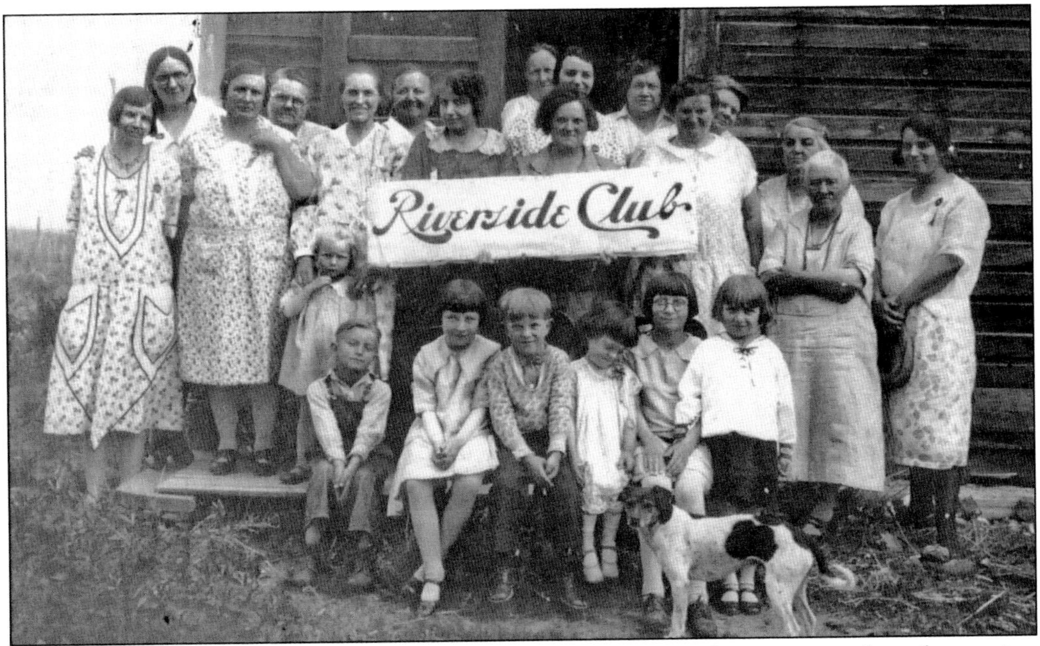

Through the support of the Park County Agricultural Extension Service, a number of extension clubs existed throughout the countryside. Pictured here is a gathering of women proudly proclaiming themselves as the Riverside Club. This extension club began in 1920 at the home of Louie and Mary Onstine. Mrs. Marie Milliken served as the first president, Mrs. Vincent Franklin as vice president, and Mrs. Kinder as secretary-treasurer. In 1923, the Riverside Club purchased an old pool hall in Garland and moved the building directly south of Powell, north of the Shoshone River. Sixteen extension clubs were formed in the Powell area. (HM.)

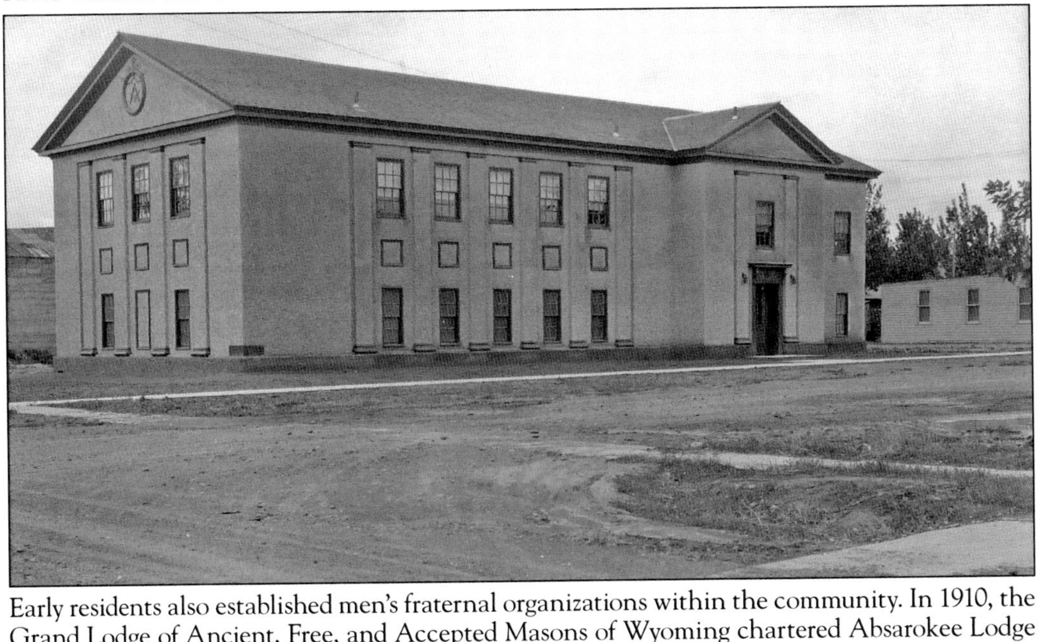

Early residents also established men's fraternal organizations within the community. In 1910, the Grand Lodge of Ancient, Free, and Accepted Masons of Wyoming chartered Absarokee Lodge No. 30. Originally the lodge brothers met in the room above the theater. In 1931, the members of Absarokee Lodge No. 30 built the Masonic Lodge seen here. (FNB.)

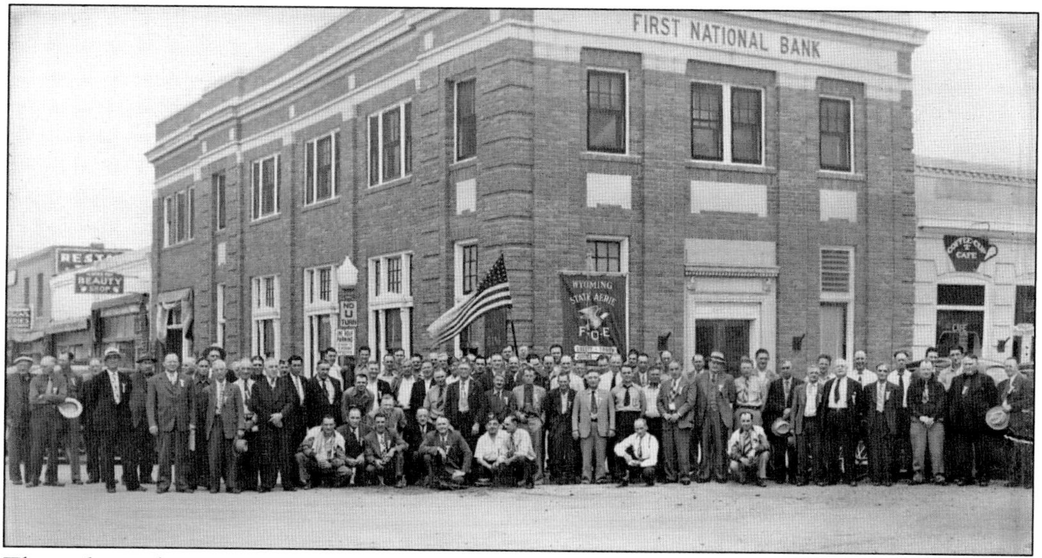

Throughout the 1940s, a number of new clubs and women's auxiliaries organized in Powell, including the VFW, the International Order of Odd Fellows, the Fraternal Order of Eagles, the Rebekahs, the Knights of Columbus, and the Heart Mountain Rod and Gun Club. Also during the 1940s, a number of service groups such as the Powell Club, the Rotary International, and the Jaycees were established. A number of these organizations hosted state conventions in Powell, as seen in this photograph of the delegates to the State Aerie Meeting of the Fraternal Order of Eagles. (Powell Aerie No. 2426 FOE.)

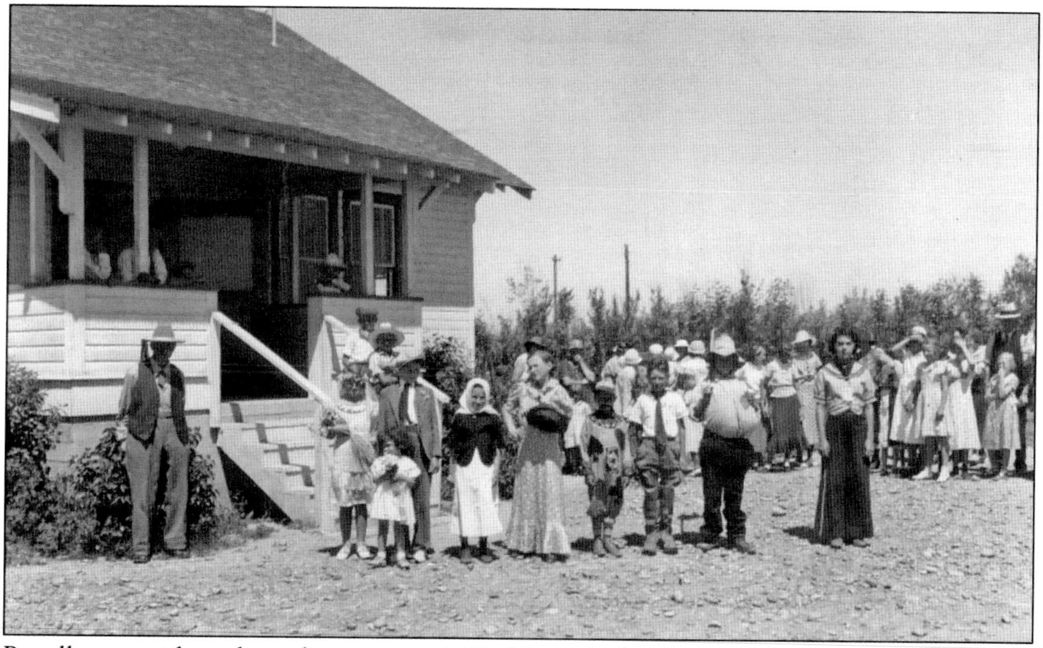

Powell-area residents formed community halls. Using the headquarters building of the Willwood Division, the Willwood settlers established a community clubhouse. The clubhouse is currently used to host community picnics, family events, an annual celebration honoring the opening of the division, and various civic functions such as serving as the polling place for voters. This photograph depicts a summer gathering at the Willwood Clubhouse in 1936. (SIDA.)

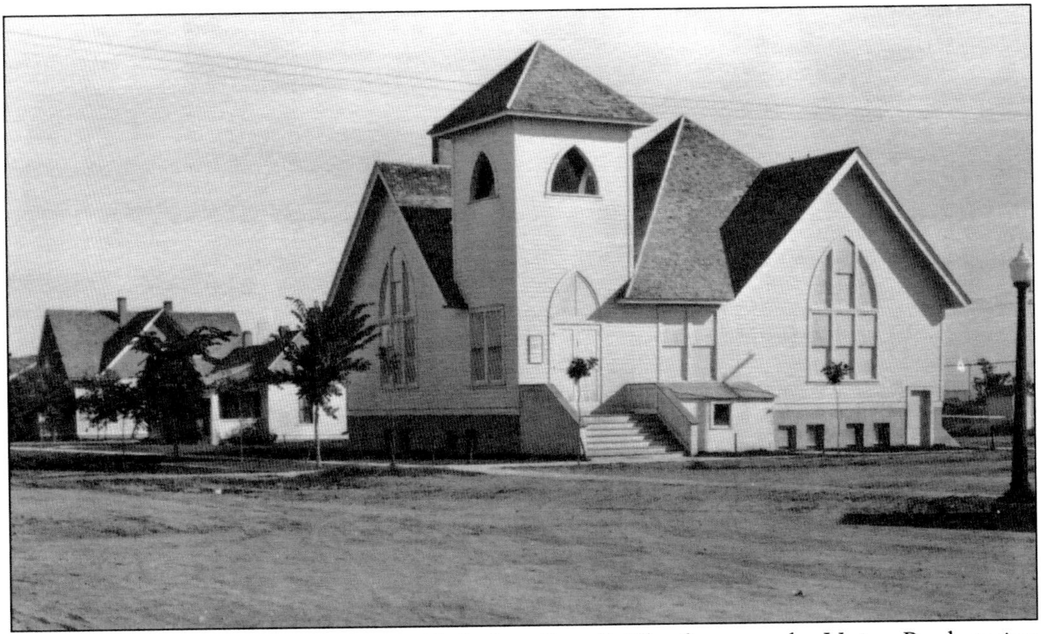

A number of churches soon were established in Powell. The first was the Union Presbyterian Church, located on the northeast corner of Bent and Third Streets. Construction of the church began on August 30, 1909, and the congregation dedicated the building on May 11, 1911. Other churches were established in Powell within its first 50 years, including the First Methodist Church, St. Barbara's Catholic Church, First Baptist Church, St. John's Episcopal Church, Seventh-day Adventist Church, Christian Science Church, Church of Jesus Christ of Latter-day Saints, Glad Tidings Assembly, Immanuel Lutheran Church, Church of Christ, Church of the Nazarene, Hope Lutheran Church, Jehovah's Witnesses, Church of God of Prophecy, Reorganized Church of Jesus Christ of Latter-day Saints, and the First Southern Baptist Church. (HM.)

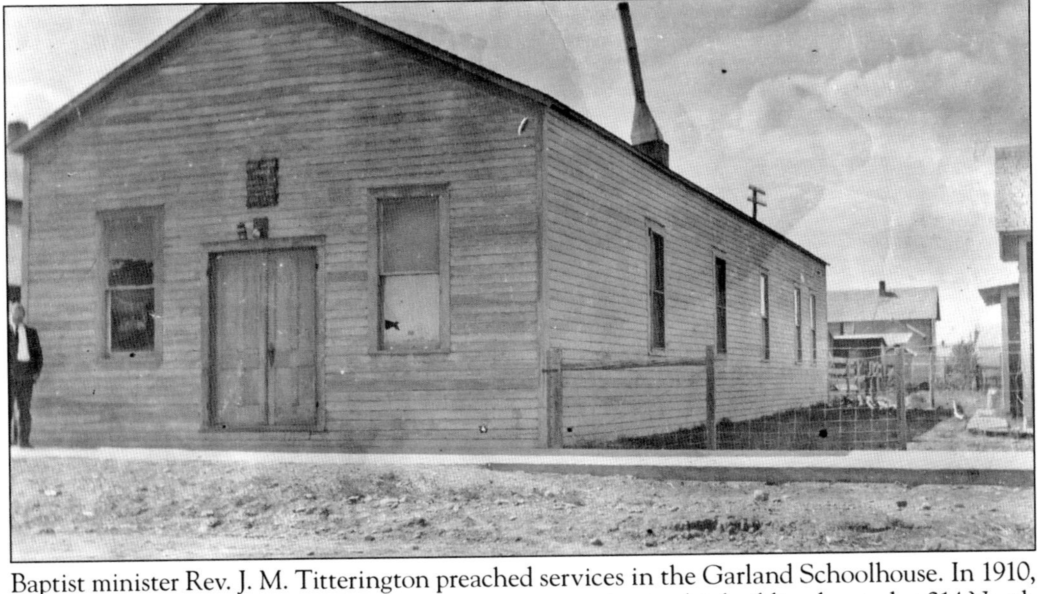

Baptist minister Rev. J. M. Titterington preached services in the Garland Schoolhouse. In 1910, the First Baptist Church offered services to its congregation in this building located at 214 North Bent Street. (HM.)

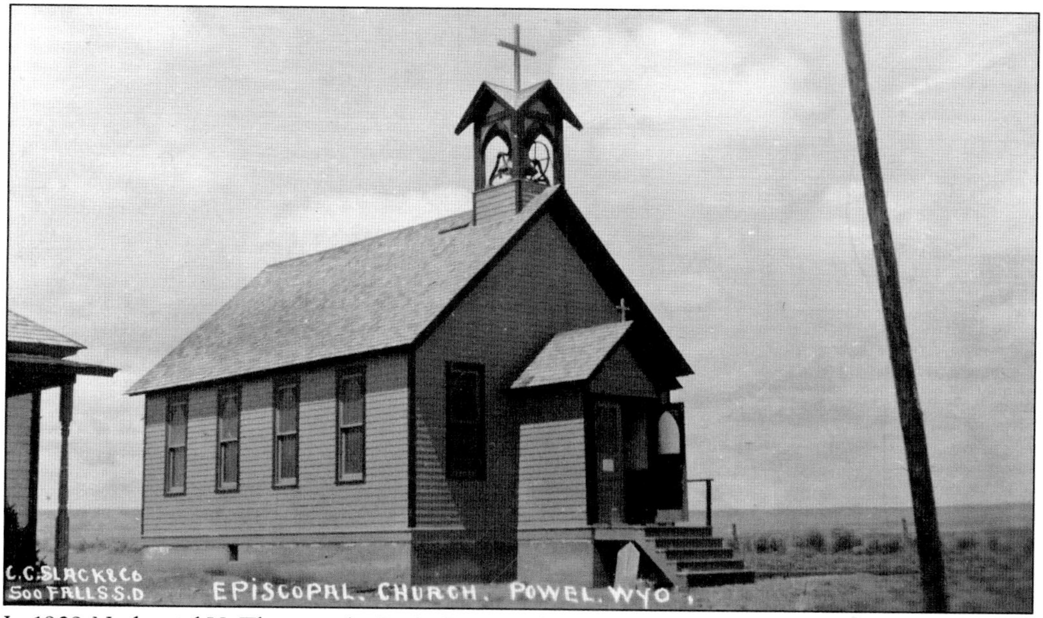

In 1909, Nathaniel H. Thomas, the Right Reverend Missionary Bishop of Wyoming, visited Powell and decided to build an Episcopal church for the community. The ground-breaking ceremony for St. John's Episcopal Church occurred in August 1910 and the building was consecrated on January 26, 1911. (HM.)

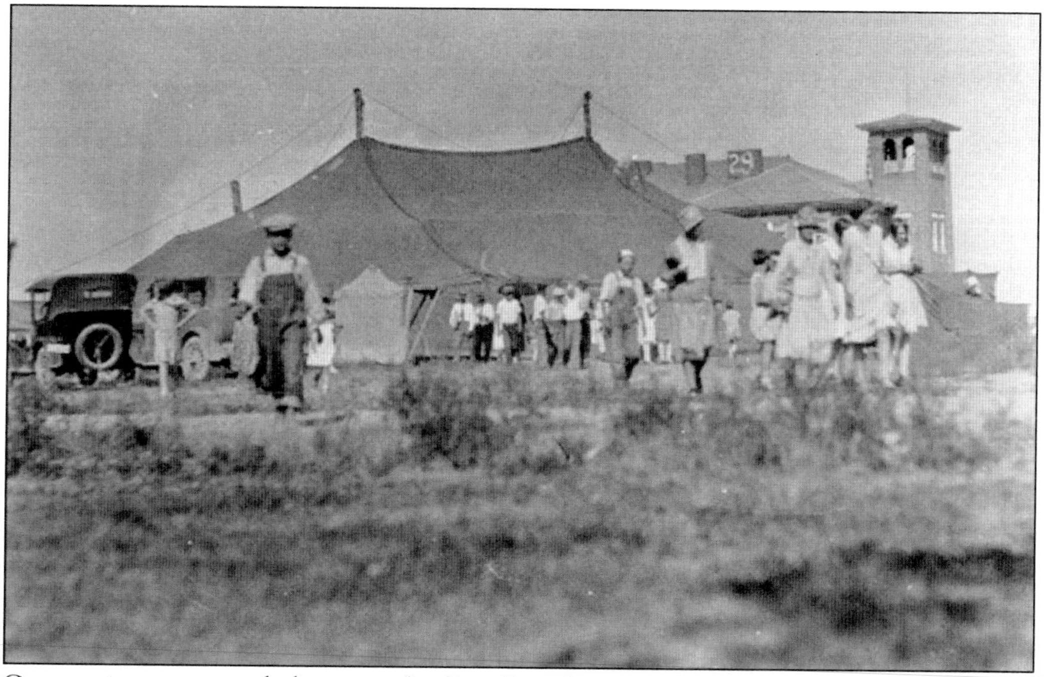

Community events regularly occurred in Powell, and concerts, picnics, and celebrations brought the many Powell citizens out to celebrate. The Chautauqua movement began in the 1870s. By the 20th century, traveling Chautauquas visited various communities and offered lectures on art, literature, politics, and science. This image depicts a 1929 Chautauqua in Powell. Note that a proud member of the class of 1929 has tagged the school's chimney. (SIDA.)

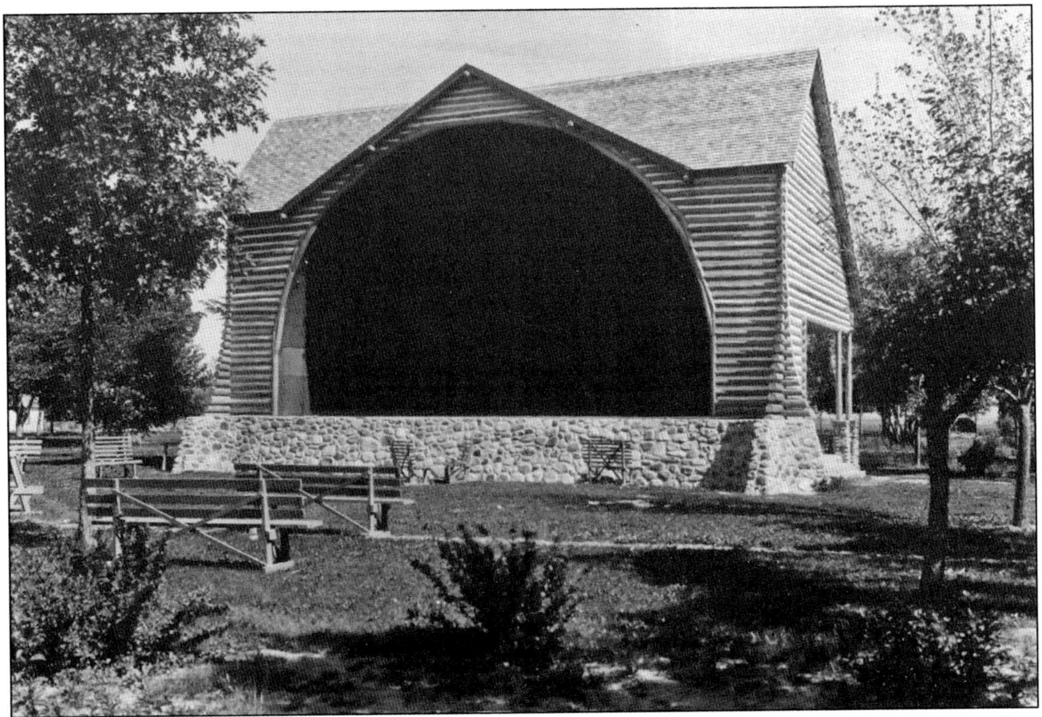

Washington Park, located between First and Second Streets and Cheyenne and Douglas Streets, has long been a gathering place for Powell residents. During the Great Depression, the Work Projects Administration (WPA) completed this band shell within the park. A number of community concerts occurred under this massive log structure. (SIDA.)

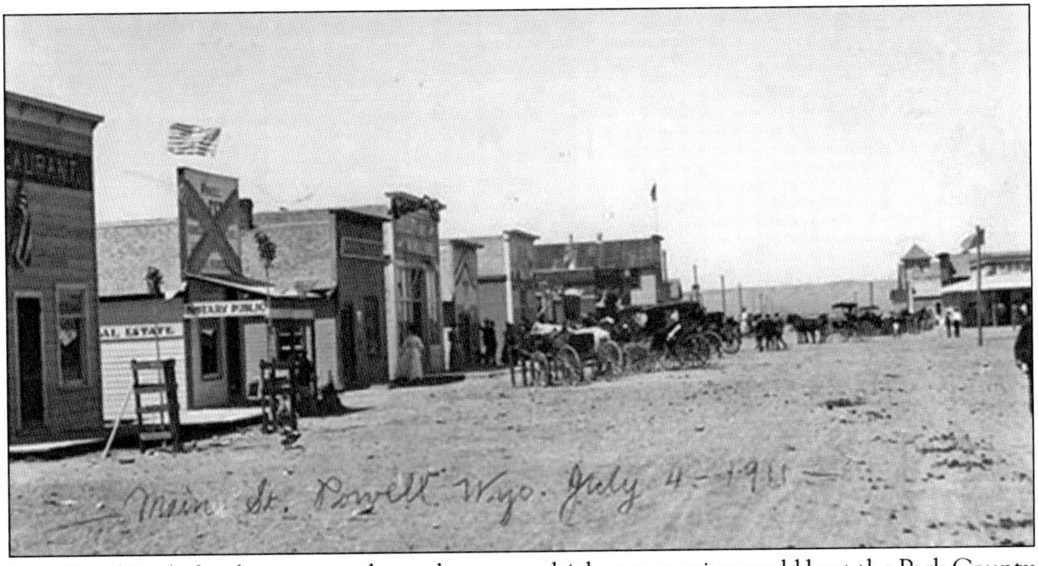

Powell and Cody fought amongst themselves over which community would host the Park County Fair. To acquire Cody's blessing to host the fair, Powell had to promise not to have a Fourth of July celebration. Today most Powell residents enjoy the parade and events celebrating the Fourth of July in Cody, but in 1911 the town clearly went all out to celebrate Independence Day, as seen in this photograph. (HM.)

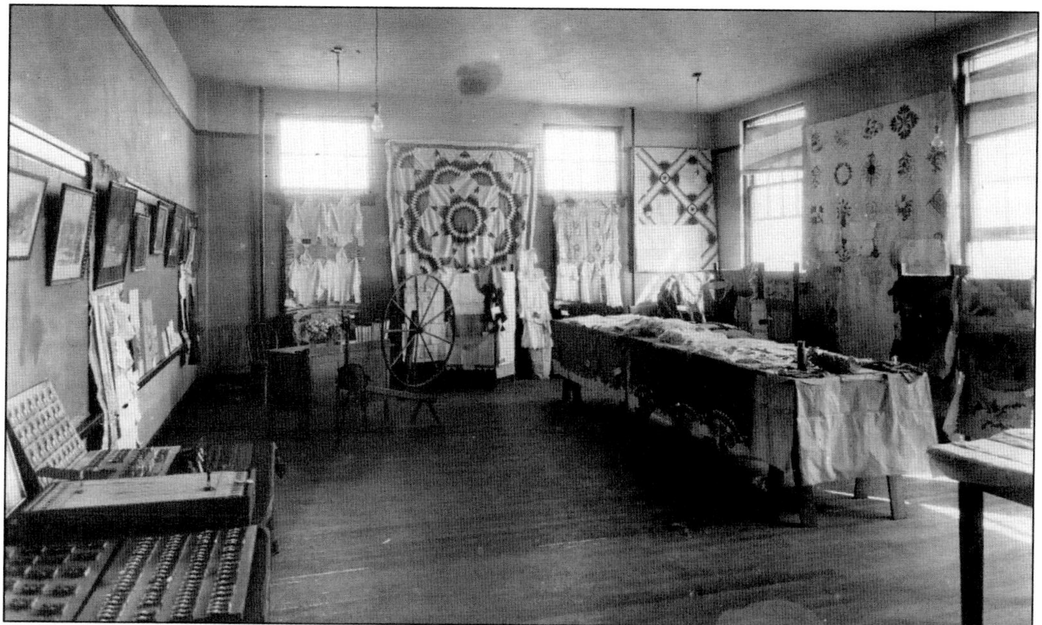

The county seat, Cody, Wyoming, originally hosted the Park County Fair. In 1921 and 1922, Powell hosted the Northwestern Wyoming Fair to promote its agricultural products and its homemade items, as seen in this photograph of fair exhibits taken in 1921. In 1923, Cody and Powell decided that Powell would host the Park County Fair and Cody would host the Fourth of July celebrations. This agreement is still observed today. (SIDA.)

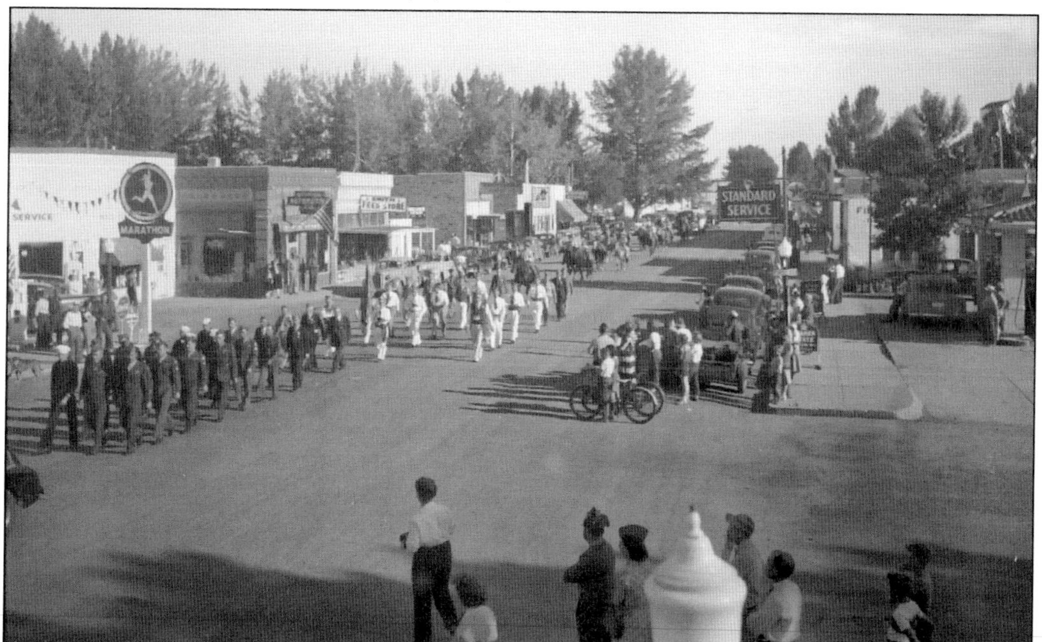

After conceding the Fourth of July celebrations to Cody, Powell hosted the Park County Fair. To kick off the fair, Powell celebrated with a parade down Bent Street. This image depicts the fair parade in 1950. The parade celebrated Powell's agricultural development and praised the success of reclamation. (FNB.)

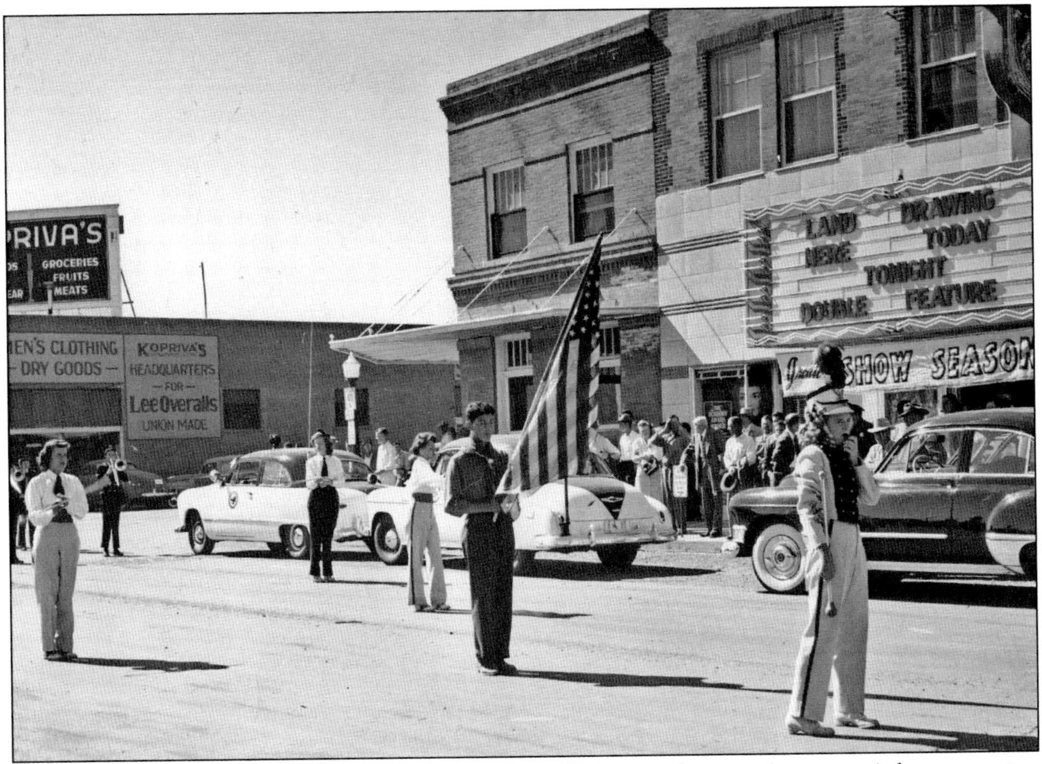

Powell also celebrates its current students and its alumni with annual events. A homecoming parade occurs in the fall, followed by the homecoming game, and then concludes with a high school dance. Every summer, Powell welcomes its alumni at Alumni Weekend. The class reunions occur at this time and all classes celebrate with a community dance. The image above depicts the Powell High School band proudly marching in front of the movie theater around 1949. The community's pride in its youth was evident from the very beginning. The photograph below proclaims the children in the wagon "our project's best product," even though whoever printed the banner reversed the "J." (Above, PCA; below, HM.)

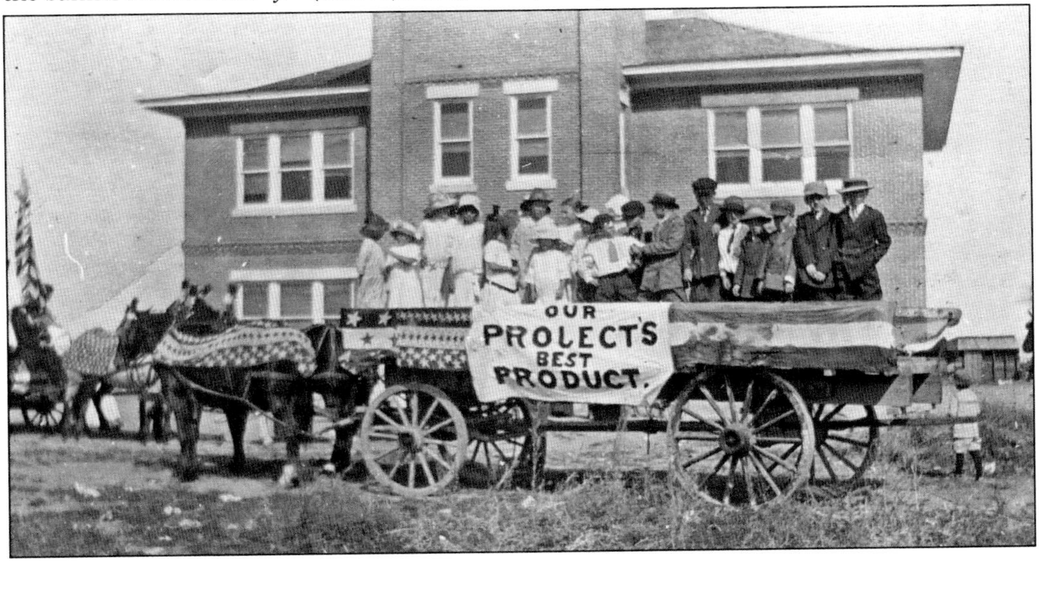

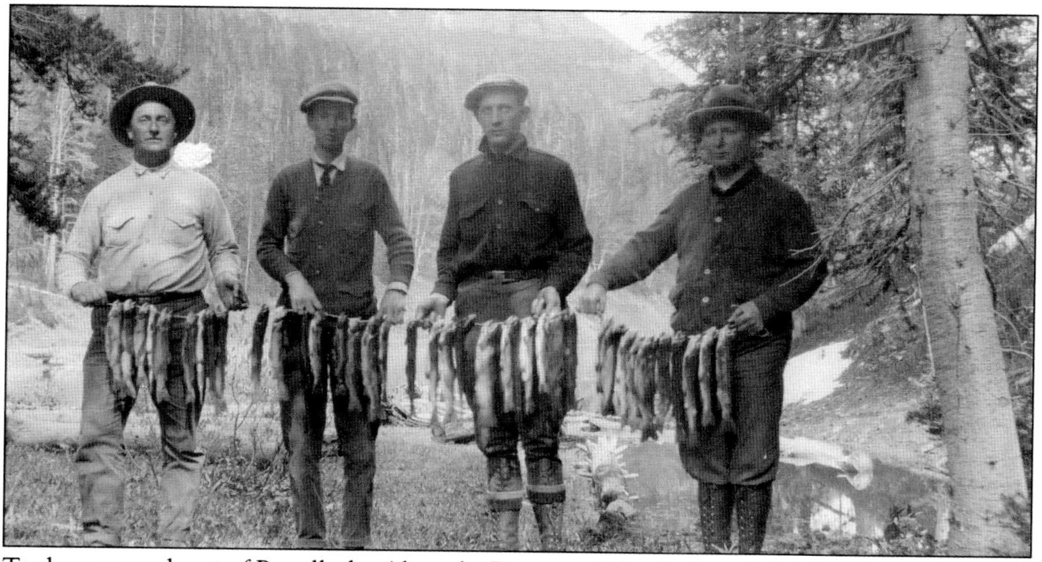

To the west and east of Powell, the Absaroka Range and the Bighorn Mountains provide Powell residents with numerous hunting and fishing opportunities. For years, Powell residents traveled the 40-plus miles to enjoy the mountain scenery and its wildlife. Occasionally Powell residents will make the 70-mile trip to Yellowstone National Park. This image shows a group of men with their day's catch of fish. (PCA.)

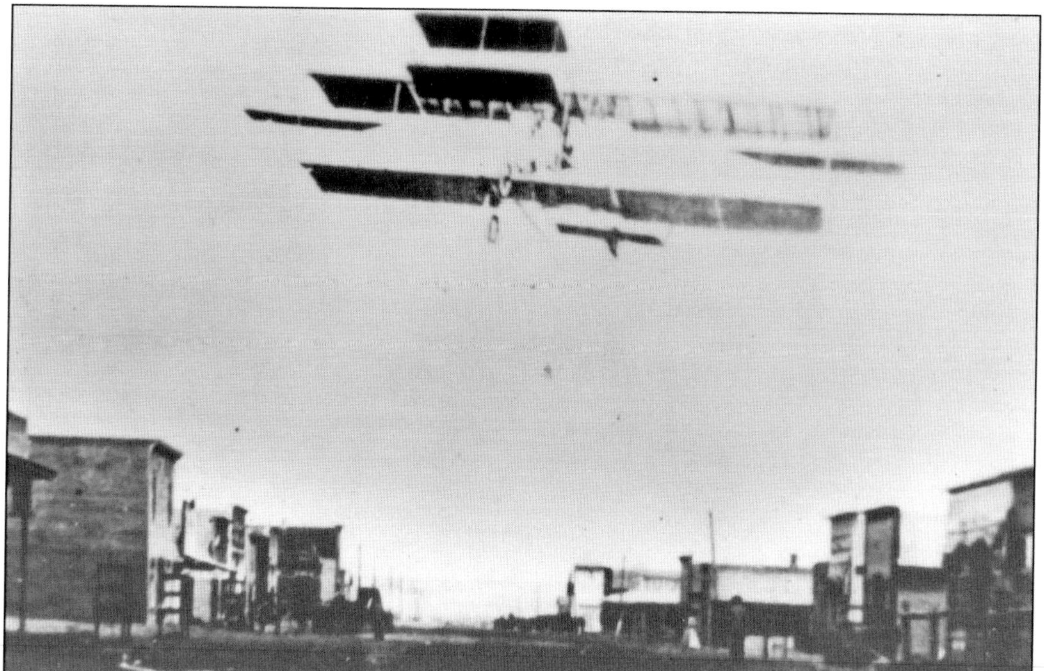

Other individuals found an escape from day-to-day life through technological advances. Pictured here is Henry Fulkerson from Powell flying along Bent Street in his airplane. Mary Elaine Bever-Housel witnessed this plane flying over her family's homestead and decided that she wanted to travel around the world, a decision that she fulfilled later in her life. (PCA.)

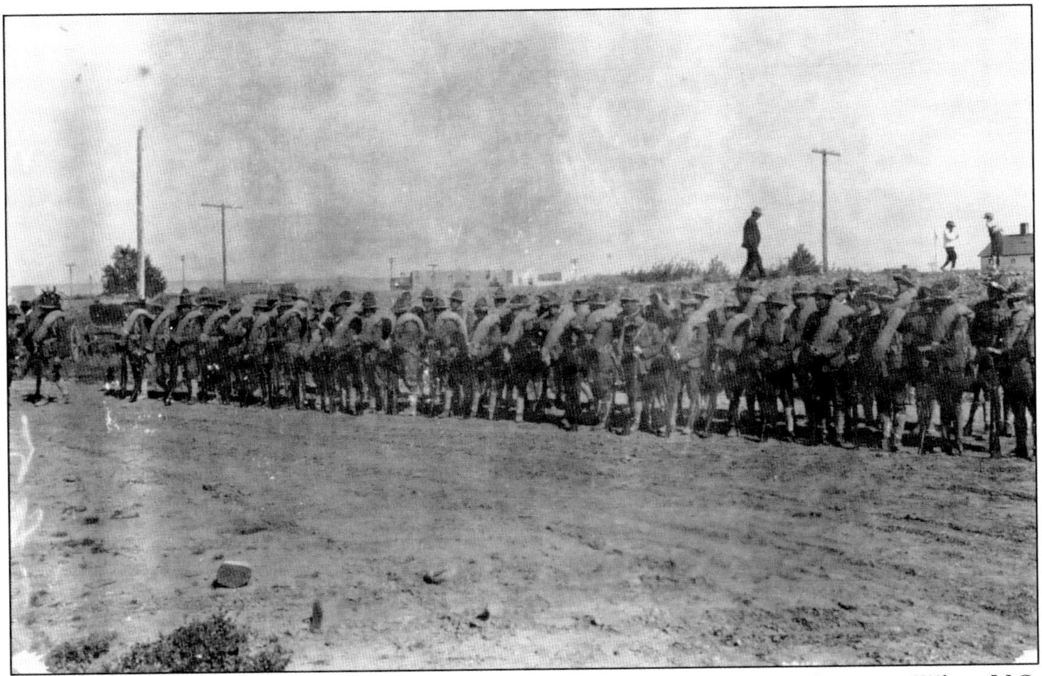

Despite its geographical isolation, Powell is still impacted by international events. When U.S. troops were called up to chase Pancho Villa in northern Mexico after his raid on Columbus, New Mexico, National Guard troops departed from Powell to assist in this military venture. Here guard troops await their departure from Powell en route to Mexico. (PCA.)

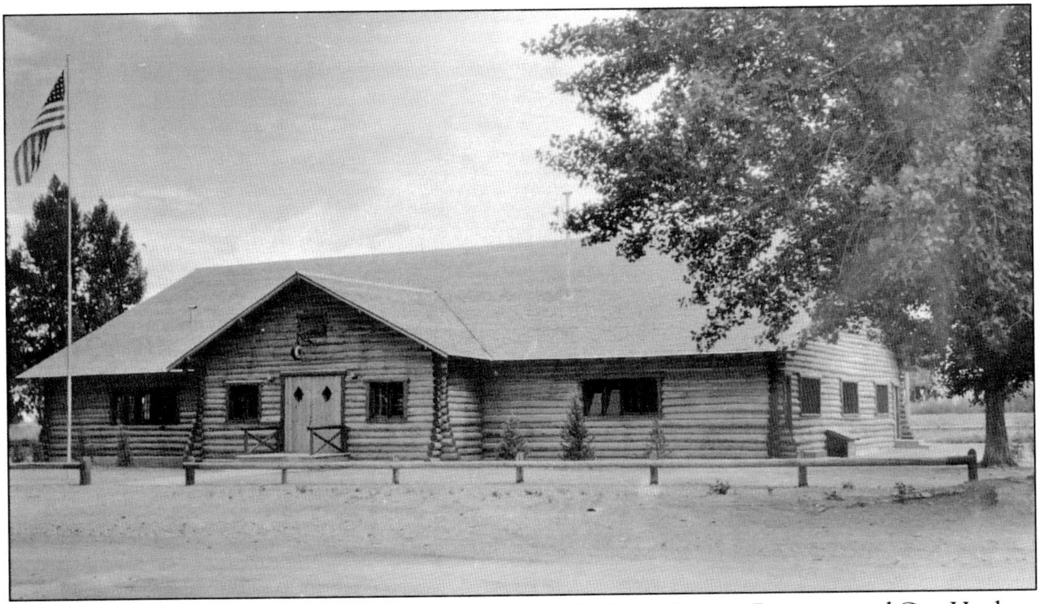

World War I claimed the lives of two Powell residents, William Francis Pittinger and Guy Hughes. The Powell American Legion Post is named in their honor. Pictured here is the American Legion Building, constructed in 1934 with logs hauled from the forests east of Yellowstone National Park. With its large dance floor, it hosted a number of dances and even served as a roller rink. Currently it houses the Homesteader Museum. (HM.)

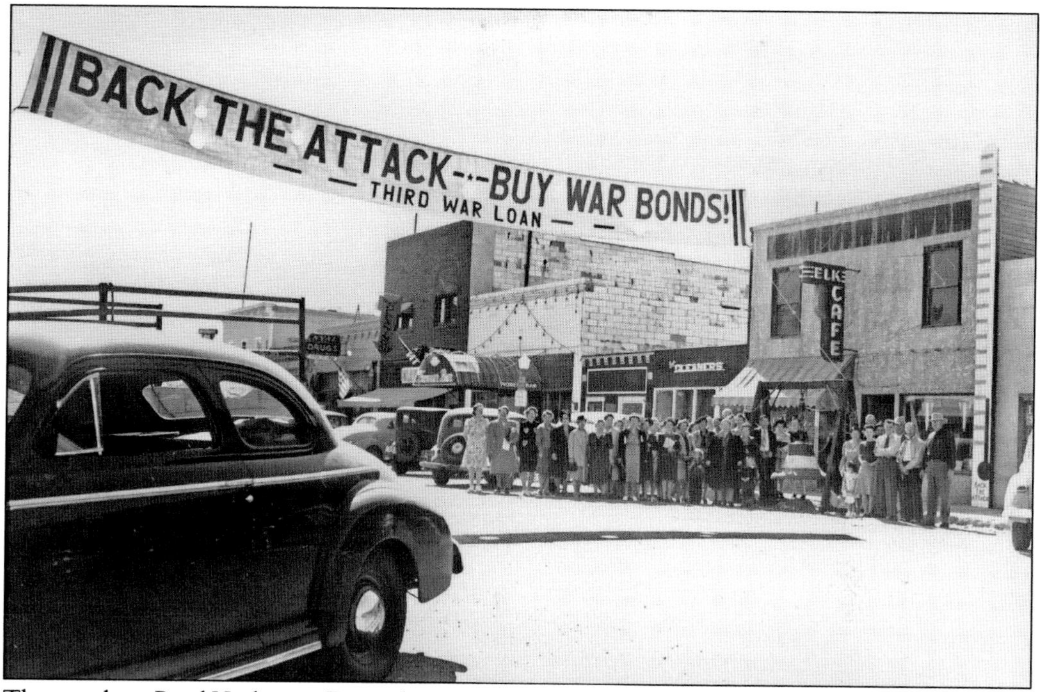

The attack on Pearl Harbor on December 7, 1941, brought out the best, and in some cases the worst, in Powell's community spirit. Powell supported the war effort by holding bond drives, as pictured above. It also had its share of recycling drives to gather scrap metal and goods for the war effort. A number of Powell's citizens, male and female, served in the armed forces during the war. Today a memorial west of town honors those individuals who were captured and held as POWs and those who gave their lives in defense of their country for all major conflicts. The darker side of Powell's patriotic fervor came out when over 11,000 Japanese Americans were interned in the Heart Mountain Relocation Center, making it the third-largest city in Wyoming. Mayor Ora Bever led an effort to ban the internees from shopping in town, but local businessmen opposed the ban. Through the duration of the war, Powell's citizens argued amongst themselves whether to welcome or shun their neighbors in the Heart Mountain Relocation Center, pictured below. (Both PCA.)

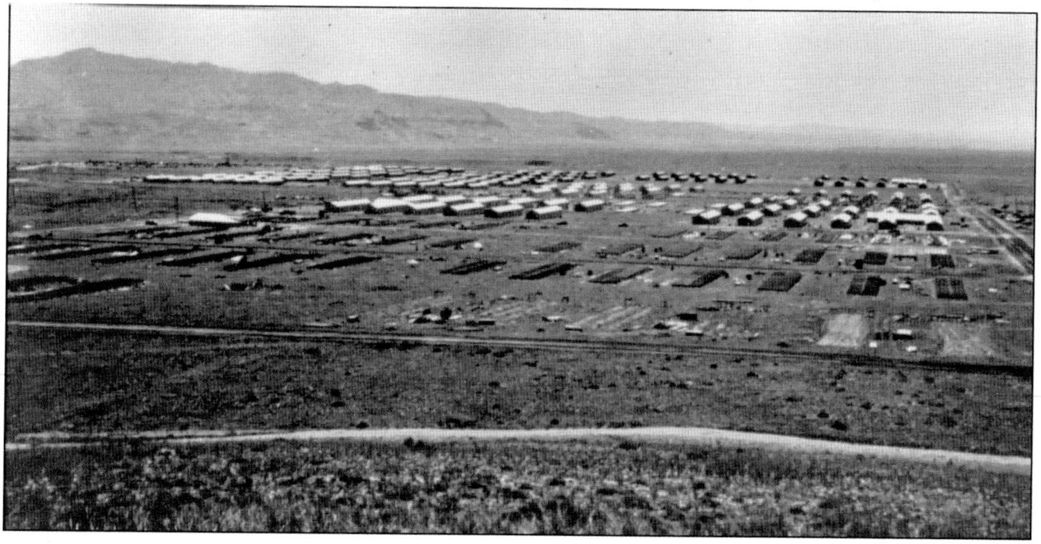

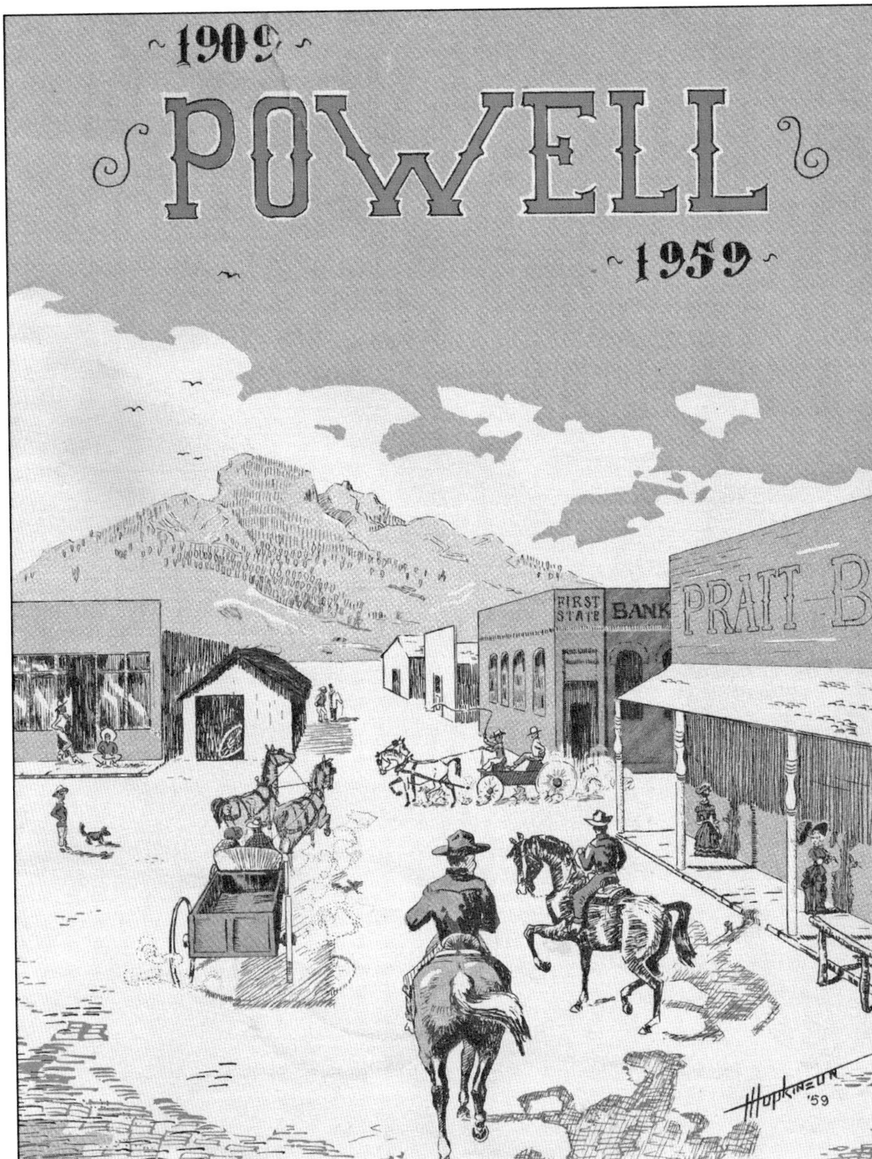

Through the bad years and the good years, Powell took pride in its past and celebrated its accomplishments and those individuals who contributed so much to the community. In 1959, Powell celebrated its 50th anniversary, its Golden Jubilee. The town hosted a skit entitled "Powellorama" to honor the its past. Men participated in a beard-growing contest, while women promised to be "belles" of the celebration by wearing long dresses and bonnets. A history of Powell, by Jane Johnstone, Betty Van Wagoner, Donna Larson, Patricia Wolsborn, and Marvel Rauchfuss, pictured here, honored Powell's past pioneers. The cover illustration was drawn by Harold Hopkinson, an artist from Byron, Wyoming, based on the photograph shown on page 45. The governor of Wyoming wrote of Powell's citizens, "So it is fitting and proper that we should pause at this 50-year milestone to take cognizance of the strides that have been made in the development of this community and its surrounding area, to acknowledge and rededicate ourselves to the traditions and principles of those early settlers to the end that the next fifty years will see comparable gains in the growth and progress of this community." (Author's collection.)

BIBLIOGRAPHY

Blevins, Bruce H. *Park County, Wyoming: Facts and Maps Through Time*. Powell, WY: WIM Marketing, 1999.

Bonner, Robert, and Beryl Gail Churchill. *Powell's First Century—Home in the Valley*. Cody, WY: Words Worth, 2009.

———. *Farm Town: Stories of the Early History of Powell*. Powell, WY: Powell Tribune, 1999.

———. *William F. Cody's Wyoming Empire: The Buffalo Bill Nobody Knows*. Norman, OK: University of Oklahoma Press, 2007.

Churchill, Beryl Gail. *Challenging the Canyon: A Family Man Builds Dam*. Cody, WY: Words Worth, 2001.

———. *The Dam Book: The Construction History of Corbett, Buffalo Bill and Wilwood Dams*. Cody, WY: Rustler Printing and Publishing, 1986.

———. *Dams, Ditches and Water: A History of the Shoshone Reclamation Project*. Cody, WY: Rustler Printing and Publishing, 1979.

———. *People Working Together: A 75th Anniversary Salute to Powell*. Powell, WY: Custom Printing, 1984.

Frison, George C. *Prehistoric Hunters of the High Plains*, 2nd ed. San Diego, CA: Academic Press, Inc., 1991.

Hendricks, Cecilia Hennel. *Letters From Honeyhill: A Woman's View of Homesteading, 1914–1931*. Boulder, CO: Pruett Publishing Company, 1986.

Plenty Coups, as told to Frank B. Linderman. *Plenty-Coups: Chief of the Crow*. Lincoln and London: University of Nebraska Press, 1962.

Johnstone, Jane, Donna Larson, Marvel Rauchfuss, Betty Van Wagoner, and Patricia Wolsborn. *Powell, 1909–1959*. A booklet of the 50th-year celebration of Powell, 1959.

Richardson, Allen G. *Polecat Bench*. Laramie, WY: Jelm Mountain Press, 1983.

Rollinson, John K. *Wyoming Cattle Trails*. Caldwell, ID: The Caxton Printers, Limited, 1948.

Turner, Lillian. "The Legendary Earl Durand." *Montana: The Magazine of Western History* 55, no. 3. Autumn 2005: 48–57.

Discover Thousands of Local History Books Featuring Millions of Vintage Images

Arcadia Publishing, the leading local history publisher in the United States, is committed to making history accessible and meaningful through publishing books that celebrate and preserve the heritage of America's people and places.

Find more books like this at
www.arcadiapublishing.com

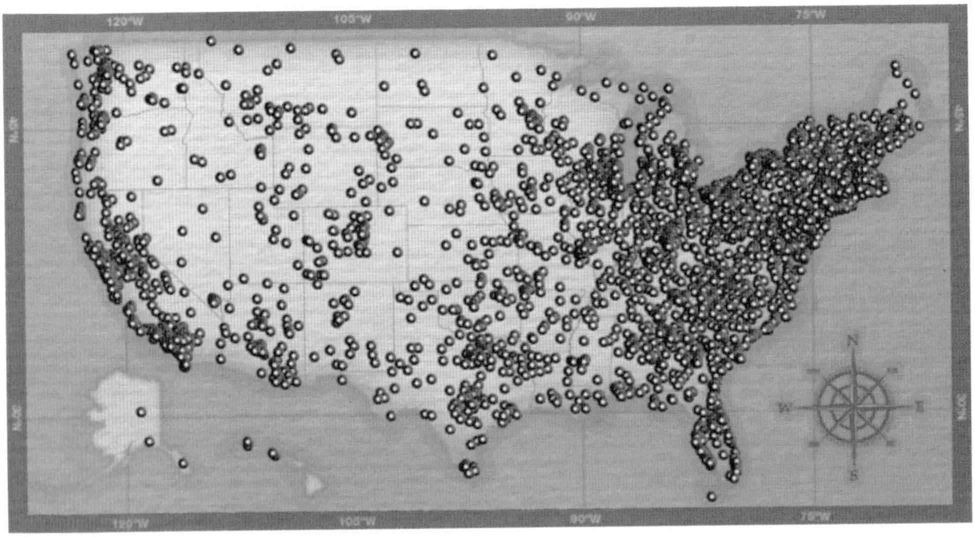

Search for your hometown history, your old stomping grounds, and even your favorite sports team.

Consistent with our mission to preserve history on a local level, this book was printed in South Carolina on American-made paper and manufactured entirely in the United States. Products carrying the accredited Forest Stewardship Council (FSC) label are printed on 100 percent FSC-certified paper.

MADE IN THE USA